PENGUIN B

A Bright & Savage Land

Ann Moyal is the author of several books, monographs and many papers on 19th and 20th century Australian science, technology and telecommunication. She has held research and teaching posts in a number of Australian universities. She is also a former honorary editor of *Search*, the journal of ANZAAS, and a well-known science communicator. She lives and writes in Canberra.

ANN MOYAL

A Bright & Savage Land

PENGUIN BOOKS

Penguin Books Australia Ltd
487 Maroondah Highway, PO Box 257
Ringwood, Victoria 3134, Australia
Penguin Books Ltd
Harmondsworth, Middlesex, England
Viking Penguin, A Division of Penguin Books USA Inc.
375 Hudson Street, New York, New York 10014, USA
Penguin Books Canada Limited
10 Alcorn Avenue, Toronto, Ontario, Canada M4V 3B2
Penguin Books (N.Z.) Ltd
182–190 Wairau Road, Auckland 10, New Zealand

First published by William Collins Pty Ltd, 1986
Published by Penguin Books Australia, 1993
10 9 8 7 6 5 4 3 2 1

Copyright © Ann Moyal, 1986

All rights reserved. Without limiting the rights under copyright
reserved above, no part of this publication may be reproduced, stored
in or introduced into a retrieval system, or transmitted, in any form
or by any means (electronic, mechanical, photocopying, recording or
otherwise), without the prior written permission of both the copyright owner
and the above publisher of this book.

Typeset in Sabon by Midland Typesetters
Made and printed in Australia by Griffin Paperbacks

National Library of Australia
Cataloguing-in-Publication data:

Moyal, Ann.
A bright & savage land

New ed.
Bibliography.
Includes index.
ISBN 0 14 017806 6.

1. Scientists—Australia—Biography. 2. Naturalists—Australia—Biography.
3. Natural history—Australia. 4. Research—Australia—History. I. Title.

509.22

For José Moyal

This book was originally published as a highly illustrated work titled '*A Bright & Savage Land*': *Scientists in Colonial Australia*, by William Collins Pty Ltd, created and produced by Mead & Beckett Publishing (1986).

This production is designed to reach a large and different audience. Various institutions have helped me with the study. My thanks are due to the National Library of Australia, the Mitchell Library and the British Museum (Natural History) for permission from their trustees to allow me to publish illustrations in their keeping.

Sources of Illustrations

Ferdinand Bauer drawing from British Museum (Natural History); Joseph Banks mezzotint by Benjamin West from Nan Kivell Collection, National Library of Australia, 26S; line engraving by G. Smith after Sydney Parkinson from Banks' *Florilegium*, British Museum (Natural History); emus by C.A. Lesueur, *Peron Voyage de decouvertes aux terres Australes 1804* from Nan Kivell Collection, National Library of Australia; native woman from *Terre de Diémen* from Mitchell Library of NSW: platypus from G. Perry's *Arcana* vol. 1 from Mitchell Library; cockatoos from Mitchell Library; black swan from Mitchell Library; koala bear from Mitchell Library; wombat from G. Perry's *Arcana* vol. 1 from Mitchell Library; Elizabeth Gould from Mitchell Library; lyrebirds from Mitchell Library; boobook owls from Mitchell Library; black-gloved wallabies by John Gould from Nan Kivell Collection, National Library of Australia; native encampment by George Angas from Nan Kivell Collection, National Library of Australia; the naturalist's cabin by Joseph Selleny from Mitchell Library; crinoid fossils by James Dwight Dana from Mitchell Library of NSW; 1880 Melbourne Exhibition from National Library of Australia; Jane, Lady Franklin from Queen Victoria Museum, Launceston; goanna by Dr James Stuart from Mitchell Library; green tree snake by Harriet Scott from Mitchell Library; butterflies by Harriet Scott from Mitchell Library: Richard Daintree from Oxley Library, Brisbane; 'the mechanical eye' from Mitchell Library: transit telescope from *Picturesque Atlas of Australia* vol. 3 from Nan Kivell Collection, National Library of Australia; illustration from Ferdinand von Mueller's *Plants Indigenous to the Colony of Victoria* from Mitchell Library; Ferdinand von Mueller from Mitchell Library: skeletal reconstruction by Richard Owen from Mitchell Library; fossil tooth from Mitchell Library: laboratory of Professor J.T. Wilson from University of Sydney Archives.

Contents

Introduction

ONE	The Great South Land	9
TWO	Under a virgin sky	28
THREE	Entrepreneurs & explorers	40
FOUR	Navigators & ship's naturalists	56
FIVE	Science, societies & the people	70
SIX	The feminine touch	90
SEVEN	The conquest of the rocks	104
EIGHT	The weather & the sky	117
NINE	Evolution in Australia	131
TEN	Colonial scientists versus the 'experts'	146
ELEVEN	Science in colonial universities	162
TWELVE	Experimenters & inventors	174
Endnotes		193
Select bibliography		214
Index		229

Introduction

Australia takes a great pride in her scientific pioneers. Consider the paper currency. On the two-dollar note we found William Farrer, agricultural experimenter, with his sheaves of wheat. The five-dollar note carried scientific progenitor Sir Joseph Banks encrusted about with many of the sturdy banksia species to which he lent his name. The 100-dollar note commemorates the Australian born 19th century astronomer John Tebbutt, at an age when his observations at his private observatory at Windsor, New South Wales, had netted him the discovery of two 'great comets' and international astronomical acclaim, together with the South Australian geologist, Sir Douglas Mawson, who thrice explored the Antarctic between 1907 and 1931. The 20-dollar note shows the remarkable aeronautical experimenter Lawrence Hargrave, who, in the late years of the 19th century, carried out his highly innovative and tireless experiments with heavier-than-air flight. With the 50-dollar note science shines again. We have entered the 20th century with two Australian scientists on either side: the medical scientist Sir Howard Florey whose work on the development of penicillin earned him a Nobel Prize, and the veterinary scientist Sir Ian Clunies Ross, Chairman from 1949–59 of Australia's great government scientific organisation, the CSIRO.

In the 20th century we live in a scientific age. The scientific enterprise and the contributors to it double with every decade. Science – pure, applied, and its applications in technology – are in a state of rapid growth. In Australia, the Commonwealth Government now spends approximately one per cent (and many urge much more) of the gross national product on scientific development and research. Science is seen as a benefactor and an unpredictable, potent force to be harnessed, a source of progress and of change.

What is the background of this development? What are the bases on which the Australian enterprise has taken root? What, in its emerging colonial period, did Australia contribute to international science? The questions are crucial to its historical record and the answers loaded with relevance and force. The newly settled continent of Australia was launched in another scientific age, and the country's first experiences were closely bound up with the important expeditions of discovery that brought key naturalists to the southern hemisphere and made the fifth continent a vital outpost for comparative insights and discoveries about the natural world.

The 19th century proved to be one of the great ages of scientific advance. From massive accumulations of data, fundamental changes took place in the biological and geological sciences; the theory of evolution and geographical distribution transformed men's understanding of the nature of species; chemical science matured to invigorate other disciplines; the physical and geophysical sciences broke down the Newtonian concept of a strictly mechanical world; and the sciences of astronomy and geography (including meteorology,

Introduction

hydrography, cartography and anthropology) made remarkable headway from the voyages of survey and scientific enquiry that characterised a century of maritime exploration.

Though the major speculative breakthroughs were made in England and Europe, these depended, particularly in the biological sciences, on science 'outside Europe' and on the body of evidence brought to light by observers scattered in the far corners of the world. British and European naturalists, travelling in distant countries, found their eyes opened by the appearance of new species and their geographical dispersal around the globe, and their observations were strengthened and extended by resident naturalists on the spot. In this, Australia played a central part. When Cook 'discovered' and charted the eastern seaboard of the new continent in 1770, the country already had a history of scientific observation reaching back to the early 17th century, though these identifications related to Van Diemen's Land and to western parts. With the *Endeavour*'s collections of natural history back in England, great was the interest generated among other powers. France, Europe's scientific leader, would rapidly send out her own scientific men, and the botanical and natural history material despatched to the Paris Museum in 1804 from Nicholas Baudin's discovery expedition became one of the major collections of Australian natural science.

Despite regular and competent scrutiny on the part of France, Australia's own scientific tradition grew up directly under the White Ensign and the personal patronage of Sir Joseph Banks. In an unexplored country, it hinged on a reconnaissance of the natural environment and on the examination and description of its unique organic forms. The sheer traffic in botanical and zoological specimens was immense. The greatest part went to British herbaria and museums although, at intervals throughout the 19th century, Australia was also penetrated, and her treasures collected, by German, Polish, Austrian and other naturalists who added to the growing store of scientific specimens and curiosities in the hands of European and American collectors and museums.

In this large-scale reconnaissance of natural history there were many participants. Naval officers, explorers, doctors, clergymen, governors, settlers, public officials and surveyors joined with trained botanists, zoologists and natural history draughtsmen to make up the working complement of science. One vital component was the artist, sometimes a professionally trained painter or, often, a self-taught amateur who, in the educated tradition of the period, used the sketchbook as an essential companion and traveller's tool. In no century more than the 19th was there so rich and rewarding an alliance between science and art. The marriage was often arranged. Banks equipped himself for the *Endeavour* voyage with two natural history 'draughtsmen', Parkinson and Buchan, and the young Sydney Parkinson became the first painter to land in Australia. His remarkable body of floral and faunal drawings at once attest to the singular importance of the visual record in conveying the discoveries and contents of a new land. Parkinson was to be followed by a diverse band of artists. Ferdinand Bauer, natural history illustrator to Flinders' *Investigator* voyage (and another choice of Banks), brought back unsurpassed portraits of Australian plants and flowers, while the many artists recruited to the French expeditions of science and discovery, with their early representations of Aboriginal subjects, marsupials, birds, and monotremes, both illustrated their venturesome journeys and enhanced their scientific results.

Early governors added to the pictorial record. Hunter and

Introduction

Bligh were able illustrators. Hunter sketched some hundred drawings of flowers, birds, fish and the indigenous inhabitants while Bligh caught the fleeting poses of Tasmanian birds. Colour and form filled out the rough initial content of science. Thomas Watling, the convict artist, found in exile that flowers, shrubs and plants were 'ringed with hues that might baffle the happiest effects of the pencil'. As time went on, surveyors and explorers would add their informal sketches of new regions and landscapes, of rocks and caves and natural history to the growing illumination of the country's science. Ships' captains and their officers were sometimes trained in art. Captain Owen Stanley, commander of HMS *Rattlesnake* on her Australian journey, was such a one whose delicate watercolours caught the very essence of the life of maritime survey and of the scientific activities they pursued. Lieutenant E.A. Porcher of the survey ship *Fly* was also a watercolourist with a keen eye, and an interest in physical science. Thomas Huxley, the *Rattlesnake*'s naturalist under Stanley, although untrained in art, proved to be a striking scientific artist who indulged his taste for sketching on his excursions ashore. Such informal drawings found their way into expedition 'Narratives', those popular and invaluable reports of 19th-century voyages of discovery, where they were sometimes upgraded by an engraver's hand. More directly, the professional productions of such naturalists and artists as John Gould and George French Angas opened up the bright beauties of the colonies to the wider world. Additionally, the land expeditions of exploration took trained artists to the remote inland to bring back rich illustrations as the century advanced.

The history of science in Australia is, hence, both visual and verbal; its documents paintings as well as words. Some of it was never intended for publication. Yet its very informality adds to its effect and reveals the keen commitment, the struggle and the enthusiasm of those involved. A number of women participated in this creative work. Some were skilled natural history illustrators; other were gentle sketchers; still others proved curious and intrepid observers of the natural world.

The life of science was shaped variously across the 19th century. At first Australia provided a hunting ground, a new source of data for science overseas. Gradually, indigenous scientists gathered, enlarged the spectrum of their interest and enquiry, and assumed fuller responsibility for the investigation and interpretation of their scientific world. For the first 50 or more years in a convict emancipist society, the community in general proved indifferent to science. Colonial governments, straining for political and economic stability, were also ready to leave the scientific enterprise largely in private hands. The period of the 1850s saw significant change. Transportation ended in New South Wales in 1850, in Van Diemen's Land in 1853 (the island was officially renamed Tasmania in 1855), and in Western Australia – a late starter in convict importation – in 1868. The gold discoveries ushered in new colonial wealth and, with it, a new commitment on the part of legislatures to a local colonial and national consciousness of science. Australia passed its first million population in 1861, the Victorian Government appointed a Science Board to advise on policy in 1858, and each colonial government emerged as a progressive, if pragmatic sponsor of science. Universities were established, astronomical and magnetic observatories erected and government finance put to the building of geological and mineralogical surveys, herbaria and museums. Buttressed by their own materials, colonial scientists struck out against the grip of British dominance and hegemony in

Introduction

different fields. Through interesting museum collections, colonial and international exhibitions, the press, libraries and Mechanics Institutes, the colonial public was drawn in growing numbers to an interest in their national science.

In the last third of the century, the 'mechanical eye' – the photographer's lens – would come gradually to replace the sketchbook. Photographic portraiture had already begun to provide the historian with the scientist's guise. The geologist Richard Daintree would introduce photographic studies into fieldwork in the 1850s, carting the cumbersome wet plate equipment to procure some pioneering studies of folded rocks and landscape and the people who inhabited it. It was a complicated art. A decade or so later, dry plate photography made field photography a less demanding tool, and its use spread productively to astronomical and anthropological fields. The elegance of the sketchbook, however, would not be overtaken for many years.

The diary, the letter, the journal, the sketch, the painting, the photograph and the portrait all form part of this history. Each medium conveys its message. Each furnishes a piece of the pyramid of 19th-century colonial science. By the century's end, Australia still depended substantially on British technology, concepts, and instrumentation for her research needs; but she was shaping a maturing scientific community of her own. The universal naturalist, whom the British natural philosopher William Whewell first captioned 'scientist' in 1839, had given way to a miscellany of biologists, physiologists, embryologists, microscopists, entomologists, conchologists, geophysicists, biochemists and many more, eager to define their professional identity and differentiate their distinctive fields. Australian scientists continued to look to Britain for their institutional and societal models and for their highest honour (the Fellowship of the Royal Society) in science. Unlike their American colleagues, they did not partake of that diversification imparted to the scientific tradition by close educational association with European science. In response to the sense of their own national growth, however, Australians established their first scientific award, the Clarke Medal, named for the geologist the Reverend W.B. Clarke and struck by the Royal Society of New South Wales in 1878 and, 100 years after settlement, began projecting their own territorial investigation in the exploration of Antarctica and New Guinea. It marked a long and significant haul from the *Endeavour* landings to the end of what could be called 'colonial science'.

CHAPTER ONE

The Great South Land

James Cook was the supreme navigator of the 18th century. When, in 1768, after seafaring around Newfoundland as master and ship's master for 20 years, he was promoted to lieutenant and appointed by the British Admiralty to lead an expedition aboard HMS *Endeavour* to observe the transit of Venus at Tahiti, he had demonstrated already his skill as a naval surveyor and solar observer; but a brilliant career lay before him in southern seas. This practical Yorkshire lad, son of a Scottish labourer, would change the known contours of the geography of the world and pave the way for a new British Empire in the southern Pacific.

Cook's instructions for the voyage were unique. Under a joint agreement between the Admiralty and the Royal Society of London, he was to observe the transit of Venus across the sun from the vantage point of Tahiti in mid-1869 and, on secret Admiralty instructions, to procced to search for the 'great south land'. Ever since Magellan and Drake had circumnavigated the world, sketching in the coasts of South America and Africa, there still lay the unknown fifth continent – 'Terra Incognita', 'Terra Australis' – touched on by the Spanish Torres, the Dutch explorers Janz, Pelsaert, Tasman and de Vlamingh, and by the English navigator, William Dampier. All brought fragments of information about localities and fauna back to Europe, while map makers filled out their own designs of an imagined continent.[1]

James Cook was sceptical of its existence.[2] But scientific men, fired by Dampier and Tasman's sightings, were eager for knowledge of the continent's contours and of the contents of a land mass at the antipodes of the globe. Hence the *Endeavour* voyage was linked directly with science. The astronomer Charles Green was appointed expressly by the Royal Society to observe the transit of Venus with Captain Cook, while the Society's Council pressed upon the Admiralty one of their most recently elected fellows, Joseph Banks, a young man 'well versed in natural history' whose presence, they believed, was likely 'to contribute to the advancement of useful knowledge' and enlarge men's understanding of the natural world.

Banks (1743–1820) was already an experienced and accomplished naturalist when he presented himself for the rare assignment. Rich, educated at Eton and Oxford, he had been tutored privately in botany and had joined an earlier expedition to Newfoundland and Labrador where he had collected fauna, rocks and plants. Fascinated by the prospect of a long and distant journey, from his private fortune he equipped himself lavishly, gathering a party of two naturalists, the Swedish (Daniel) Carl Solander (1733–1782) and Herman Spöring, two natural history illustrators Sydney Parkinson (1745–1771) and Alexander Buchan, four servants and two dogs.[3] To the large cabin allotted him amidships, Banks added his natural history library, a batch of machines for catching insects, 'nets, trawls, drags and hooks for coral fishing, a curious contrivance of a telescope by which, put into water you can see the bottom to a great depth', and innumerable cases of specimen bottles, boxes, paper and wax for the transport of fauna, seeds and plants. 'No people ever went to sea,' wrote one friend admiringly, 'better fitted out for the purpose of natural history, nor more elegantly.'[4] Banks' total investment in the expedition was estimated at £10,000.

The barque *Endeavour* sailed from Plymouth on 26 August 1768 and reached Tahiti via Cape Horn in April the following year. There the company observed the transit of Venus across the sun on 3 June and, breaking their elaborate camp, sailed westward to circumnavigate and chart the islands of New Zealand, which Tasman had discovered, and search for the southerly continent. On 19 April 1770, the shore of 'Terra Australis' loomed into view. 'I have named it Point Hicks,' Cook recorded the first sighting in his journal, 'after the lieutenant who first perceived the land.' As the *Endeavour* turned northward, sailing up the coastline, Cook scored his chart with the names of bays and promontories – Ram Head, Cape Howe, Mount Dromedary, Bateman's Bay, Point Upright, the Pigeon House, Long Nose, Red Point – while pounding surf sheltered the slopes from landing by the visitors.[5] Banks meanwhile minuted his not very flattering judgment. 'The countrey tho in general well enough clothd,' he wrote of the region round Jarvis Bay, 'appeared in some places bare: it resembled in my imagination the back of a lean Cow, covered in general with long hair, but nevertheless where her scraggy hip bones have stuck out farther than they ought accidental rubbs have intirely bard them of their share of covering.'[6] Two days later, Cook, with Banks and Solander, tried unsuccessfully to land a yawl, but on 28 April they found a sheltered bay, which Cook initially called Stingray Bay, and dropped anchor. Because of the importance of its discoveries, Cook would soon rename it Botany Bay.

There, with his botanist and naturalist and the native Tupaia acquired at Tahiti to act as interpreter, Cook landed to find water and make contact with the 'Indians'. But the Aborigines' reaction was, not surprisingly, anxious. 'As we approached,' Cook noted of this historic meeting, 'they made off, except 2 Men who seemed resolved to oppose our landing . . . As soon as we put the boat in again they came to oppose us, upon which I fir'd a musket between the 2, which had no effect than to make them retire back, where bundles of their darts lay, and one of them took up a stone and threw it at us.' Cook fired again and 'Altho' some of the shot struck the man, yet it had no other effect than making him lay hold on a Target. Immediately after this we landed . . .'[7]

The *Endeavour* remained at anchor within Port Jackson for more than a week and there, under blue skies, Banks and Solander eagerly roamed the foreshore collecting plants. The trees abounded with lorikeets and cockatoos. They saw, too, the first strange fauna, 'a quadruped the size of a Rabbit' and the dung of a large animal that fed on grass. But their own haul was botanical.

'Our collection of Plants has now grown so immensely large,' Banks noted of his Pacific and Australian assortment, 'that some extraordinary care had to be taken of them.' He accordingly carried ashore all the drying paper 'nearly 500 Quires of which the large part was full' and, spreading them upon a sail in the sun, kept them exposed the whole day, turning them and sometimes moving the quires inside out. 'By this means,' he reported with satisfaction, 'they came aboard at night in very good condition.'[8]

Cook's instructions had carried clear and liberal advice for dealing with the native people.⁹ But his first overtures yielded dismally little in Australia. The Aborigines, seen in small groups, kept their distance. Firmly ignoring the beads and trinkets left by the visitors in their huts, they appeared, Cook remarked, 'to want nothing more than for us to be gone'. 'The natives often reconnoitred us,' Sydney Parkinson noted, 'but we could not prevail on them to come near us to be social; for, as soon as we advanced, they fled as nimbly a deer.'[10]

After the ship's departure on 6 May, Banks and his party occupied themselves preparing and describing their rich collections.

We sat at the great table with the draughtsman [Parkinson] *directly across from us* [Banks wrote in his journal]. *We showed him how the drawings should be depicted and hurriedly made descriptions of all the natural history objects while they were still fresh. When a long journey from land had exhausted fresh things, we finished each description and added the synonyms to the books we had. These completed accounts were immediately entered by secretary Spöring in the books in the form of a flora of each of the lands we had visited.*

Six days out from Botany Bay, Parkinson had completed his delicate drawings of the new flora, which Banks kept fresh for the purpose arranged in wet cloths and tin chests. They would attempt no further landing for another 17 days. Cook made his second Australian landing in present-day Queensland at Bustard Bay. Again Banks and Solander accompanied their captain in blustering winds to the high hilltop, but as there was no water available in that marshy area, the *Endeavour* moved on, keeping prudently outside the shoals that encompassed the coast. Their passage was now hazardous, threading through the unseen, and to them unknown, outcrops of the Great Barrier Reef. At night they anchored often in those perilous waters. Drinking water was crucial to them. They found none at Thirsty Sound, where they landed on 29 May, but there were other rewards. A maze of butterflies, velvet black and blue, coloured the scene. 'The air,' wrote Banks, 'was for a space of 3 or 4 acres crowded with them to a wonderful degree. The eye could not be turnd in any direction without seeing millions and every branch and twig was almost covered with those that sat still. Of these we took as many as we chose, knocking them down with caps or anything that came to hand.'[11]

On 4 June, the *Endeavour* steered serenely through a broad deep passage, which Cook named Whitsunday for the Anglican Church festival celebrated on that day. He named Cape Upstart the following day and Rockingham Bay after a former British Prime Minister. They were still having extraordinary good luck tacking among the coral reef, of which they were unaware. On 10 June, Banks and Solander landed at Green Island, already known in Cook's chart. Cook passed and named Low Island, rich in coral, and, still unconscious of the reef, entered latitudes discovered by Quiros. But their luck had run out. In the darkness of night on 11 June, the *Endeavour* struck the sharp coral surface at high tide. They were off Cape Tribulation, and the names Cook scattered thereafter on that landscape – Mount Sorrow, Weary Bay, Hope Island – bore testimony to the peril and isolation of their plight. Sails were pulled in, everything that could be spared thrown overboard, and anchors put out. But as the tide receded, the ship heeled to starboard. Everyone was at the pumps. 'All the time the Seamen worked with surprising cheerfulness and alacrity,' Banks' journal recorded, 'no grumbling or growling was to be heard throughout the ship, not even an oath (tho' the ship in general was well furnished with them).' They were not off the reef and safely into harbour for six days. And there, at the Endeavour River, the site of present-day Cooktown, the company remained to repair the menacing gashes in their ship until 4 August.

Fate had favoured science. Cook's voyage had been dedicated primarily to surveying. Banks had reason to envy the time allowed by later ships' captains for the shore interests of natural science. Now, at Endeavour Bay, he and his assistants, far more than at their first Australian landfall, could devote themselves to the study of the plants and fauna of the region. Their six-week period marked a concentrated assault on the unknown contents of the fifth continent. Zoology and botany engaged them. Camped by the river mouth, rising early 'almost devoured by mosquitos', 'these indefatigable insects' as Banks described them, they spent the days scouring the landscape for plants, shells and animals. A 'kangaru' was sighted several times and finally shot and eaten. Its skull was taken back to England together with Parkinson's sketches of it, and presented to John Hunter, surgeon and anatomist. Banks himself also took a female opossum and two young.

By 16 June the *Endeavour* was ready to depart. Cook, thoroughly cautious now, had plotted his route out from the bay from the high vantage point of Grassy Hill. He would creep past the shoals, reefs and islets, landing and naming Lizard Island and finally reach the northern tip of the continent that had brought him and his expedition desperately close to death and destruction in the southern seas. 'I have engaged more among the Islands and Shoals upon this Coast,' he confided to his Journal, 'than perhaps in prudence I ought to have done with a single ship, but if I had not I should not have been able to give any better account of the one half of it, than I had never seen it; at best I should not have been able to say whether it was Main Land or Islands & as to its produce, that we should have been totally ignorant of.'[12] On 22 August at Possession Island, off Cape York, Cook took possession of the whole of Eastern Australia, in the name of the British Government, calling it New South Wales.

By early October 1770, the *Endeavour* reached Batavia for major repairs. It proved a disastrous interlude. Both the crew and the scientific company were decimated by illness. The astronomer Charles Green and Sydney Parkinson died as a result of fevers contracted there. The topographical draughtsman John Buchan had already died at Tahiti. Grimly reduced, the ship's company reached England on 12 July 1771. Captain Cook, however, was a maritime hero, and Banks an instant leader of international science. Since by far the largest part of his collection of plants had been gathered in Australia, Europe's botanical luminary, Carl Linnaeus, recommended that the new land should be named 'Banksia'. Both Banks and Solander won wide acclaim: they received the honorary degree of doctor of laws from Banks' alma mater, Oxford University, while their rich collections excited the admiration and interest of naturalists in Europe. Yet, despite the excellence of their materials, Banks' grand plan for the botany of the expedition did not mature, and, to the disappointment of colleagues, he contributed little to the journals of science.

His contribution to scientific knowledge was to flow by other routes. Centred at his home in London's Soho Square, with Solander as his librarian and secretary, Banks opened the *Endeavour* collections to men of science. His house became the repository for the *Endeavour* collections, as well as for his earlier Newfoundland and Labrador collections and for materials gathered in England, Scotland, Iceland and Europe, to all of which he added continually by large-scale purchase and exchange. The illustrations, invaluable depictions of the living species, of which some 1163 were made on the *Endeavour* voyage, were also assembled, while the impressive array of Australian flora, described by Solander on the journey home, was bound and arranged for scientific reference. Banks personally supervised the preparation of the engravings to be made from Parkinson and Buchan's drawings and the work of other artists who were engaged to complete the drawings from the pressed and dried specimens. Some 740 copperplates were made from Parkinson's watercolours between 1771–4. However, over 200 years would elapse before these remarkable botanical illustrations were printed.[13] Why? In one sense, Banks' own fame from his remarkable exploits yields the clue. The sheer pace and range of his public activities diverted him from the steady scholarship necessary to get his data into print, and Solander, who had been cataloguing the collections and constantly revising the difficult classification of the many new species, died of a stroke in 1782.

Joseph Banks, however, was to exert a powerful influence on Imperial and Australian science. In 1772 he was nominated director of the King's Royal Botanic Gardens at Kew, and six years later elected president of the Royal Society of London, a post he held with singular continuity and authority for the next 42 years. He was created baronet for his scientific services in 1781.

From these various positions of vantage, Sir Joseph Banks now came to exercise a powerful patronage in natural science. His unrivalled herbarium and library became the Mecca for British and foreign naturalists, while he personally enlisted the help of the Admiralty in adding to the existing collections and in building up the resources at Kew. In 1779, recalling the varied vegetation of Australia's eastern coast, Banks gave important testimony before a Select Committee of the House of Commons for the choice of a penal settlement at Botany Bay and, for the next 30 years from the settlement in 1788, inspired and dominated scientific investigation in the Australian colonies until his death. With the despatch of the First Fleet to Sydney, Banks corresponded with governors, issued clear directions to ships' captains for collecting and preserving specimens, forwarded useful plants for cultivation from Kew and set in motion the traffic in botanical and zoological specimens that laid the foundation for the study of Australian natural science.

In 1798, Banks sent his own botanical collector, George Caley (1770–1829), trained at Kew, to begin the systematic collection of Australian plants. Self-educated and discerning, Caley proved an adroit collector, moving out progressively from his depot at Parramatta and consigning diverse packets of plants and fauna to his patron at Kew. Aware of the advantages, he was the first of the early naturalists to enlist the help of Aborigines in his work. 'Every inch of ground I consider sacred,' the diligent Caley wrote Banks in 1800, 'and not to be trampled over without being noticed.'[14] Natural history also formed part of his province. Banks particularly urged him to attend to that most bizarre of Australian discoveries, the platypus. 'Our greatest want here,' he wrote Caley in April 1803, 'is to be acquainted with the manner in which the Duck Bill Animal & the Porcupine Ant Eater which I think is of the same genus, breed, their internal structure is so very similar to that of Birds that I do not think it impossible they should lay Eggs or at least as Snakes & some

Fish do Hatch Eggs in their Bellies.[15] Banks was not far wide of the mark, though it would take more than the assiduous efforts of Caley and the Aborigines he engaged for the task of collecting specimens to resolve a puzzle that was not finally sorted out scientifically until 1884.[16]

Banks' initiative stirred other exploits. It was largely due to his zeal and influence that the British Admiralty commissioned Lieutenant Matthew Flinders (1774–1814) to sail the *Investigator* and survey and open up Australia's southern and western coast. Banks, who kept his mind, and finger, on all things Australian, had been greatly impressed by Flinders' charts of Van Diemen's Land, made when he circumnavigated the island with George Bass in the *Norfolk* in 1798. But the voyage of 1801 was to have particular consequences for Australian science. Throughout the lieutenant's chequered career, Banks kept closely in touch with Matthew Flinders, whose charts of the Great Australian Bight and Spencer's and St Vincent's gulfs dispelled the notion that a passage cleaved the great continent from Carpentaria to Bass Strait. Banks also selected the ship's naturalist, Robert Brown, its botanical illustrator, Ferdinand Bauer, and the landscape artist, William Westall.

Of all Banks' protégés, Robert Brown (1773–1858) had the most seminal influence on botanical science. Brown was the first of the interpretive botanists to land in Australia. A former surgeon's mate in the Scottish Fifeshire Fencibles, he had become deeply interested in natural history while studying at Edinburgh University for a medical degree, and after meeting Banks in London, readily accepted his recommendation for the scientific post on HMS *Investigator*, which Banks himself financed at a salary of £490 a year.

The ship made its first Australian landing in December

1801 at King George's Sound, where Brown and Bauer, challenged by the astonishing floral richness of the area, botanised widely and collected some 500 species, all new to science. No adequate guide existed for the arrangement or classification of these plants. Brown, of course, had familiarised himself with the Banksian collection before he set forth. But the very strangeness of Australian flora presented difficulties. 'When a botanist first enters . . . so remote a country as New Holland,' the British botanist and collector Sir James Smith had pointed out acutely in 1793, 'he finds himself in a new world. He can scarcely meet with any fixed points from whence to draw his analogies. Whole tribes of plants which first seem familiar . . . prove on a nearer examination, total strangers, with other configurations, other economy, and other qualities; not only the species that present themselves are new, but most of the genera, and even natural orders.'[17] More than all others, Brown appreciated the point. His approach to the problem was professional and new. His method of collecting a range of plants during their various stages of development as well as in their mature state led him to adopt a system of classifying plants into families and genera. This moved him away from the Linnaean classificatory system, which was based on reproductive organs (the stamen and pistils) as the criteria for a basic division into classes, orders, genera and species, and towards the natural system of Jussieu, founded on the anatomy and physiology of parts. Bauer's detailed illustrations of floral and seed structure, made as he and Brown laboured, revealed the striking influence of Brown's approach.[18]

As the two men botanised, Flinders mapped the southern coastline, making 17 anchorages between King George's Sound and Port Phillip, including Kangaroo Island and King

The Great South Land

Island, Bass Strait. Seeds were sent to Kew and, clearly delighted with the pickings, Banks himself could not but reflect on Cook's more hurried passage up the eastern seaboard and the good luck experienced by his protégés in having a captain who made such great provision for 'landing and botanizing'.[19] Fortune would continue to favour botanists. While Flinders surveyed the northern Australian coastline in a leaky vessel, Brown and Bauer remained behind: Brown to spend ten months in Van Diemen's Land and later in New South Wales; Bauer sketching in Norfolk Island. In all, Robert Brown spent three and a half years in Australia, and when the unlucky Flinders was imprisoned by the French at Mauritius on his homeward journey, both botanist and illustator made their way to England on the repaired *Investigator*.

Like Banks, Brown devoted his life to science. On his return to England he became secretary of the newly formed Linnean Society in December 1805, and five years later librarian and private secretary to Banks. In 1811, Brown published Part 1 of his classical *Prodromus Florae Novae Hollandiae et Insulae Van-Diemen*, which covered 464 genera and 2000 species of Australian plants. The work, based on and extending the natural system of Jussieu from a great diversity of plants, embodied many profound observations on the anatomy, physiology and function of plants, and together with Brown's later essay, 'General Remarks, Geographical and Systemic, on the Botany of Terra Australia', published as an appendix to Flinders *Voyage to Terra Australis* in 1814, helped to transform botanical classification and to launch the new study of plant geography.

Throughout his long career, Brown exercised a powerful influence in botanical circles. World botanists sought his advice, not always with profit, for he was generally thought to be 'the driest pump imaginable'. His close control of his own and Banks' material proved even more obstructive after Banks' death, when Brown inherited a life interest in the Banksian collections and carried them off in 1827 to his new post as keeper of the Botanical Collections at the British Museum. Though he published only one part of the *Prodromus*,[20] he continued to write on Australian plants and to offer penetrating studies of the morphology, embryology, organic function and distribution of species until his death.

Banks' interest in natural history found many disciples to enhance and serve it. His contacts spanned the world. Allan Cunningham (1790–1839) was the last of his Australian collectors – a botanist trained at Kew who Banks originally sent to Brazil but ordered on in 1816 to join Phillip King's survey to complete the circumnavigation of the Australian coast. Cunningham had frequent occasions to land and botanise on the four voyages of circumnavigation that King undertook between 1818–21, and in June 1819 had the unexpected experience of collecting on the Endeavour River almost 50 years after Banks and Solander had made their rich excursions there. 'Much pleasure was derived,' Cunningham wrote the ageing Banks, 'in tracing your steps . . . and in detecting many plants then discover'd, which in all probability have never been seen in a living state since that period . . . You may with pleasure call to remembrance the remarkable fruited Grevillea in flower and fruit, so prevalent on the rocky Hills; the beautiful bluish-flowering Mymphaea . . . expanding its flowers and leaves on the surface of the Chains of Stagnant Pools in the Lowerlands; and the truly ornamental Melastoma clothing the muddy shaded margins of these small ponds.'[21] Cunningham would remain in the colony throughout the 1820s, botanising and exploring widely, and would return, after an English interlude, as Government Botanist of New South Wales in 1837. A well-informed and enterprising man, Cunningham provided a link between the era of British-inspired botanical discovery and an emergent colonial botanical science.

In an age when natural history was still the preserve of a few and where men of means and influence could lend it great prestige, Banks was the impresario of colonial science. Under his management, Australia became the centrepiece of a vast collecting empire whose boundaries stretched from South America to the Pacific, India and Africa, and whose hub was Kew Gardens and Banks' home in Soho Square. Throughout the 19th century, specimens collected in these outposts would change the structure of biological science. In Australia itself, the thrust that Banks imparted to the study of botany and zoology set the stage for the great natural history reconnaissance that, for the length of the century, characterised and dominated the development of Australian science.

The French investigators

The riches revealed by the *Endeavour* could not fail to impinge on Europe's scientific leader, France. Even as internal revolution rumbled, successive governments – Monarchical, Revolutionary, Napoleonic and Restoration – prepared a series of elaborately equipped expeditions to chart the new continent, investigate the nature of its fauna and human inhabitants, and collect specimens for the Paris Museum. To the considerable surprise of the British enclave at Port Jackson, which was still making its first raw acquaintance with the country, Comte de la Pérouse sailed into Sydney Harbour a mere three weeks after the first settlement, in February 1788. Sponsored by King

Louis XVI, the two vessels *La Boussole* and *L'Astrolabe* carried no less than two astronomers, a naturalist, a botanist, a mineralogist-meteorologist, a geographer, a gardener, botanical and landscape draughtsmen and two chaplains who were experienced naturalists. The exploring party spent over two weeks on the northern shores of Botany Bay, which now bears their captain's name, before they sailed on 10 March to vanish 'trackless into the blue immensity'. The wreckage of the two ships was finally discovered off Santa Cruz, New Hebrides, 40 years later, in 1828.[22]

With so signal a loss of men and equipment, the French National Assembly despatched Admiral Bruny D'Entrecasteaux (1739–1793) in 1791 to search for La Pérouse in vessels named, appropriately, *La Récherche* and *L'Esperance*. D'Entrecasteaux carried out cartographic surveys around the Australian coast between 1792–3, while the skilled botanist to the expedition, Jacques-Julien Houton de La Billardière, made large collections of botanical specimens, most notably from Van Diemen's Land, and recorded observations on the Aborigines. While the expedition found no trace of its lost compatriots, La Billardière's two-volume botany of the voyage, *Novae Hollandiae Plantarum Specimen*, published in Paris from 1804–7, linked Australia directly to the European scientific enterprise, and provided a major early tool of Australian botany.

Both La Pérouse and D'Entrecasteaux' expeditions were completely outranked, however, by the splendidly equipped entourage commissioned in 1800 by Napoleon aboard *Le Géographe* and *Le Naturaliste* under the command of Nicholas Baudin (1754–1803). Napoleon Bonaparte approved of science. It is also probable that, together with his agreement to the Institut de France's proposal to extend man's knowledge of the habitable regions of the earth, he saw the advantage of having accurate hydrographic surveys made by his own cartographers of the Australian coast. Whatever the motive, the two ships set sail from Le Havre in October 1800 and, travelling via the Cape of Good Hope and Mauritius, reached Cape Leeuwin in May 1801 and sailed northwards along the Western Australian coast. From Timor, the two vessels surveyed part of the north Australian coast and sailed around eastern Australia to Van Diemen's Land. By chance or design, *Le Géographe* met HMS *Investigator* at Encounter Bay, South Australia, early in April 1802, and despite the war that locked their nations in conflict at home, Flinders and Robert Brown boarded the vessel to meet Baudin and members of his civilian scientific corps.[23] They totalled, Brown wrote Banks, 'an uncommon number' when they left France.[24] Among them were the naturalist François Péron (1775–1810), the second-in-command, cartographer and naturalist Louis de Freycinet (1779–1842), the mineralogists Louis Depuch and Charles Bailly (the first geologically trained observers to reach Australia), the botanist Jean Baptiste Lechenault (1773–1826), the painters Charles Alexandre Lesueur (1778–1846) and Nicholas Martin Petit, and a number of astronomers, zoologists and anthropologists. It was the most significant concentration of scientific talent to be directed towards the Antipodes, though the expedition would suffer considerable losses of its scientific members along the route.

Focusing notably on Van Diemen's Land and its offshore islands and on Kangaroo Island, South Australia, the naturalist Péron and his assistants made impressive inroads on the unknown zoology of the region and collected large numbers of specimens of animal life. The artist Lesueur depicted the most striking fauna to furnish the plates of the atlas of the

Voyage de découvertes aux Terres Australes 1800–4, which Péron, and on his death Freycinet, published in France between 1807–1816.[25]

Dysentery and scurvy kept the French expedition in Sydney Harbour for several months in 1802. In November, *Le Naturaliste*, under Freycinet, embarked for France carrying the scientific collections, many live animals, and a number of the scientific corps who had become ill. Baudin, after a further sojourn in Van Diemen's Land until March the following year, would himself die at Mauritius on the journey home. Bad management, bad teamwork and inadequate supplies or knowledge of sound rations underlay the expedition's trials. But its scientific output was immense. The collections delivered to Paris numbered 100,000 specimens of animal life, including 2500 species and a vast array of botanical material. Péron's work alone marked a fundamental contribution to Australian zoology and strongly influenced the leading French comparative anatomist and systematist, Lamarck. At the same time, French observations of the Aborigines of Tasmania – their physiognomy, dwellings, weapons, implements and customs; their ceremonies, the sex and age of tribal 'bands', and their vocabulary – were of primary importance in providing some of the earliest detailed descriptions of the original inhabitants of the Tasmanian mainland and offshore islands in their natural state before white settlement in 1803.[26]

It fell to Captain Louis de Freycinet to continue his country's post-Napoleonic penetration of the Pacific. Chosen by the restoration government in 1817, he was given command of the corvettes *L'Uranie* and *La Physicienne*, and charged to circumnavigate the globe and conduct research into terrestrial magnetism, meteorology, and the shape of the earth. This time, his scientists were drawn from the ranks of his own officers. The problems of linking a group of civilian scientists with a naval expedition had caused well-remembered difficulties for Baudin.

Three thousand plant specimens were brought back to France from this Pacific cruise, a significant number being gathered at Shark Bay, Western Australia, and New South Wales. Although cases of natural history specimens were lost when *L'Uranie* struck a rock off the Falkland Islands on the journey home, French scientific leaders praised highly the work of the surgeon naturalists Jean René Quoy and Joseph Gaimard, whose observations were published in the zoological volume of the Narrative of the voyage and in scientific papers.[27]

In the last two decades of the 18th century and the first two of the 19th, science followed the flag. Both Britain and France established substantial collections of Australian species: both contributed significantly to early knowledge of Australian science. As a visiting naval power welcome in peace and war, France's long continued presence in colonial waters was the clearest pointer to the extraordinary importance of the great south land. Henceforward, the White Ensign rather than the Tricolour would dominate these parts, and the British Navy would serve as a persistent and influential foster-parent of colonial science.

CHAPTER TWO

Under a virgin sky

Australia was a botanist's paradise and an ornithologist's delight. From the earliest days of settlement, the educated members of the small community looked about them at the new landscape and began to collect and record their impressions of its natural life. Early governors and ship's surgeons scattered their journals with observations and with delightful, impressionistic drawings of birds and flowers. Captain John Hunter (1737–1821), second-in-command of the First Fleet, and from 1795–1800 the second governor of the colony of New South Wales, was a keen amateur naturalist who left 100 drawings of Australian flowers, birds, fish and natives, while John White (1756–1832), chief surgeon of the First Fleet, included 65 drawings of the colony's products and natural history in his *Journal of a Voyage to New South Wales*, published in 1790. In the first decades of the new century their ranks were joined by an expanding number of pastoralists, surveyors and settlers eager to dispel the loneliness of their raw existence with the study of natural science, who readily collected and arranged specimens and forwarded them to botanical correspondents and experts abroad.

Under a virgin sky

Astonishment and wonder accompanied these early observers along with their collecting bags, sketchbooks, compass, perhaps a knife or rifle, and their butterfly and insect nets. 'No country,' the marine surveyor and naturalist P.P. King enthused, 'ever produced a more extraordinary assemblage of indigenous productions – no country has proved richer than Australia in every branch of natural history.'[1] Certainly Australia, cut off by long geological ages from the other continents of the world, offered a unique ecological retreat for the unusual species of marsupials long extinct in other regions of the globe. It also supported, as observers were quick to note, some of the most primitive and grotesque forms of botanical and zoological life. 'In point of animated life,' George Bass reflected after his early navigation along the eastern coast and across Bass Strait, 'nature seems to have acted so oddly with this and the neighbouring islands that were their stores ransacked, the Departments of Natural History would be enlarged by more new and valuable specimens than could be acquired from any land.'[2] Australia was, indeed, as one observer saw it, 'a bright and savage land'.

Almost an entire century lay ahead in which its treasures and rare specimens were to be located, large collections made of new genera and species, the ethnology of the Aborigines investigated, the remote inland regions combed for their challenging revelations, the minerals and geology of the country discovered, and a tonnage of specimens shipped to England and Europe to be fitted within classificatory and taxonomic systems being consolidated at the centres of research. Yet despite this widespread curiosity about the natural environment and the activity it engendered, the science from the colonies that was to make the most significant impact, marking the achievement of local investigators and adding new comprehension to man's knowledge of the physical world, was the science of astronomy in Australia.

Astronomical pioneers

Of all the sciences inherited from the 18th century, astronomy was the most prestigious and advanced. In the first quarter of that century, the noted British astronomer Edmund Halley (1656-1742), in addition to identifying the famous comet, had determined the proper motion of certain stars. In the last quarter of the century, the remarkable work of William Herschel FRS (1738-1822) in enlarging and refining the scope of the reflecting telescope, initiated the science of stellar astronomy and made the exploration of the cosmos, the discovery of new planets, nebulae and galaxies the central undertaking of astronomical science. At first the focus was on northern skies. Herschel himself discovered the planet Uranus – the first addition to the classical list of planets – in 1781 and undertook the elaborate counting of the northern stars. In the southern hemisphere, Halley recorded observations of about 300 stars in 1677 while the French astronomer Abbé Nicholas da Lacaille (1713-62) determined the position of 10,000 more, using a small transit instrument during a visit to Cape Town in 1751-53. Otherwise, the southern heavens were totally unexplored. The point was not lost on Sir Thomas Makdougall Brisbane FRS (1773-1860), who was appointed to the governorship of New South Wales in 1821.

Brisbane was devoted to astronomy. Born in Ayrshire, Scotland, and educated at Edinburgh University, he was commissioned in the army, did service in the West Indies, rose to brigadier-general under his friend the Duke of Wellington in the Peninsular War where he 'kept the time of the army', and in 1808, during a lull in his military career, he erected

Under a virgin sky

a private observatory at Brisbane House, Ayrshire. He accepted the Iron Duke's nomination to the colonial post and, looking forward to the sublime study of *un ciel vierge* (a virgin sky), he rounded up the best instruments Troughton and Ruchenbach of London had to offer and took them, together with two astronomical observers, Carl Rümker and James Dunlop, hired and paid by himself, to Sydney to begin the exploration of the southern heavens. 'What,' he wrote excitedly from Sydney, 'may not be achieved?'[3]

By May 1822, the small observatory that Brisbane built at Government House, Parramatta, was working around the clock. Using the 'sweeping' technique employed by Herschel, Brisbane and his assistants made observations of stars, recorded eclipses, observed the transits of planets, kept records of the winter solstice, and in 1822 earned the distinction of becoming the first astronomers to mark the reappearance of Encke's comet. Initially, Rümker and Dunlop shared much of the observational work, while Brisbane supervised their researches and communicated the Australian findings to scientific peers. Readings and observations were sent to Edinburgh and London, reports were published in the *Philosophical Transactions*, and meteorological and astronomical data brought to the attention of observers abroad. Alive to the need for accurate weather records in a country where agriculture was of first account, Brisbane also used his office to eastablish a network of weather stations at Parramatta, Sydney Heads, Newcastle, Port Macquarie, Bathurst, Macquarie Harbour and the Derwent River. These stations were placed in the charge of convicts, and systematic records of wind, rain, temperature and climate were kept.

Brisbane also found time to preside over the colony's infant scientific society, the Philosophical Society of Australasia, to conduct meteorological researches on his country excursions and, importantly, to bring the Australian settlement to the attention of scientists abroad. In a remote convict and growing emancipist society, it was of inestimable advantage to have a governor who was an active patron of science. Yet these scientific activities were pursued against a background of intense political infighting; some among the leading colonists considered that the governor's 'stargazing' enjoyed precedence over his governance of men. Brisbane, however, conducted all his scientific activities from his private purse, and his stimulus to astronomy was immense. So impressive were the attainments of his small observatory that the New South Wales Government purchased Brisbane's instruments and scientific library when the governor returned to England in November 1825. Two years later, Brisbane's senior assistant, the German Carl Rümker (1788–1862), was appointed first government astronomer of New South Wales; James Dunlop (1783–1848) was subsequently made superintendent upon Rümker's departure for Europe in 1831.

Rümker published *Astronomical Observations at Parramatta in New South Wales* in 1829, a *Preliminary Catalogue of Fixed Stars* in 1832 and recorded the appearance of several new comets in addition to Encke's, for which he received the silver medal of the Royal Astronomical Society. However, a disagreement with the president of the society over the authorship of some of Rümker's work at Parramatta led to his dismissal as government astronomer in 1830. Much put out,[4] Rümker returned to Germany to become successively director of the Hamburg School of Navigation and director of the Hamburg Observatory in 1833.

James Dunlop, his successor, was a man of different stamp. A practical Scot, clever with instruments, it was Dunlop who contributed the major part of the meticulous observations for the Parramatta Catalogue of Stars,[5] made observation of the length of the pendulum (to determine the value of gravity) and produced a catalogue of southern nebulae, star clusters and double stars which won him the gold medal of the Royal Astronomical Society in 1828. He had gone to England with Brisbane two years earlier to help found an observatory at Makerstoun in Scotland, but, returning to New South Wales as superintendent in 1831, he was active in publishing material on the asteroids, planets and comets he observed on the now somewhat obsolete instruments at Parramatta. All three men won accolades from the elite Royal Astronomical Society. When that body conferred its highest honour, the gold medal, on Brisbane in 1828, it was honouring a remarkable scientific achievement in Australia. 'Our first triumphs in those fair climes,' observed the society's president, the distinguished astronomer John Herschel, 'have been the peaceful ones of science . . . and you will be identified as the founder of her science.' Brisbane's contribution, in effect, transcended the colonial convict stain in international eyes, and planted the physical sciences in Australia.

Enterprising collectors

With astronomy, the New South Wales Government, backed by the Imperial Exchequer, became involved in the direct funding of Australian science. It was a commitment begun modestly enough a decade earlier with some support of botany. In 1816, Charles Frazer (1788–1831), a former soldier, was put in charge of a small botanic garden at Sydney and, five years later he was given the title of colonial botanist. In Hobart Town, in 1828, William Davidson was made superintendent of gardens, while the following year, James

Drummond (1784–1863), arrived in Western Australia to plant a government garden on the Swan River.

Both Drummond and Frazer were enterprising botanical collectors. They made excursions from their coastal depots to seek rare inland species and exchanged dried and living specimens with herbaria abroad. Frazer accompanied the explorers Surveyor-General John Oxley (1785–1825) and Allan Cunningham on several journeys around New South Wales, in the course of which he established a small botanic garden at Moreton Bay. Drummond, first as government botanist and later privately from his farm in the Toodyay Valley, for 20 years ranged widely over the south-west and north-west regions of Western Australia collecting the strikingly colourful flora of that colony and consigning it for sale to botanists and herbaria overseas.

For the first four decades of the 19th century, botany rather than zoology dominated scientific enterprise in the colonies. The reasons for this are not hard to find. Banks put his thrust behind botanical researches, and there was less encouragement given to zoological science. Collecting sets of plants, moreover, was simpler than collecting fauna. Visiting naturalists and naval officers might draw the local birds and fauna, but, in collecting specimens around the coastline, their pickings were of necessity random, and they were not in a position to assemble representative types. The procedures for preparing zoological specimens were also more complex and demanding than those required for preparing plants. Faunal specimens had to be skinned and dried, organs preserved in solution, and precautions taken against decay and mildew on the long journey to England and Europe. In the absence of determined backing from the British Museum, it was not, perhaps, surprising that the richest and most diverse collection of

Under a virgin sky

Australian fauna remained for years that made by Baudin's expedition and deposited in the Paris National Museum.

Even in botany, collectors contended with special needs. Reams of paper were required for laying out and wrapping specimens. The expert, Robert Brown, was specific about the kind most suited to the colonies. 'Imperial Brown paper,' he advised Banks firmly in 1802, was 'much superior both for drying and preserving specimens, especially the rigid shrubs of this country; & what is no small advantage in our station, mice do not eat it.'[6] For many years, the accoutrements of collecting – the paper and seed boxes – had to be obtained from Britain. Colonial collectors were also hampered by a lack of scholarly resources. Reference books were hard to come by, libraries were assembled slowly, and for long periods there were no herbaria or museums where comparative suites of specimen could be seen. For decades, then, taxonomic work could not be handled in the colonies. The Banksian and Kew centres were where new species were named and classified, affinities determined, and nomenclature registered. Until his death in 1820, Banks was the patron of these botanical pursuits.

With Banks' departure, the role of coordinator and promoter passed to another gifted enthusiast, Sir William Jackson Hooker FRS (1785–1865), from 1820–41 regius professor of botany at Glasgow University. When he was appointed director of the Royal Gardens at Kew in 1841, Hooker had already amassed a large private herbarium based on his own gatherings in Scotland and Europe and on materials from a circle of collectors. He would push the fortunes of the Royal Gardens very far. 'Rising early, going little into society, and retiring late,' he not only managed to develop the gardens (reconstituted as a national institution in 1839) from a modest

11 acres under cultivation to 75, adding hothouses and 270 acres of arboretum exhibiting plants and shrubs from every quarter of the globe, but he made his own herbarium into one of the richest ever accumulated, and placed it at the disposal of the nation. Additionally, Hooker found time to publish numerous volumes and papers of his own researches,[7] prepare and edit 100 volumes of systematic and economic botany, and promote and assist the publication of the local floras of British North America, the British West Indies, Cape Colony and the African continent, and Australia. Sir William Hooker ran his botanical empire on a blend of charm, personal enthusiasm and tact. He was also generous in supplying books of reference to his collectors in the colonies.[8] Charles Frazer and John Drummond were his early collectors in Australia. Hooker published several of Drummond's long, descriptive letters on Western Australian flora in his *Journal of Botany*. He was also in touch with the young Tasmanian pastoralist and botanical enthusiast Robert William Lawrence (1807–1833), who collected for him widely around his Formosa estate on the Lake River. When Lawrence died in 1833, the breach was filled by the talented botanist R.C. Gunn (1805–1881), who collected Tasmanian flora for William Hooker and his son Joseph for 40 years.

Ronald Campbell Gunn was the most eminent resident botanist in the colonies. A one-time clerk with the Royal Engineers in Antigua, he arrived in Hobart in 1830 and, during the course of a diverse career, became successively assistant superintendent of convicts, justice of the peace and police magistrate at Launceston, police magistrate and superintendent of the Male House of Correction at Hobart, private secretary to the governor, Sir John Franklin, managing agent of the Formosa and other estates, a member of the Tasmanian

Assembly, deputy commissioner of Crown Lands for northern Tasmania, a member of a New Zealand Commission to determine the capital of that colony, and, towards the latter part of his life, deputy registrar of births, deaths and marriages, and, finally, coroner. Throughout these heterogeneous undertakings, Gunn devoted himself to collecting flora, and though, as he first wrote to Hooker, he was 'ignorant of botany', he quickly showed a flair for recognising new genera and species and developed perfect techniques for preserving plants. He read widely, became acquainted with the natural system through the works of Brown and others,[9] and with Hooker's ready help from London, built up his own scientific library while he collected tirelessly for the Kew herbaria and assembled a valuable herbarium of his own. In time, Gunn developed his own local circle of collectors and became the most knowledgeable botanist in Tasmania. Yet despite his skill as systematist and collector (he published *Observations on the Flora of Geelong* in 1842), he remained by choice the pragmatic observer, content to arrange and systematise and to leave the advancement of theory to botanists at the centre of research.

In this, however, Gunn had an unexpected role to play. In August 1840, Joseph Dalton Hooker FRS (1817–1911), Sir William's 24-year-old son, reached Tasmania as assistant surgeon and botanist of HMS *Erebus*, the command ship of the British Antarctic expedition of research and discovery under Captain Ross. Gunn and Hooker became firm friends, and from August to October 1840, and for a period of weeks when the expedition returned from the Antarctic in 1841, the two explored the countryside collecting for what became Joseph Hooker's famous *Flora Tasmaniae*, which was published in two detailed and beautifully illustrated volumes as

Part III of *The Botany of the Antarctic Voyage of the Discovery Ships Erebus and Terror* in 1859. Gunn and other Tasmanian collectors contributed substantially to the completed work, their roles reflected in the names of many genera assembled there. Gunn's role was pivotal. Hooker, in his important introductory essay to the *Flora*, paid elaborate tribute to Gunn, his Tasmanian mentor, for his knowledge of the vegetation they explored. He could, he said, recall 'no happier weeks in my various wanderings over the globe, than those spent with Mr. Gunn, collecting in the Tasmanian mountains and forests, and studying our plants in his library'.

Over the intervening years, Gunn continued to supply material for what Hooker cheerfully called 'a Flora of Gunn's collections upon the elucidation of which I bring my little personal experience to bear'. Hooker was also busy producing a Flora of the Antarctic and another on New Zealand plants, and between his return to London and the publication of the final volumes, he battled strenuously to sort his complex data. 'I almost wish I never had taken the thing in hand,' he wrote, venting the author's lament in a letter to Gunn full of affection and gossip in 1844, 'however I shall push on till I sink . . . I want grasses & *Cyperaceae* from V.D.L. very badly indeed & all cryptogamae but ferns . . . What would I give to have you here, old friend, for one little day?'[10] Although the young Hooker's letter to Gunn in Tasmania gave no express intimation of the turn his mind was taking from his Voyage researches on the geographical distribution of species, it was his Tasmanian *Flora* that became Hooker's vehicle for enunciation of his belief in the theory of descent by natural selection as exemplified in plant geography, which Darwin welcomed as 'the greatest buttress to the theory of evolution'. Thus Gunn's substantial supply of data and the enormous variations in species found by himself and other explorers and collectors in Australia served to challenge the concept of permanence and fixity in species and to shed new light on the origin and diversity of organic life.

Gunn's attitude and conduct mirror the early botanical experience in Australia. Confronted with a new environment, colonial botanists were happy to pick and fossick, comb forests and climb mountains, and devote their leisure to drying and preparing specimens for Kew[11]. To do so drew them into active participation in the wider scientific world. In return, overseas experts identified and classified their specimens, established their priorities (often putting the colonists' names to new species), published new genera and species in the journals of botany and, not unimportantly, gave the remote colonial botanists information on advancing scientific frontiers and a shared sense of collaborative exchange. With the rise of independent work and knowledge, this link with distant leaders would prove less sustaining in later years.[12] For the first half century, however, the relationship the Hookers established with colonial botanists created a strong tradition of cooperation, which set the scene for major botanical reconnaissance and laid the groundwork for the ongoing systematic study of Australian plants.

CHAPTER THREE

Entrepreneurs & explorers

In the zoological sciences, the man who was to popularise and give wide dissemination to Australia's bizarre and brilliant species was the British ornithologist and zoologist, John Gould (1804–1881). Gould was one of that rare breed of 19th-century researchers – the natural history entrepreneur. Born in Dorset, the son of a gardener, Gould acquired an early grounding in botany and developed an interest in stuffing birds. In 1827 he was appointed taxidermist to the Zoological Society of London and with a speed that was to become his hallmark, brought out two multivolumed works – *Birds from the Himalayan Mountains* in 1832 and the *Birds of Europe* in 1837 – which were illustrated by his wife Elizabeth Gould (1804–1841).

During the 1830s, Gould's interest focused on Australia where his wife's brothers, Charles and Stephen Coxen, were settled as pastoralists in the Hunter River Valley of New South Wales. Basing his work on the Linnean Society's bird collection and some specimens received from the Coxens, Gould issued a four-part synopsis on *The Birds of Australia and Adjacent Islands* in 1837–8, but, dissatisfied with the existing materials, he himself sailed for Australia with his wife, a small child, and the zoological collector John Gilbert in 1838.

Gould spent 18 months in the colonies, collecting first in Van Diemen's Land and its adjacent islands, later in South Australia, and then ranging out from the Coxen property on the Hunter River in New South Wales. He noted the manners and economy of Australian birds, assembled species, and observed and collected mammals. Elizabeth Gould was kept occupied continuously, making some 600 drawings of birds and animals. 'The country is very fine,' she wrote her mother from Hobart where the Goulds spent their first year, 'teaming with beautiful natural productions, both in the animal and vegetable kingdom.'[1] With her husband absent on field trips, she found herself much occupied sketching the native plants and tree branches as a background for her delicate and accurate depictions of the specimens he would amass. Her skill as an artist was of the first rank. Some of the birds she drew were reared in captivity; likenesses of others she caught from rapid depiction in the field. Gould depended heavily upon her tireless work and careful presentations for his important contribution to Australian science. Elizabeth Gould was the first professionally qualified woman natural history artist to draw in the colonies, and after her death in 1841, within a year of her return to England, her fresh sketches passed to other artists whom Gould engaged to bring out his brilliant publications on Australian animals and birds.

Gould's own part was far-sighted and diverse. He himself was an indefatigable planner and, together with his own field work, he employed a range of agents and collectors in the colonies. These included the naturalists Dr George Bennett and Charles Coxen in New South Wales, the botanists James

Drummond and his son Johnston in Western Australia, and naval officers surveying widely around the coast. His most notable assistant was John Gilbert (1810–1845), whom he met through the Zoological Society of London and brought to Australia on a salary of £100 a year. Gilbert began his collecting in Tasmania but soon moved to Western Australia where he gathered specimens in all departments: quadrupeds, reptiles, insects, fish, shells, crustacea, birds and their nests and eggs. He wrote to Gould enthusiastically from Perth at the beginning of September 1839,

Since I last wrote to you I have increased my collection to 150 Species of Birds; 13 Species of Quadrupeds; about 70 Skeletons; 7 Bottles of Reptiles &c; a few Fish; 500 insects; 400 Shells; a few Crustacea; and 3 or 4 hundred Plants.

I have been in the Interior as far as any Europeans have been settled, but unfortunately at the time I was there, the Natives committed several frightful murders on the white people, who to punish them killed several of the Blacks in return . . . It was considered very dangerous to move far away from the settlers houses . . . I was therefore obliged to work myself in the best way I could, but although my efforts in this respect were crippled, I still succeeded in obtaining many Birds not found at Perth . . . Among the more striking examples of my additions are, three more species of the Honey Sucker *tribe making now 15 Species in my collection, two species of* Nanodes, *differing from* venustus, *or* pulchellus, *I think, a different species of* Cinclosoma *from that we obtained in V.D.L., the* Bell Bird, *a singularly interesting bird, its note, as its Colonial name implies, resembling the tinkling of a sheep bell at a distance . . . an* Eagle *nearly as large as* fucose *but having a short tail; a* Falcon *like* Gyrfalco; *a* Swallow *with white throat and crown; a* Flycatcher *very similar to the* Tyrannidae *of America; a* Bird *nearly allied to the* Shorttailed Pheasants *of India;* Himantopus palmatus; Rrythrogonys cinctus; *a species of* Calamanthus, *a large* Reed wren *&c.&c.&c.*[2]

Gilbert followed Gould to Sydney in 1840, only to find, to his considerable disappointment, that his employer had already set out for England in April that year. But a diligent servant, he would, he wrote, now get on with Gould's 'List of Desiderata', which Gould had left for him in Dr Bennett's care. Though, as Gilbert pointed out, 'from the want of a knowledge of Latin I must remain in utter ignorance of a great many of them . . . I shall notwithstanding this be as zealous in collecting everything I meet with and study their habits, as if I knew them.'[3]

Zealous he was. By a series of chances which he was always quick to seize, Gilbert found himself at the northern station of Port Essington (near Darwin) where he collected extensively from July 1840 until March 1841. Though, as his letters suggest, his education was fairly limited, Gilbert paid close attention to the habits, food, nesting and migration of birds; he kept vivid notes on all the fauna he assembled; he recorded observations made by settlers and other visitors, and always noted whenever possible the animal's Aboriginal name. At Port Essington, he encountered several British naval officers collecting specimens for Britain's Haslar Museum. The news greatly alarmed his competitive employer, who sent Gilbert urgent instructions not to accompany any of the surveying ships calling at the station and to keep his treasures to himself. 'It will be better for you,' Gould warned from England, 'to be quite independent of Government assistance at least in that quarter for I have reason to believe we are both looked upon with very jealous eyes by the officers of the present Surveying vessels in consequence of the numerous valuable discoveries we, private individuals, have brought under the notice of the scientific [world] while Government officers go out and return without having achieved any of these pleasing results . . . I therefore put you on your guard; keep your discoveries quiet and also the direction of your future researches; in fact "put on the Scotchman" with respect to the purpose of your mission.'[4]

Gould could not but be highly delighted with the rich collections Gilbert's efforts procured. He praised him, commented on his new additions, and waited eagerly for all news. An assiduous employer, he also sent Gilbert lively instructions for further gains. 'In a word,' he exhorted, 'collect everything from the locality . . . If you are satisfied you can do no more, leave at the end of the breeding season of the birds . . . Collect all the Insects you can by sweeping and beating; do not pin them out as that can be better done at home: fill chipboxes or even phials, seeing that they are properly dried before closing them up or they will breed mites.'[5]

Later in 1841, Gilbert returned to London laden with specimens but, 'dreaming of kangaroos and cockatoos', he was soon back in Western Australia where from July 1842 until December 1843, he added 432 new bird species and over 300 new reptiles and mammals to what had become the finest collection extant of Australian wildlife. Early in 1844, at Gould's request, Gilbert moved to Queensland at Moreton Bay and, acting on his own initiative, there joined Ludwig Leichhardt's overland expedition to Port Essington, a journey by which his collecting in Australia would have encircled almost the entire continent. It was Gilbert's last service to

Entrepreneurs & explorers

science. Still actively collecting on 27 June and perceptively noting the behaviour of the Aborigines, he was speared to death near the Gulf of Carpentaria on June 28th. The last entries in his diary, which Leichhardt saved and sent with his collections to Gould in England, showed the persistent and careful nature of Gilbert's work.

Fri. 27 . . . Peristera again met with in large flocks, Brown in three shots killed 22 birds. During the day's march I again met with Myzomela nigra, *being a male bird in the change of plumage I did not recognise it until I shot it. The* Milvus isurus *is on the increase as well in numbers as in boldness. In the afternoon while sitting at the entrance of my tent skinning birds I had a tin case with specimens between my legs the lid of which I had opened to air the specimens enclosed, among which was the only specimen of my last new Honey-sucker. This was lying on the top and had deceived the bird so much that he darted down, and to my surprise and vexation fairly carried off my specimen . . . As yesterday native fires all around us. While out with my gun I shot* Monarcha trivirgata *or a nearly allied species for the first time in the expedition . . .*

Sat 28 . . . Today we passed another of the singular constructions of the natives which the Dr [Leichhardt] thinks are houses. This like the former had its detached platforms which have no marks of fires. During the day we passed many rings of fires made by the natives, doubtless for the performance of some of their extraordinary ceremonies, the inner space in all are perfectly bare, and the small fires forming the ring are about a foot apart, in some I counted ten and in other 12 fires. Round them at a little distance are round heaps of stones sunk in a slight hollow in the ground . . . But what the thing is for would be very interesting to know, perhaps in some way connected with their superstitions.[6]

Gould was to make extensive use of Gilbert's specimens and notes. In London he immediately embarked on the first of 36 parts of *The Birds of Australia*, which he completed in seven volumes in 1848. In this large-scale publishing venture, Gould employed a team of artists and continued to amass specimens from his far-flung collectors in Australia. Capable and determined, Gould himself described and systematised the species, supplied information on their economy and manners, supervised the drawing (often from his own rough sketches), colouring and preparation of the stone engraving and printing, submitted notes on new species to British scientific journals, and carried on a bird-stuffing business on the side. *The Birds of Australia*, a magnificent production of hand-coloured lithographs, which cost Gould £15,000 to publish, proved a financial success, and Gould followed it with an *Introduction to the Birds of Australia* in 1848. In 1855, he brought out his *Handbook to the Birds of Australia*, an invaluable two-volume reference of all known types, while his *Supplement to the Birds of Australia*, based largely on rare species from Queensland and North Australia, was issued from 1851–69. His last Australian work, *Birds of New Guinea and Adjacent Islands*, was completed and published posthumously from 1881–88.[7]

Gould also turned his attention to marsupials, and in 1842 published *A Monograph of the Macropodidae; or Family of Kangaroo*, much of it drawn from Gilbert's fieldwork and containing 30 plates. This he followed with *The Mammals of Australia*, with 130 illustrations in colour, published in 13 parts between 1845 and 1863.

Given this productivity, what was the measure of Gould's scientific work? By any estimate it was impressive and in the 19th century it had no rivals in the field. Though Gould's Australian publications represented little more than a quarter of his total work,[8] they marked the area of his special expertise. In ornithology his observations were thorough and scientific and were supplemented by original and, at the time, innovative information on the migratory habits of birds. In addition, Gould's experience as a bird stuffer led him to find clear relations between the structure and habits of birds. His work on Australian mammals, supported by careful field notes, was the first attempt to bring these unique fauna under review. Importantly, though his work was centred in London, Gould had seen the species in the field. As an entrepreneur in natural history, Gould himself was unique. Audubon,[9] the naturalist-illustrator and salesman and Gould's near contemporary in America, worked exclusively on American species, and while his paintings were more vivacious than Gould's, Gould outshone the American as a taxonomist and systematist.

Enterprising, shrewd, persevering, and a hard taskmaster, Gould kept one eye on his colleagues and the other on the marketplace. He rapidly gained acclaim as a zoologist and became a fellow of the Royal Society of London and president of the Zoological Society. However, his lavishly illustrated productions were not uniformly well received. There was criticism of his tendency to overcolour and of a certain static quality in his representational work. To the emerging band of professional scientists he was 'not quite a scientific man', and the botanist J.D. Hooker judged wrongly that the time 'for those gorgeous works of his has altogether gone'.[10]

Yet Gould conferred large benefits on Australian science. His pioneering works of reference combined scientific accuracy with aesthetic appeal, while his influence reached down into the present century with the formation of the Australian Gould League of Bird-Lovers and the re-publication of his splendid books on Australian birds and mammals, which continue to stimulate community interest in ornithological and zoological science. His publishing centre in London served as a clearing-house for zoological specimens, which he sold and distributed to British museums, while the network of collectors Gould subsidised in Australia encouraged the business of natural history and supplied important suites of specimens to the local museums. John Gilbert, in turn, represents the most able of the early naturalist-collectors in Australia; a discerning and assiduous observer whose excursions dug deeply into the remote regions of the colonies and whose record of detailed field work was carried to his last hours of life.

Science & exploration

Gilbert's association with a major journey of exploration typified one important aspect of 19th-century science. In a vast and untrodden country like Australia, the quest for geographical and scientific knowledge went hand in hand. No history of the botany, natural history or meteorology of Australia is complete without reference to the land explorers and surveyors who, lured by fresh pastures, broad rivers and perhaps an inland sea, moved inwards from the coastal settlements and penetrated the continent from all parts of the compass as the century advanced. These men made up the forward guard of observational scientists, and their notes and specimens, secured often against daunting hardships, greatly extended the knowledge of the country's physical and organic life. At first, individual explorers assumed responsibility for registering and collecting facts. Charles Sturt (1795–1869), George Grey (1812–98) the colony's successive surveyors-general, John Oxley (1783–1828) and Thomas Mitchell (1792–1855), the European visitors Paul de Strzelecki (1797–1873) and John Lhotsky (1800–?), with their varying degrees of scientific competence, made records of fauna, flora, rocks and climate on their inland journeys, and all brought back specimens for overseas collectors, and for the opinion of experts abroad. Some of the earliest descriptions and classifications of Australian rocks and species are found in the appendices of the published journals of these exploratory expeditions.

Many of the explorers were skilled writers, capable of communicating their encounters with the landscape and of translating their informal notes and sketches into publications that brought them recognition and acclaim abroad. Major Thomas Mitchell was a competitive and ambitious figure, who surveyed deep into Australia, bent on discovery, but he was also a gifted scientist who combined a knowledge of geology, palaeontology, mineralogy, zoology and botany with his surveying and artistic skills. Mitchell made a name for himself with his discovery of the 'Breccia Caves' at Wellington, New South Wales in 1831, from which he extracted fossilised bone specimens of remarkable, extinct marsupials. He despatched them to Britain's major comparative anatomist, Richard Owen.[11] Mitchell's *Three Expeditions into the Interior of New South Wales*, published in London in 1838, won him a knighthood. Strzelecki, a self-styled Polish count, explored widely across New South Wales, Victoria and Tasmania, propounded on the mineralogy, geology and climate of the colonies, and published competent findings in his *Physical Descriptions of New South Wales and Van Diemen's Land* in London in 1845. The more eccentric Czech-born Lhotsky produced an incomplete but highly perceptive work, *Journey from Sydney to the Australian Alps*, which shed light on natural history and man.

One of the most remarkable figures of the period was F.W. Ludwig Leichhardt (1813–1848), a German emigrant, who landed in Sydney in 1842 with the express intention of exploring the continent and opening its treasures to the world of science. Leichhardt had studied in Europe and England, was proficient in botany and zoology, and took a knowledgeable interest in meteorological science. From his graduate work he had come to perceive 'underlying connections' between all the sciences and saw himself as a 'discoverer'. Essentially, he had a dream: to explore the vast land mass of Australia, open up a land route from Moreton Bay in Queensland to the Swan River in Western Australia and unite geographical discovery with natural science. Between 1842 and 1844 he made a number of excursions between Sydney and Moreton Bay, collecting and reporting on the botany of the region, and in 1844 he set out with a party from Moreton Bay on an expedition paid by public subscription to attempt to link the eastern seaboard with Port Essington on the far northern coast. On the journey, which claimed the life of the naturalist John Gilbert, Leichhardt made extensive collections of flora some of which he consigned to experts in Germany and France. But collection and preservation in these rugged circumstances – common to inland explorers – was difficult.

'You may easily imagine,' Leichhardt wrote a European colleague, 'that I lost no opportunity of collecting everything new in botany. The length of time 14½ months enabled me to render the collection very perfect as I remained long enough within the two floras (that of the Eastern Interior, and that of the Gulf of Carpentaria, and of Arnhem's Land) to see the flower, the fruit and seed of almost every one. As my collection increased, I surrounded the different packages with green hide, which when dry, formed a fine box round them, and protected them from the hard usage to which they were exposed . . .

'But the time came when I had to open all my fine green boxes, to make a poor choice of the dried plants, and to throw the greatest number of them away unable to carry them any further, as 4 of my pack horses drowned, and the means of carrying my collection of plants and geological specimens were destroyed. I fully lost by this 4,000–5,000 specimens. There are however still some very interesting remnants which I shall send to have them determined, I shall do the same with my Moreton Bay plants, for I wish very much to establish a good well-named herbarium in the Museum in Sydney, that we have some means of ready comparison. Unique specimens you should of course send back.'[12]

Eager to link his great overland search for a land route to the Swan River with ever rarer findings for science, Leichhardt and his party disappeared without a trace on his third expedition from Moreton Bay in 1848.

Despite losses, exploration and the quest for scientific evidence went on. As the century advanced, colonial legislatures and scientific societies were quick to see the advantage of attaching qualified naturalists to exploring teams. From the 1850s onwards, the major expeditions combined the enterprise of collecting and reporting scientific data with the geographical objective of marking overland routes. In 1855–6, Victoria's government botanist, Ferdinand von Mueller, joined Augustus Gregory's North Australian

Exploring Expedition, which traversed the continent from the mouth of the Victoria River in north-west Australia to Moreton Bay, and collected new genera and species that formed the basis of his 12-volume work in Latin on new Australian plants.[13] A few years later, George Waterhouse (1815-1898), curator of the South Australian Museum, accompanied John McDouall Stuart as naturalist on his pioneering expedition from 1861-3 across the continent from Adelaide to the north-west coast and added important specimens of all varieties to the Museum in Adelaide he had helped to found.

Such penetrations of the continent were immensely beneficial to the growing local museums and, as Leichhardt had planned, provided suites of reference material by which colonial scientists, for long dependent on overseas examination, could begin to make their own systematic analysis of genera and species of all kinds – marsupials, reptiles, spiders, insects, rocks, fossils, crustacea, molluscs and birds – on home ground. Together with the natural sciences, ethnology assumed an important place; the Aborigines were a constant presence in the scientific reconnaissance of 19th-century science. They were, after all, the original inhabitants of the territory into which the naturalists plunged. Sometimes they were welcoming and friendly figures, ready to share information with their visitors, convey their names for plants and animals, and reveal their artifacts and customs to the observers' eyes. At other times, they were hostile forces, plundering the explorers' stores, threatening the parties, and killing a number of scientists who entered their domain. Gilbert in the Northern Territory, New South Wales government botanist Richard Cunningham killed on the Bogan River exploring with Thomas Mitchell, and Edmund Kennedy in

Entrepreneurs & explorers

North Queensland – all fell victim to Aboriginal spears.[14]

By the last decade of the century, scientists were attempting to make the Aborigines a specialist field of study and expertise. One expedition to attempt such a task was the Elder Scientific Exploration Expedition of 1891, which was fitted out at the private expense of South Australian mining and pastoralist magnate Sir Thomas Elder, and arranged by the South Australian Branch of the Royal Geographical Society of Australia. With three scientists and 44 camels, its aim was to cover a million square miles of Central Australia, collect and record extensive data, and acquire ethnographic material and photographs of the scattered Aboriginal tribesmen from those arid parts. But the expedition was no great success. Four thousand miles on, and 11 months later, it ground to a halt.

Speedier, better organised and equipped, and more productive in every way was the famous Horn Expedition of 1894, sponsored by another mining magnate, camel farmer and entrepreneur, William Austin Horn. This expedition was to direct its manpower and research to the eroded landscape of the red interior of Australia, from Oodnadatta above Lake Eyre, north to Charlotte Waters and the Finke River, and on via Alice Springs and Hermannsburg to the sandstone ridges west of the high MacDonnell Ranges. The area had been opened up: a telegraph repeater station on the Overland Telegraph Line tapped away in the lonely silence of Charlotte Waters, and there was a mission station at Hermannsburg; but the region was new to science. Moreover, the expedition positively glittered with scientists, 12 in all, including three academics: the university anatomist and director of the South Australian Museum, Professor (Sir) Edward Stirling (1848–1919); the Professor of Geology and Botany from the University of Adelaide, Ralph Tate (1840–1901);

Walter Baldwin Spencer, Melbourne University biologist and photographer to the expedition; J.A. Watt, a mineralogist; two naturalists and taxidermists, F.W. Belt and G.A. Keartland, and several more. Their purpose was to do a systematic appraisal of the geological structures and mineralogical resources of the region, its fauna and flora, and to learn as much as possible of its inhabitants.

Spending only three and a half months and covering 1200 rugged miles, the expedition proved a stunning success. New botanical species were added to the record, many more, known to science, were found in previously unexplored arid Australia, and 171 new species of beetles, spiders, reptiles and molluscs came to light. Baldwin Spencer made important discoveries of small marsupial species round Charlotte Waters and, with his camera – a new tool for ethnographic exploration – added significantly to existing knowledge of Australian anthropology. Spencer talked with Aborigines, sketched them, recorded their names for plants and animals (as men like Caley and Gilbert had done before him), learnt their topographic and tribal terms, and gratefully accepted their pickings of small marsupial specimens – the bandicoots, pouched mice and marsupial moles of the region – which added to his store. With Spencer's editorship at its core, the three-volume *Report of the Horn Expedition*, published in 1896, constituted in the words of his biographers 'one of the most substantial contributions to 19th-century Australian exploration'[15] and provided a major springboard for further ethnographic research.

Baldwin Spencer's conclusions about the Australian Aborigines, however, proved rooted in 19th-century thought. When, towards the end of his long and productive life, he wrote about them over a quarter century later, he emerged as a disciple of the Darwinian interpretation of the Aborigine as an Australian evolutionary form. 'Australia,' Spencer contended in 1927, 'is the present home and refuge of creatures often crude and quaint, that have elsewhere passed away and given place to higher forms. This applies equally to the aboriginal as to the platypus and kangaroo. Just as the platypus laying its eggs and feebly suckling its young, reveals a mammal in the making, so does the Aboriginal show us . . . what early man must have been like . . . It has been possible to study in Australia human beings that still remain on the culture level of men of the Stone Age.[16]

Whatever their conclusions and misjudgments within the limitations of intellectual frameworks of the time, these explorers and seekers were intrepid men, armed with a strong motive to learn and comprehend. Their struggle for knowledge, for clues and pieces of the faunal, topographical and floral pattern, offered a promising window on Australian science. The window's landscape was peopled by another race. The tentative probe of Western understanding reached into their environment and, at first eager, simplistic and crude, built upon a body of recorded observations that would yield keener perception and wider understanding as the next century advanced.

CHAPTER FOUR

Navigators & ship's naturalists

Possibly no single factor exerted as much pressure upon both the physical and biological sciences as did the expeditions of maritime research and survey that probed the southern and northern hemispheres in the first half of the century. Acting on a tradition that began with the first *Endeavour* voyage of Captain Cook, the British Admiralty increasingly assumed the task of pushing out the boundaries of hydrographic survey and of gathering geographical, meteorological and other scientific information about the oceans and continents of the world. Its exploits spanned the globe. Through the 1820s a number of Arctic voyages explored the north Canadian coastline and determined the position of the north magnetic Pole.[1] In the southern hemisphere, from 1818–22 Captain Phillip Parker King carried out the Admiralty's commission of completing the circumnavigation of the Australian continent, begun by Flinders, and later initiated the survey of the South American coast. In 1831, the Admiralty commissioned HMS *Beagle*, under Captain Robert Fitzroy, to complete this survey of South America's coastline and to carry a chain of chronometrical stations around the world.

Australia itself, through the 1840s and 1850s, became the target of a series of British hydrographic surveys that were aimed at opening up an easterly trading route across the northern coast and at marking a safe passage through the Great Barrier Reef. Three of Her Majesty's Ships, the *Beagle*, the *Fly* and the *Rattlesnake*, surveyed in those waters between 1837–50. The *Beagle* visited north Australian waters on her second expedition to Australia in 1837;[2] HMS *Fly* conducted hydrographic surveys from south-east New Guinea to Raine Island from 1842–6, while in the 1840s, HMS *Rattlesnake*, under Captain Owen Stanley, explored the north-east coast, conducted scientific experiments and charted the treacherous channels of the Reef.

In all these ventures science followed the flag. The alliance between geography and geophysics developed naturally in a naval service where knowledge of astronomy, meteorology, and magnetism were pivotal to navigational skills. But since Banks' successful collecting forays, the British Admiralty had also given encouragement to the study of natural science. From the late 18th century, the practice of adding a naturalist, often doubling as ship's surgeon or financed privately, to the ship's crew, was adopted readily by the Navy as an extension of its surveying role. It was a powerful lure to young scientific men. Some of Britain's most brilliant researchers cut their scientific teeth as naturalists at sea, and it was their observations and data that threw crucial light on the origin and distribution of species and ushered in concepts that changed man's thinking about organic life.

In this, Australia had a central part to play. Charles Robert Darwin (1809–1882), appointed unpaid naturalist to HMS *Beagle* on its world navigation from 1831–6, landed in Sydney in January 1836 and marvelled at the advances of a colony stained by crime. 'On entering the harbour,' he wrote his sister from Sydney, 'we were astounded with all the appearances of the outskirts of a great city – windmills, forts, large stone white houses, superb villas . . . This is really a wonderful colony; ancient Rome, in her Imperial grandeur, would not have been ashamed of such an offspring. My first feeling was to congratulate myself that I had been born an Englishman.'[3]

Darwin had won the coveted place of *Beagle* naturalist through the influence of Professor Henslow, who had introduced him to both botany and geology at Cambridge. Now it was principally as a geologist that the youthful Darwin inspected the Australian landscape and reported his observations in the summer of 1836. He had been greatly influenced on the voyage by his reading of Charles Lyell's *Principles of Geology*, a gift for the trip. The volumes were to provide important stepping stones for Darwin's acceptance of the infinitely long and gradual process of geological, and hence, organic, change; they were also to alert him to keen observations of the slow, progressive transformations shaping the contours of the earth.

Riding out to the Blue Mountains in the Great Dividing Range, he recorded his speculations on the origins of the steep sandstone valleys which, from a close inspection, he concluded were original escarpments carved out of the sandstone by the action of a former sea. At Emu Plains where the Great Dividing Range rises he wrote: 'About a mile and half from this place there is a view exceedingly well worth visiting . . . The point of view is situated as if at the head of a bay, the line of cliff diverging on each side, and showing headland behind headland, as on a bold sea-coast. These cliffs are composed of horizontal strata of whitish sandstone; and are so absolutely vertical, that in many places a person standing on the edge and throwing down a stone, can see it strike the trees in the abyss below . . . About five miles distant in front, another line of cliff extends, which thus appears completely to encircle the valley; and hence the name of bay is justified, as applied to this grand amphitheatrical depression . . .'

Darwin's first impression, on seeing the correspondence of the horizontal strata on each side of these valleys and great ampitheatrical depressions was that they had been hollowed out by the action of water. But he discarded this viewpoint in favour of 'the action of strong currents and of the undulations of an open sea'.[4]

He was wrong in these speculations. Nonetheless, his detailed observations offered the first serious analysis of the geological structure of the country and generated local investigation and research. The surveyor-general, Sir Thomas Mitchell, sought his advice, while Darwin's Australian Journal entries reveal his keen eye for significant detail and his capacity for generalising from one territory and set of physical circumstances to another.

After three weeks in Sydney, the *Beagle* sailed for Hobart, where Darwin again went ashore, geologising and botanising, climbing Mount Wellington, and making a brisk study of the Aborigines. Though he freely confessed that 'nothing but sharp necessity' would cause him to emigrate, and he left the shores of King George's Sound in Western Australia 'without sorrow or regret', he later found fundamental support for his evolutionary theory in the unique flora and fauna of the country and discerned in the Aborigine a pertinent illustration of his thesis of natural selection.

The arrival six years later of another young British geologist, J.B. Jukes, naturalist to HMS *Fly*, was to bring a further, and more lasting, geological perspective to the colonies. Jukes, trained in geology at Cambridge, contributed to early investigations of the rock formations of Australia[5] and was the first naturalist to seriously examine Australia's coral reefs. The *Fly*, accompanied by the schooner *Bramble*, set off from England under the command of Captain Blackwood in April and arrived in Sydney in October 1842. The ship would make two circumnavigations of Australia in the following three years, but the main purpose of the expedition was to survey and chart the channels of the Great Barrier Reef and to erect a warning beacon at the southernmost tip on Raine Island. 'On January 7 1843,' young Jukes began his *Narrative*, 'I landed for the first time in my life on a coral islet, in the northern part of the Capricorn group which is an assembly of islets and reefs on the north-east coast of Australia.' He was at once enthralled by the brilliant waters and the brightly coloured clams he could see from the surface; 'rich velvety blue or green spotted with black, and light brown spotted with yellow'. At Heron Island, whose structure he perceived as of great 'importance to the geologist' in typifying the Barrier Reef islands, and at neighbouring Swains Reef, Jukes got a closer look at living coral and the delicate beauty of its forms. A chunk of coral, hauled up on an anchor, showed 'a vast variety and abundance of animal life'; one block 'a perfect museum in which its outside glared with beauty from the many brightly and variously coloured animals and plants'.[6]

Little descriptive information about coral reefs was available when Jukes was making his study in 1843. Darwin had published his broad theoretical paper on 'The Structure and Distribution of Coral Reefs' in 1842. But Jukes was gathering increasingly precise and discerning information as the expedition moved from reef to reef. 'The coral appeared principally rounded masses of astraea and maeandrina, covered with their green coloured animals in a state of expansion,' he wrote. 'There were finger shaped madrepores of beautiful purple colours and leaf-like expansion of . . . branching corals.' In all, it resembled 'a great submarine cabbage garden'.[7] In the event, Jukes' chapter on the Great Barrier Reef included in his *Narrative of the Surveying Voyage of the Fly* became a classic of early Australian geology, the first published record of the reef, while its detailed evidence from field work among the coral afforded strong support for Darwin's hypothesis on the formation of coral reefs.

For Thomas Henry Huxley (1825-1895), nicknamed 'Darwin's bulldog', the period he spent in Australian waters on board HMS *Rattlesnake* proved the most formative and influential in his life. But, curiously, he found little to attract him among the exotic marine fauna when he toured the Great Barrier Reef between 1847-9. No voyage of British survey in the 19th century so felicitously combined the two strands of science and art. Commissioned under Captain Owen Stanley in December 1846, the purpose of the *Rattlesnake* expedition was to make a hydrographic survey of north Queensland waters from Port Curtis to Cape York and a survey of the Louisiade Archipelago and the southern New Guinea coast. Stanley (1811-1850), a physical scientist, astronomer and artist, had already served once in Australian waters as commander of HMS *Britomart* when he oversaw the first settlement at Port Essington, north Australia in 1838. He returned now on what would prove his last journey, but one in which his artist's pen would capture the atmosphere and the human and scientific activities of these long, demanding voyages of discovery.

The *Rattlesnake*, sailing via the Cape, dropped anchor in Sydney Harbour in July 1847. And it was there that Huxley began his researches on the structure of the delicate hydroza, tunicates and mollusca that float near the surface of the sea and prepared his memoir 'On the Anatomy and Affinities of the Family of Medusa' that was to transform the study of animal morphology and win Huxley election to a fellowship of the Royal Society of London at the age of 26.

Even more important to the young traveller, Huxley met his future wife, Henrietta Heathorn, in Sydney. 'We spent three months in Sydney,' he reported in a letter to his sister on 21 March 1848, 'and a gay three months of it we had – nothing but balls and parties the whole time. In this corner of the universe, where men-of-war are rather scarce, even the old *Rattlesnake* is rather a lion, and her officers are esteemed accordingly.' Out and about among Sydney society, he met and fell speedily in love with Henrietta. 'I think you will understand,' he wrote his family, 'how happy her love ought to and does make me. I fear that in this respect indeed the advantage is on my side, for my present wandering life and uncertain position must necessarily give her many an anxious thought . . . Three years at the very least must elapse before the *Rattlesnake* returns to England, and then unless I can write myself into my promotion or something else, we shall be just where we were. Nevertheless, I have the strongest persuasion that four years hence I shall be married and settled in England.'[8]

It took, in fact, twice that time. The Huxleys were married in London, and ready to found a dynasty, in 1855, when Huxley was already making a distinguished name for himself among the scientific fraternity. 'My scientific career,' he acknowledged later, 'practically commenced with work done in Australian seas and the strongest ties of my life were formed in Sydney.'[9] Struggling for position, Huxley would cheerfully have made his career in Australia. While there, he formed a stimulating friendship with one of the colony's most renowned resident scientists, William Sharp Macleay FRS (1792–1865). A graduate of Cambridge, Macleay had worked in the Paris laboratory of Cuvier and won considerable acclaim for himself in the 1820s for his classificatory work on species, *Horae Entomologicae*, which espoused the quinary or circular system founded on affinity and analogy between species. In 1836 he emigrated to Australia to join his father, the entomologist and former Colonial Secretary, Alexander Macleay. Huxley viewed W.S. Macleay as his mentor. He approved of his classificatory thesis, used him as a sounding board for his own philosophical and scientific thinking, and sought his help in gaining appointment to the chair of Natural History at the new University of Sydney. The plan fell through. 'As you *won't* have a Professor of Natural History at Sydney – to my great sorrow,' he wrote his old friend in November 1851 when plans for the university changed, 'I have gone in as a candidate for a Professorial chair at the other end of the world, Toronto in Canada.'[10]

Fortunately for science perhaps, and for Huxley's dynamic and influential leadership of the evolutionary cause, neither of the colonies took him up. Instead, he was appointed to the Royal School of Mines in London and subsequently became Hunterian Professor of Comparative Anatomy at the Royal College of Surgeons, London.

On his Australian visit, however, he was much engaged. He had, he wrote his sister on 1 March 1848, 'sent two or three papers home already to be published, which I have great hopes will throw light upon some hitherto obscure branches of natural history, and I have just finished an important one [the Medusa], which I intend to get read at the Royal Society.

The other day I submitted it to William Macleay (the celebrated propounder of the quinary system), who . . . I hear, werry much approves what I have done.'[11]

The *Rattlesnake* also visited Melbourne and Van Diemen's Land where Assistant Surgeon Huxley watched the first operation carried out under ether in Hobart Town. In April 1848, the ship set out on its first survey of the Great Barrier Reef, stopping at Brisbane where Huxley rode out on horseback to the Darling Downs. His curiosity would attract him to more dangerous exploits as the tour advanced. The barque *Tam-o-Shanter* had sailed with the *Rattlesnake* from Sydney, carrying the exploring party and equipment of the surveyor Edmund Kennedy (1818–1848). Kennedy, attended by a large party including the botanist William Carron and naturalist Thomas Wall, planned to carve a route from Rockingham Bay in central Queensland to the tip of Cape York. Huxley wished to accompany him and spent a lively few days with the party when they landed at Rockingham Bay journeying with them a short distance through the surrounding rainforest, sketching as he went. Again fortunately for science, Captain Stanley's orders brought Huxley back to safety: Kennedy was killed by an Aboriginal spear near his planned rendezvous point with Huxley at Cape York's Albany Passage, while only three of the party of 17, including the Aboriginal Jackey Jackey, survived the rigours of that terrible journey.[12]

During the next two years, the *Rattlesnake* made two cruises northward, pursuing its task of charting and observation along the Great Barrier Reef to Port Essington, through the islands off the south-east coast of New Guinea and along the Louisiade Archipelago. But Stanley would also fall victim to the hazards of navigational survey and scientific exploration: he died on board his ship in Sydney Harbour in March 1850, from an illness contracted in the Louisiade Archipelago and the stress of the arduous voyage.[13]

Huxley's journey to Australia spurred him to a life in science. Darwin, slowly accumulating his evidence for evolution, would keep Australian data tenaciously within his sights. When, finally, he published *The Origin of Species* in 1859, Huxley, one-time upholder of the quinary system, would exclaim, 'It was like a flash of light which, to a man who has lost himself on a dark night, suddenly reveals a road which, whether it takes him straight home or not certainly goes a long way.'[14] For the next quarter of a century, he would serve as an articulate advocate and spokesman for the evolutionary view.

Of the three major evolutionists who visited Australia in their youthful years, it was undoubtedly Joseph Hooker, the botanist, who worked most directly on Australian evidence and whose *Flora Tasmaniae*, published in the same year as *The Origin of Species*, both buttressed Darwin's evolutionary thesis and related Australia's biological material to the mainstream of scientific ideas.[15]

In addition to biological evidence, Australia was to provide a focus in the early 1840s for important developments in physical science. Commissioned by the British Admiralty under the command of Captain James Ross and Francis Crozier in 1838, the expedition of HMS *Erebus* and *Terror* had as its objective the establishment of a chain of magnetic observatories around the world, and the determination of the position of the south magnetic Pole. In its performance of these tasks, the expedition also brought the study of terrestrial magnetism to Australia. During one stay at Hobart Town, its men assisted in the erection of the Rossbank Observatory in 1840 in the grounds of Government House, with the active encouragement of the Lieutenant-Governor of the Colony, Sir John Franklin. Lieutenant Joseph Kay (1815–1875) stayed on to run the observatory, maintain detailed magnetic and meteorological readings, and to cooperate in programmes of international geophysical science.[16] Kay became Australia's first geophysicist and won election to the Royal Society of London in 1846 for his work on geomagnetism. His uncle, physicist John Franklin, gave it the highest praise. 'A more complete set of observations,' he wrote the expedition's coordinator in Britain, Sir Edward Sabine, 'was never, I will venture to say, forwarded from any observatory. I scarcely ever examine attentively the observations now in progress here, without receiving some new idea which I have not leisure or means of working out.'[17] Meanwhile, Ross and his ships reached the Antarctic towards the close of 1840, where he named several landmarks and was credited with marking the position of the south magnetic Pole.

British navigators and their naturalists were not the only scientific visitors to Australia as the 1840s dawned. In a period of burgeoning nationalism and scientific enterprise at home, the United States Exploring Expedition sailed in 1838 under Lieutenant Charles Wilkes and, after exploring the North American coast and the Pacific, reached Sydney in November 1839. Local residents were indeed surprised to awake one morning and see an array of foreign vessels riding at anchor in the harbour. Sydneysiders, nonetheless, were quick to take these ebullient visitors to their hearts. 'Our vessels,' Wilkes wrote later, 'were much visited by all classes, and a great many enquiries made respecting our accommodations etc. They inquired whether we had compartments on our ship to prevent us from sinking? How we intended to keep ourselves warm? . . . and where were our great ice saws? To all these questions

I was obliged to answer in that we had none . . . They saw us as cheerful, young and healthy and gave us the character . . . of recklessness of life and limb. Altogether, as a gentleman told me, most of our visitors considered us doomed to be frozen to death.'[18]

As befitted a venture designed to give America a higher international profile in navigation and exploration, the US Exploring Expedition carried a strong contingent of scientists. These included two naturalists, a mineralogist, a botanist, a conchologist, a philologist, two draughtsmen and a horticulturalist.[19] Wilkes himself attended to the physical sciences. He quickly established headquarters at Fort Macquarie, Sydney, and made pendulum, magnetic and meteorological observations, wondering as he did so why the Australians were not more interested in 'that glorious occupation – astronomy'. The mineralogist-geologist, James Dwight Dana, was destined to become a major figure of American science. He had published already his classic *System of Mineralogy* shortly before he embarked for Australia, and during the several months he stayed in New South Wales while the Expedition ventured on its Antarctic survey, he was to make positive contributions to Australian science. He explored the coal beds of the Illawarra and Hunter River, made collections of Australian fossils, and drew together a series of observations that would form the basis for important early generalisations on the geology of New South Wales.[20]

It was Dana who challenged Darwin's assertion on the shaping of valleys in New South Wales and rightly ascribed their formation to the continuing effects of running water eroding the sandstone over long periods of geological time. In the small scientific community of Sydney, he formed a warm friendship with the geological clergyman, the Reverend

W.B. Clarke who, acquiring his geological skills in Cambridge, had arrived recently in New South Wales. Dana found him 'somewhat more interested in geology than theology'. Together the two men explored around Prospect and Parramatta, and in the month of January 1840, rode forth on horseback to examine the rocks of the Illawarra district south of Sydney. They made rich hauls of fossils, which Dana would write up in his volume on the geology of the US Exploring Expedition. Nonetheless, he was sensitive to the position of a visitor invading a local scientist's domain. 'I hope you do not consider my observations, or intentions of publishing at all interfering with your plans,' he wrote Clarke cordially as he prepared to leave Sydney. 'I must satisfy our Commodore that I have not been idle and of course am expected to do something . . . Moreover the findings or facts of one will corroborate those of the others and afford double satisfaction to friends at home.'[21]

If Lieutenant Wilkes' exploration and survey of the Antarctic proved less spectacular and productive than his government had hoped (Ross cast doubt on the existence of land at the longitude and latitude Wilkes described and Wilkes faced court martial and discredit on his return home), the work of the civilian scientists published through the 1840s made a notable addition to natural and anthropological science. Dr Charles Pickering, the zoologist, bestowed substantial collections of Australian specimens on the American Academy of Science; the philologist Horatio Hale included observations on the Australian Aborigines in his *Ethnology and Philology* published in 1846; while Dana's output was substantial across geology and crustacea, and he corresponded with Clarke for many years on geological findings in both their countries. 'I should enjoy very much another ride over the hills and through the valleys of the country,' he wrote his old friend some years later. 'Will you never come to Yankee land? . . . Australia is a land for queer things, and therefore a grand place for Scientific Exploration . . . My time there was short, but it was spent most agreeably and instructively to myself; and that Illawarra District is a perfect gem of a place for Geology as well as for landscape beauty. It is one of the loveliest spots on the Globe. I shall look forward with great interest for the published account of your Labours, in which you have made so many important discoveries.'[22]

Scientific visitors would give international resonance to Australian science. But if the distant colonies offered an exciting collecting ground for the touring naturalists, the traffic was by no means one way. Contact with these naturalists – often brilliant scientists on the edge of notable careers – brought an invigorating breath of life to colonial workers, enlivening their efforts and linking them with the currents of research abroad. In turn, the colonial scientists encouraged the visitors, assisted them with local data, joined them on expeditions, and reaped collaboration and friendship in return. Ships' officers and naturalists collected specimens for them around the coastline, wrote for colonial journals, and donated specimens to local museums. Most importantly, the lines of communication established by the visitors remained open and fruitful when the voyagers sailed for home.

CHAPTER FIVE

Science, societies & the people

The new world of Australia was a source of science for countries at the centre of research. Britain and Europe represented 'metropolitan science': Australia 'science at the periphery'.[1] At first, the colonies were an exploring ground into which such patrons as the British Admiralty, the French Academy of Sciences, the Paris Museum of Natural History, the Haslar Museum in Britain[2] and Sir Joseph Banks sent their collectors and observers, drew out scientific trophies, and added them to the intellectual capital of their nation. New material gathered at the Antipodes strengthened scientific knowledge, augmented the growing systematisation of biological data and consolidated man's picture of the physical world.

Even so, quite early in the 19th century there were moves within the Australian colonies to establish a nucleus of Australian science. In the light of local zoological evidence, where the laws of Nature seemed reversed, a few enlightened colonists saw it as their duty to study and unravel this important evidence on the spot. In June 1821, therefore, a small group of prominent Sydney citizens[3] joined together to

Science, societies & the people

found the Philosophical Society of Australasia under the presidency of their newly arrived Governor, Sir Thomas Brisbane. Their purpose, set down in the first minutes of the Society, was both practical and oriented to research: 'to collect information with respect to the natural state, capabilities and resources of the country and the adjacent regions' and to publish, from time to time, 'such information as may be likely to benefit the world at large'. Despite clear challenges and the nice suspicion that, with the various taxonomic and classificatory systems being settled in Europe, 'Nature had been leading us through a mazy dance of intellectual speculation only to laugh at us at last in this fifth continent,'[4] the group accepted stringent conditions of membership, and agreed to contribute regular papers and to catalogue their libraries for collective use. But their major goals, conceived with vision, proved short-lived. A number of exploratory papers on astronomy, geology and meteorology were read,[5] but the Philosophical Society fell victim to the rancorous political atmosphere of Sydney and expired in August 1822.

The experience of neighbouring Tasmania was no less precarious. There, Dr John Henderson, a former surgeon in the Indian Army, inaugurated the Van Diemen's Land Scientific Society under vice-regal patronage in 1829 and drew a keen initial audience. His society attracted the attention of visiting British scientist Matthew Friend, who arrived in Sydney in April the following year to locate correspondents for British scientific societies. He addressed the Tasmanians and emphasised the importance of the materials they might bring to light. Their mysterious country, he reminded them, 'would tend much to illustrate many of the most abstruse and important questions in the history of organic life'.[6] Henderson himself attempted to postulate a mathematical system for the classification of plants, animals and minerals based on 'permanent and intrinsic qualities observed in the specimens'. But his society vanished unceremoniously within two short years.

Motivated colonials recognised the importance of fostering science. Yet the broader colonial community was unsympathetic to scientific pursuits. 'Zoology, Mineralogy and Astronomy and Botany, and other sciences,' one Sydney newspaper declared firmly in 1833, 'are all very good things, but we have no great opinion of an infantile people being taxed to promote them.'[7] The attitude was widespread. Society put a heavy emphasis on practical arts. Those who flocked to join the Van Diemen's Land Society were drawn more by the presence of the governor than by an interest in scientific advance, and the papers given showed a marked bias towards the useful arts. This failure to find a cultural foothold inhibited the growth of science. Books were hard to obtain; journals devoted to the arts, science and religion suffered precipitate eclipse,[8] and local scientists experienced difficulty in publishing papers in the colonies.

The most vital encouragement to the scientific community came from the presence of interested governors. Sir John Franklin FRS (1786-1847), who arrived as Lieutenant-Governor of Van Diemen's Land in 1837, spurred considerable scientific action in the colony. A physicist and Arctic explorer who had first spent time in Australia as midshipman on the *Investigator* at the beginning of the century, he lent support to the founding of a magnetic observatory in the grounds of Government House,[9] and soon after his arrival, stimulated the formation of the Tasmanian Society of Natural History from a handful of working naturalists in the colony. The Society grew, and through its *Tasmanian Journal of Natural Science*,

Science, societies & the people

it attracted membership and contributions from other colonies. Franklin's hopes were fittingly realistic, as one letter to a colleague showed: 'We are endeavouring to get up a small scientific society,' he wrote, 'composed first of only 6 or 8 members, as many individuals I believe as we can muster who take any lively interest in anything but what relates to party politics, wool and oil . . . Nevertheless, if it should tend to excite an interest and disseminate anything like a taste for pursuits which have no tendency to excite the inflammatory propensities of our oddly constituted community, it will have a moral advantage . . . of which we are greatly in want.'[10]

Three volumes of the *Tasmanian Journal* were published between 1842–48, under the principal editorship of Ronald Gunn, and, with a leaven of reportage of scientific discoveries overseas, it provided the first scholarly journal of Australian science. The *Journal* ranged widely over questions of Australian palaeontology, botany, zoology, conchology, ornithology, meteorology, and the more practical problems of irrigation and hydrology, and secured a considerable roster of resident and corresponding contributors. Jane, Lady Franklin lent her support. She participated in the society's activities, toured the colony taking an interest in its botany and natural history, and personally established an elegant classical building near Hobart to serve as a cultural museum. When, during 1838, Elizabeth Gould stayed with the Franklins at Government House during her husband's collecting tours, it became the meeting place of two of the earliest scientifically-minded women in the colonies.

With the Franklins' departure from the colony in 1843, the Tasmanian Society's affairs passed largely to Gunn in Launceston and, for a period, the association functioned alongside the Royal Society of Van Diemen's Land for Horticulture,

Botany and the Advancement of Science, which the new lieutenant governor, Sir John Eardley-Wilmot, founded on his arrival in the colony. Though this more popular association became the first royal society in the colonies in 1844 (and the first royal society outside England), the advancement of scientific investigation continued to come from the Tasmanian Society until it was amalgamated with a revitalised Royal Society of Van Diemen's Land, under the active patronage of another scientific governor, Sir William Denison FRS (1804-71) in 1849.

In striking contrast, the 'senior' colony of New South Wales possessed no scientific society of its own. Leading naturalists pursued their own researches and contributed specimens to the Australian Museum. Some joined the Tasmanian Society and sent occasional papers to the *Journal of Natural Science*. But for the most part, they looked to British colleagues for stimulus and published their findings in the journals of science abroad.

The geologist the Reverend W.B. Clarke was one scientist who became a notable publicist for Australian science. Throughout the 1840s, in newspaper articles and editorials, he railed against the intellectual apathy of the colony and worked to alert public interest in the findings of Australian science.[11] In 1850, two Sydney doctors, Henry Douglass and William Nicholson, founded the Australian Philosophical Society, but it achieved stability only after Sir William Denison arrived as Governor of New South Wales (1855-61). Under him, the newly styled Philosophical Society of New Wales emerged in 1856, and after ten years of practical investigation and research, provided the foundation of the important Royal Society of New South Wales.

These colonial societies, struggling from uncertain bases,

found their institutional matrix in models overseas. British science and British institutional influences strongly permeated colonial science. Colonial scientists, however, both took pride in their contribution to the international community and cultivated a growing expertise and confidence of their own. There were two impulses behind their work: to keep contact and collaborations with metropolitan science, and to stimulate local scientific activity and discussion.

One important centre for scientific discourse was the home in Elizabeth Bay, Sydney, of the colonial secretary, Alexander Macleay FRS. Macleay had been a dedicated collector of exotic insects before taking up his administrative post in 1826 and brought his collection to the colonies. There he found time from government duties to build a beautiful garden on the shores of Sydney Harbour and, with his son William Sharp (W.S.) Macleay, provide hospitality for the colony's visitors and resident scientists. Young Joseph Hooker declared it a 'botanist's paradise' and wrote to his father nostalgically of the smell of camphor and specimens in W.S. Macleay's workshop, 'reminding me strongly of olden times especially as I found everything in the inevitable mixture of confusion and order'. The explorers Charles Sturt and Thomas Mitchell were frequent guests, P.P. King was an intimate, while the visiting scientists Darwin, Gould and Huxley, and the US Exploring Expedition scientists, found a handsome welcome there.

The quiet and learned W.S. Macleay became a key figure in the scientific community and formed strong bonds of friendship with other scientists. Clarke often journeyed across the harbour with fossils in his pocket, and much lively discussion of the palaeontology and stratigraphy of the colony filled Macleay's book-lined study or the drawing room at

Elizabeth Bay House. The two men also assailed each other with letters, digging into the evidence of the 'Book of Nature' or indulging in the exercise of shifting and stretching the literal account of Creation to fit man's growing knowledge of geological facts. William Sharp was himself an eclectic scientist with a special interest in marine biology which Thomas Huxley valued highly in his research. Another biologist who enjoyed his friendship was Dr James Stuart (1802-1842), an army surgeon employed as superintendent of the Quarantine Station at Sydney's North Head. Stuart, an artist as well as a naturalist, recorded a range of marine and other specimens from his seaside station and was a frequent caller upon his neighbour around the harbour. Stuart died young from typhus contracted at the Quarantine Station, leaving his valuable collection of drawings and specimens to Macleay.

The Macleay dynasty played a unique role in colonial science. Through several generations, they were catalysts and contributors. Alexander was the driving force behind the annual grant of £200 made by the Imperial Government to the Colonial Legislature in 1827 to found a Colonial Museum. The small enterprise took shape in June 1829 when a zoologist, William Holmes, was appointed by the Governor as custodian, while Macleay, as Colonial Secretary, directly administered the small Museum until a governing Committee of Superintendents was appointed in 1836 to run both the Botanic Gardens and the newly named Australian Museum. Dr George Bennett, a Sydney naturalist, was appointed Secretary and Executor the following year. Fifteen years later, the value of the collections had so increased that the Australian Museum was incorporated by Act of Parliament in 1853 and placed in charge of a Board of Trustees.

With the death of W.S. in 1865, the Macleay mantle passed to his younger cousin, W.J. (later Sir William) Macleay (1820–91), who emigrated from England to join the family in 1839. A pastoralist and politician, William Macleay developed great skills as a cataloguer and collector and cultivated an enterprising interest in science. He helped found the Entomological Society of New South Wales in 1862 and the important Linnean Society of New South Wales in 1874, and, the following year, privately funded and fitted out the *Chevert* expedition to explore the New Guinea coast – the first venture from the colonies to science beyond their borders. Inheriting the family scientific treasures, he bequeathed them with his own rich collections, strong in vertebrates and invertebrates, to the University of Sydney as the Macleay Museum. 'As a whole,' he summed up the gift, 'it may be regarded as one of the finest and most valuable in the world.'[12]

Museums

The other Australian colonies may have lacked influential dynasties, but they too, during the burgeoning 1850s, founded important museums of their own. The discovery of gold in New South Wales and Victoria in the early 1850s filled the colonial coffers and encouraged new governmental initiatives in science. The South Australian Museum was established under naturalist curator George Waterhouse (1815–1898) in 1856, and its shelves and drawers expanded steadily with gifts from explorers and collectors. There was also fruitful cross-fertilisation between colonial museums. The naturalist and painter George French Angas (1822–86), who collected and illustrated natural history on three major exploring expeditions in South Australia in the 1840s, later became curator of the Australian Museum (1835–60), where he supervised the classification and arrangement of the first public collection of Australian specimens.[13]

The greatest museum builder in Australia, however, was Victoria's Frederick McCoy (1817-99). A fiery and dogmatic Irishman whom colleagues in Britain seemed anxious to export to Melbourne to fill the new university's first natural history chair, McCoy had no degree but arrived in Victoria in 1855 with a background of appointments as curator of the Cambridge Woodwardian Museum, a member of the Irish Geological Survey, professor of natural science at Trinity College Dublin and authorship of several works on palaeontology. A grant from the Victorian Legislature had already created the nucleus of a museum associated with the Philosophical Society of Victoria in 1856, and its official zoologist, Wilhelm Blandowski, added substantially to its initial collections from an exploring trip along the Murray and Darling Rivers in 1857-58, financed by the government. Meanwhile, at Melbourne University, established on the outskirts of Melbourne in the mid-1850s, McCoy built up an impressive economic and mining museum which attracted great attention from the public. Fired by this success, and already negotiating with the governor of Victoria on the housing of the national collection, McCoy, in the summer of 1856, unceremoniously carried off the natural history collections, despite protests from the Philosophical Society. His action brought reward. McCoy was named both palaeontologist of the Victorian Geological Survey in 1856 and gazetted director of the National Museum of Victoria in 1858.

Such an act of brigandage was characteristic of McCoy's administration of the Victorian Museum. For a remarkable 40 years he carried on a spirited battle with the government to retain the collections within his care and as a resource for the teaching at the university of natural science. Despite considerable opportunism, his testimony was sound enough. Moreover, McCoy conspicuously outshone his contemporaries in enriching the resources of his museum. Under his directorship a number of large and important zoological and entomological collections came within his care, and he cultivated a network of correspondents to secure the finest materials from private collections abroad. McCoy was not above bullying his overseas agents to keep them on the go, but he was ready to use his own finances, when Government funds were not forthcoming, to ensure that valuable specimens should not be lost. Relentlessly tracking down rare specimens 'in first-rate condition only' from abroad, he also added to the display collection from dead specimens from the local zoo. Stubborn, resourceful, frequently devious in the cause of science, McCoy never shrank from applying pressure to capture an important gift or from wresting a relic from an acquisitive rival, as his correspondence shows. He spoke with disapproval of the 'ostrich-like gluttony' of the British Museum.

When, by Act of Parliament of 1869, the combined administration of the Victorian Museum, the Melbourne Public Library and the Victorian National Gallery passed to the trustees, the museum's transfer was largely one in name. McCoy remained the aggressive, articulate and immensely jealous guardian of his domain. Despite his many commitments as a professor, his museum activity remained central to his scientific work. His *Prodromus of the Palaeontology of Victoria*, written from the museum collections, was published from 1874–82. With the transfer of the mining and economic exhibits at the university to the new Industrial and Technical Museum (later Museum of Applied Science) in 1870, McCoy stepped up his demand for funds and pressed for enlarged accommodation for the growing collections of natural science. His long siege marked a triumph for one man. By 1889, through donation, purchase and some sleight of hand, McCoy had amassed a collection valued at nearly £48,000 and created a museum regarded as the richest in the southern hemisphere. He was knighted for his scientific services in 1891. Yet with his death in May 1899, the Government undoubtedly heaved a heartfelt sigh. Indeed, the breath was scarcely out of McCoy's body before the legislature closed down the university exhibits and whisked the entire collection, then numbering over 510,000 specimens, to the present site of the National Museum.

McCoy was the arch example of the architect of the colonial museums. With appropriate modifications of method, with the help of explorers and collectors, Government funds, trustees and able curators, other museums in other Australian cities were able to attain the standards his labours achieved.

At the Australian Museum, Gerard Krefft (1830–81), a German emigre, followed Angas as curator in 1861 and developed a museum that was both scientific and an attraction to the public. Krefft exported knowledge of new Australian species to the centres of the learned world. His pioneering work *The Snakes of Australia* (1860) was published at his own expense; he went on to write *The Mammals of Australia* (1871); *A Short Guide to the Australian Fossil Remains in the Australian Museum* (1870) and *A Catalogue of the Minerals and Rocks in the Australian Museum* (1873), and he ventilated many scientific issues and new information in the Sydney press. A competent researcher, now generally regarded as the best vertebrate zoologist of his day, Krefft believed ardently that new scientific knowledge should be informatively presented in the Museum. 'It stands to reason,' he wrote a friend on the matter, 'that a single accumulation of all kinds of bugs, beetles, butterflies and cockroaches without explanation is about as good a vehicle to education [as] . . . the dressed window of any large grocery establishment.' He particularly hated the mouldy 'preserved' specimens so dear to some of his trustees' hearts and wrote roundly on the subject of the exhibition of fishes to the premier, Sir Henry Parkes: 'I rely on the splendid illustrations which can now be purchased for a mere song, a thorough well coloured series with a few aquaria and plenty of explanation will teach people more and is far cheaper than all the rotten fishes crammed into bottles and covered by a brown fluid.'[14]

Krefft's aggressive nonconformism and outspoken opinions did not endear him to his museum's trustees, nor for his part, did he conceal his contempt for their tendencies to feather their own nests and collections at the museum's expense. Inevitably, their disharmonies put them on a collision course. In September 1874, in the midst of several inquiries, one parliamentary and one mounted by the trustees, Krefft – accused of crimes that ran from occasional intoxication to the wilful smashing of a fossil jaw – was asked to show cause why he should not be dismissed. Believing the government to be on his side, and with the two scientists George Bennett and W.B. Clarke whom Krefft respected newly resigned from the imbroglio as trustees, the embattled curator locked himself and his family into their residential quarters at the museum. He clearly expected to sit it out. Not so. He was outflanked by the remaining trustees who, hiring the services of two prize-fighters, wrenched open Krefft's door, picked him up as he sat in his chair, and dumped him in the street outside. It was an undignified end to a wrangle that centred on proper management and the trustee's acceptable degree of authority at the museum, and a vivid example of bigotry and animosity in science. For Krefft, his turbulent expulsion ended his career. He died in 1881. 'If he had been as much at home with men as with animals or could have charmed his Trustees as clearly as he did his snakes,' one newspaper commented wisely, 'his fate would have been a much fairer one.'

It was Krefft, however, who put his finger on the pulse of the museum as a forum of people's science. His successor, Edward Pierson Ramsay (1842–1916), the first Australian to be appointed as curator, would carry the tradition forward. A visitor to the Australian Museum shortly aftet Ramsay's appointment was delighted by the display. 'All the collections,' he reported, 'are well and distinctly named. Perhaps nowhere in Australia is there anything approaching the magnificent collection of Australian marsupial mammalia here exibited, and the specimens are so well preserved, and most of them mounted in such picturesque attitudes, that there is none of the formal stiffness we usually see in museum collections. Many of these marsupials are now very rare, and in a few years many more will be completely extinct. It is therefore a fortunate thing for Australian naturalists that such a good collection as this has been made in time.'[15] It was a long step from the small crowded room of 1827 and from the crowded packages that exported so many of the newly found products of Australian natural history to display cases abroad.

By the mid-1850s, several colonies boasted a scientific museum of their own. The Brisbane Museum threw open its doors in 1855, Western Australia followed considerably later in 1892, while Tasmania's second city, Launceston, opened the Queen Victoria Museum in 1891. Men, women and children flocked to these repositories of natural science. There they saw exhibited not only Australian species, great and small but, most excitingly, the huge fossil specimens of extinct marsupials which pastoralists, sinking their artesian wells, dug up from the deep strata of the old continent. Public debate over the origin and fate of these huge animals filled columns of the press and the colonists streamed to view their artful reconstructions. Like the Botanic Gardens which, in Sydney, were opened to the public in 1831, the museums filled a special cultural need. They stimulated the minds of people far flung from similar displays 'at home', and, as the colonial clergy hoped devoutly, acquainted the poorly educated inhabitants with the Australian evidence of God's universe of design.

The people's science

This popular quest for scientific knowledge found other outlets. During the 1830s and 40s the egalitarian Mechanics Institutes sprang up in the eastern colonies; at Newcastle and Sydney, in Hobart and Launceston, later in Melbourne and Ballarat, and in such country towns as Goulburn and Singleton in New South Wales and Ipswich in Queensland. Framed on a British model, their aim was to 'contact all men through education'; and women, too, were allowed through their doors. Their origins, however, were essentially working class. The Sydney School of Arts and Mechanics Institute was founded, for example, in 1833 by a group which included a saddler, John Reilly, a bootmaker, William Hipkiss, a builder, David Taylor and J.R. Fenwick, a boy. The biggest of the Mechanics Institutes offered evening lectures in a range of scientific subjects – as well as in literature and the arts – and included courses in botany, astronomy, cosmology, geology, physics, chemistry and anthropology, while more technical subjects were developed at the mining centre Mechanics

Institute at Ballarat. With their growing libraries and laboratories, into which the colonial legislatures dropped modest funding, the Institutes afforded considerable opportunities for public education in science.[16]

On a less routine basis, but on a grander and more exhilarating scale, the International Exhibitions of science and technology attracted a large and enthusiastic public. Following in the wake of Britain's Great Exhibition at the Crystal Palace in 1851, exhibitions mounted in colonial capitals become a form of advertising to the world. After the Prince Consort gave the imaginative start to British science and technology, similar exhibitions followed in Paris in 1854 and in the 1860s and 1870s, and in Vienna in 1873. London competed with another great exhibition in 1862, and the cities of Sydney and Melbourne set out to air their growing industrial, scientific and technological resources in International Exhibitions staged in 1870, 1879, 1880 and 1888. In one respect, these fairs represented an aspect of the foreign policy of the colonies. The world's exhibitions, as one observer noted, were 'the nineteenth century's official visiting cards'. Certainly the great buildings erected for the displays exuded a strong sense of state occasion and largesse. Commissioners were appointed; exhibits poured in from countries round the world, and every kind of object – grown, mined, designed and manufactured, from blocks of coal to steam hammers – was presented for examination. With this wide window on the world, colonists responded eagerly to the new sights and to the accomplishments and offerings of their colony. Sydney's great exhibition of 1879 drew over one million people; a year later the International Exhibition sponsored in Melbourne attracted at least 300,000 more. At Melbourne's Centennial Exhibition of 1888, attendance climbed to two million. On a population basis such figures led the world. Governments, parsimonious in supporting investigative scientific matters, did not stint the display case of technology and science. The Centennial Exhibition, with its enlargement of Melbourne's great glass Exhibition Building, cost the Victorian Government over £250,000. Similar, though smaller, International Exhibitions were also mounted in Adelaide (1881 and 1887), Perth (1881), and Hobart (1894–5), together with the no less competitive Intercolonial Exhibitions in Melbourne (1866–7), Sydney (1869, 1870 and 1877), and Brisbane (1877). Science and technology emerged in a new context of economic progress, commerce and trade. Medals were struck, symbolic artistic tableaux assembled, papers and essays published, and the colonies stood with growing confidence among the nations of the world.[17]

By the mid-1850s, the Australian scientific community was maturing. Both quantitatively and qualitatively that decade brought notable changes to the community of science. The gold discoveries attracted many scientists to the colonies, to be absorbed, when gold proved fickle, into government surveys and museums. Government geological surveys arose in response to the search for metals; museums and observatories followed in the wake of prosperity and self-government, and the universities of Sydney, Melbourne and later Adelaide, founded for the training of professional men and scientists, brought qualified candidates from British universities to fill scientific chairs. These infusions fortified the scattered communities of science. In the newly formed colony of Victoria (which had separated from New South Wales in 1852) two societies with closely related objects, the Victorian Institute for the Advancement of Science and the Philosophical Society of Victoria, emerged in 1854 to link the dual purposes of disinterested scientific enquiry and ultilitarian application of science. Such concepts were paralleled in other colonies. A maturing concern to collect facts and examine and evaluate theory was written alike into the constitution of the Adelaide Philosophical Society formed in 1853 and the Queensland Philosophical Society which emerged soon after the separation of that Colony in 1859. A decade later the Adelaide Philosophical Society became the first forum for the ventilation of Darwinian theory in Australia.[18]

The institutionalism of science, begun in the 1850s, advanced directly in the next decade. The philosophical societies and their increasingly important journals provided the foundations for the growth of a number of royal societies, beginning with the unscientific Royal Society of Van Diemen's Land (renamed the Royal Society of Tasmania in 1911), and carried over into the Royal Societies of Victoria (1859), New South Wales (1866), South Australia (1880), Queensland (1884) and Western Australia (1914). The term 'philosophical' was a misnomer, as the vice-president of the Royal Society of New South Wales, the Reverend W.B. Clarke, advised. He summed up the purposes of them all when he urged,

We must strive to discern clearly, understand fully and report faithfully . . . to abjure hasty theories and unsupported conjectures; where we are in doubt not to be positive; to give our brother the same measure of credit we take to ourselves; not striving for mastery, but leaving time for the formation of the judgment which will inevitably be given, whether for or against us, by those who come after us.[19]

Under this banner, descriptive and systematic work in the natural sciences gathered pace; subcommittees sprouted to meet specialist needs, and a growing professionalism came to replace the earlier preoccupation with the 'useful' arts. Though the colonial royal societies (despite having a less exclusive membership than their London model) continued to express a basic identifications with British science, they also fostered a developing sense of national science. There was still the isolation and some lack of overseas recognition to be endured, but there was a growing local audience for science. Governments had established the principle of some scientific funding: the Victorian Government had appointed a Science Board of leading scientists and bureaucrats to advise it on scientific, mining and technological policy in 1858; and there was a growing institutional infrastructure and network of science. The diversification of scientific disciplines also spurred the growth of specialist societies and periodicals – the Entomological Society of New South Wales, the influential Linnean Society of New South Wales and, later, the Geological Society of Australasia were cases in point – while 'acclimatisation societies' importing foreign species to Australia catered to an eclectic and dilettante element of the scientific set.

By the last quarter of the century, a strong nucleus of working scientists was emerging in every capital. Basically they tended to be state-oriented, separated by distances, and with a certain overlapping in their work. Stateism, indeed, died hard in the evolution of Australian science. In the mid-1880s, however, Archibald Liversidge, professor of geology at Sydney University, dealt it a substantial blow. Liversidge argued publicly for a national organisation of science based on the tenets of the British Association for the Advancement of Science, to give a more systematic direction to scientific enquiry and to promote the greater intercourse of Australian scientific men. His advocacy led in 1886 to the formation, at a meeting of delegates representing 34 scientific societies, of the Australasian Association for the Advancement of Science, an association which included fellow workers in New Zealand. At the inaugural meeting of the association in 1888, an initial membership of 820 was listed.

'The Australasian Association,' announced H.C. Russell, the New South Wales Astronomer in his presidential address to that first meeting in 1888, 'is for the advancement of science, and if it fails in that, it will fall to pieces. It is not the hobby of a few individuals, or of one Colony; it takes in all who wish to advance science in all the Colonies; it meets here this year, in Melbourne, probably, next year, gathering up the enthusiasm of each Colony in turn, and will come back to us when we are glad to receive it. By its charter the Association is bound to promote the intercourse of scientific men and lovers of science; to . . . obtain a public recognition for the claims of science, and to endeavour by every means in its power to promote scientific advancement of this portion of the British dominions.' The word science, said Russell, was used essentially in its comprehensive sense. 'Each branch must be pushed forward in its own special direction, and in – what is just as important – its relation to all other branches of science. Science stands or falls as a whole . . . This Association stands as a protest against the shortsighted and utilitarian policy of those who would cultivate only what they characteristically call the bread and butter sciences. Our purpose is the advancement of all the sciences, believing, as we do, that the true advance of one is inseparably connected with that of all the others . . .'[20]

It was a charter, hammered from new perceptions, that would provide a sound foundation for the thrust and diversification of a new century of science. From small beginnings the Australian scientific community had come of age. If Liversidge's ancillary plan for the creation of a national academy to shape scientific policy and advise governments on scientific matters proved to be 50 years before its time,[21] by the late 19th century the Australian community of scientists had achieved a maturity and authority in the colonial environment that allowed it to influence legislatures, sponsor research and exploration, stimulate specialisms, encourage scientific and technical education, and, with their resources of locally trained, and permanent scientists, to shape the contours of a national science.

CHAPTER SIX

The feminine touch

In a strongly male-dominated society, it was hardly surprising that only the smallest handful of women enjoyed the opportunity to pursue an interest in scientific study or to make a creative contribution to science. Many well-educated women immigrants from England were skilled sketchers, alive to their new landscape, and eager to depict the brilliant colours of flowers and plumage that delighted their eyes in a new land. Many cultivated horticultural and botanical interests; attended the Colonial Exhibitions, spent leisure hours in the museums and Botanic Gardens, and used the ladies' reading rooms of the Mechanics Institute libraries to discover more of the natural world in which they lived. Popular science reached colonial women as well as men.

Given contemporary mores and the confining preclusions of Victorian life, it was singularly rare for a woman to be drawn, even peripherally, into the scientific reconnaissance of colonial men. One such, and the earliest yet recorded in Australia, was the gentle botanical collector Georgiana Molloy (1805–1843), whom historian Manning Clark has dubbed discerningly 'the Madonna of the bush'.

The feminine touch

Georgiana, the wife of Captain John Molloy, arrived in Western Australia in 1830 in a raw corner of the continent where settlement had hardly begun. Born and reared in Cumberland, and aged 24, Georgiana knew little of botany but anxious 'not to be without flowers' on their portion of rural land, she brought with her seeds, a light rake, trowels and watering pot, for she was not to know that the wilderness would have flowers of its own. In May 1830, the Molloys settled in the newly opened region of Augusta on the Blackwood River. There, Georgiana planted her domestic garden and, with the second spring, began to note the native beauty as delicate white bells and stars, and the purple creeper erupted into view. Four years later, in 1836, Mrs Molloy was drawn into a network of collectors through a request from Captain James Mangles RN, a retired Naval Officer and Fellow of the Royal Society who had visited the Swan River from 1829–31. Already in communication with the West Australian botanist John Drummond, Mangles heard of Georgiana's interest, wrote, invited, and won her with a hortus siccus (herbarium) and a box of seeds. 'I much fear,' Georgiana replied to him modestly, 'you have bestowed your liberality on one whose chief pleasure is her garden, but who does not enter the lists as a Florist, much less as a Botanist.' She was, she wrote, 'not even acquainted with the names of native plants', but she agreed to enclose a leaf and description of the flower in each paper she sent.[1] She proved a discerning student. Walking out with her two small children – their eyes so much nearer to the ground, she noted, that they detected many minute specimens she might miss – she began gathering flower specimens and fresh brown seeds, drying, pressing and labelling her plants and leaves, and mounting them in her hortus siccus.

Through Mangles' enterprise, the seeds which Georgiana gathered at Augusta found their way into a number of public and private horticultural collections in England, including a 'perfect set' for the Horticultural and Zoological Societies of London, the Duke of Devonshire's famous garden at Chatsworth, and other show places. Within a few months, the vivid red and green of the kangaroo paw (*Anigozanthus manglesii*) was reported blooming lustily in several English gardens. Mangles was delighted with his correspondent. Her boxes of plants, collected over many months, 'set out with delicacy' and complemented with seeds from the same species, impressed him with their professionalism and care. He forwarded Georgiana's specimens and letters to Dr John Lindley, professor of botany at London University and secretary of the Horticultural Society. 'That many of the plants are beautiful,' Lindley replied, 'you can see for yourself, and I am delighted to add, that many are quite new.'[2] Devonshire's horticulturalist, Joseph Paxton, proclaimed the seeds 'far superior to any we have received at Chatsworth'. 'The examination of your dried plants,' he told Mangles, 'has afforded great pleasure and will cast off the gloom which generally is attendant on raising unknown seeds, but now there is a stimulus – we know they are good and from a good quarter.'[3]

Georgiana's education as a botanist grew from her own demand for precision. At her request, the descriptions and identification of her numbered specimens were returned to her together with copies of the *Botanical Register*, reference works on botany, and books on gardening, flower arrangements and philosophy, which Mangles sent her. She was unfailingly grateful and sought small additions to her supplies of paper, ties, and brown muslin for seed bags. During 1839, while her

The feminine touch

seeds germinated in Britain, the Molloy family moved from Augusta to the Vasse River, 60 miles to the north, where, in less beautiful surroundings, the arduous business of homemaking from rough and basic structures and of building a garden from uncleared scrub began again. Yet there were compensations with new country and new flora to be explored. Georgiana called her new home Fair Lawn and, after a period of some illness, began her sorties. 'I never set out,' she wrote to Mangles in August 1840, 'that it is not on your account.'[4]

During 1840 she invited the German naturalist, Ludwig Preiss, who had been collecting in Western Australia for two years, to the Vasse. Preiss stayed a month, botanising and augmenting his collections and traversing with his hostess her botanical collecting grounds. But his visit complete, he communicated no further with Georgiana and left for Europe, with his collection of 2,700 specimens of Western Australian flora, without sending her the promised specimens and seeds.

Through her ten years of botanising, Georgiana Molloy acquired what was for the time an encyclopaedic knowledge of the flowers of the south-west of Western Australia. Modest as she was about this 'pleasant and consonant work' and amused that her husband and sister 'laugh at this all-engrossing theme', she was deeply engaged in contributing to the process of scientific communication and exchange. Her seeds bloomed in showpiece English gardens: 'Not one in ten thousand who go into distant lands', Paxton praised her, 'have done what she did for the Gardens of her Native Country.' And her precise, carefully ordered plant specimens were an important source of information to botanical taxonomists at Kew. Several of her specimens are in the herbarium at Kew, while the plants from her notable first collection, despatched in 1838, are described in Lindley's 'Sketch of the Vegetation of the Swan River Colony' published as an Appendix to Edward's *Botanical Register* in 1839.

Sadly, her early death eclipsed her record. Neither Mangles nor Lindley acknowledged her in their publications and it remained for the blunt Western Australian botanist James Drummond to secure her some immortality. At his request, a scented boronia, 'as tall as the shoulders of a man riding on a horse' *Boronia molloyae*, commemorates her and the diligent additions that she made. 'I believe,' she wrote Mangles before her death, 'I have sent everything worth sending.'

Only a rare kind of woman could make a more conspicuous impact. One such was Konkordie Amalie Dietrich (1821–1891), a German collector employed by the famous, privately owned Godeffroy Museum of Natural History in Hamburg, who, from 1863–72, virtually alone in the Queensland bush, amassed one of the most outstanding collections made by a single person. Amalie had already collected botanical and natural history specimens in Germany, Belgium and Holland when she sought employment with the Pacific trader G.J. Godeffroy. Before despatching her to wilder pastures, Godeffroy, convinced of her enterprise and professionalism, offered her a ten-year contract and had her taught how to handle firearms, to skin and eviscerate birds and mammals, and – with a view to Aboriginal relics – how to pack human skulls and skeletons. He also fitted her out with a workmanlike 'trousseau', which included a pocket lens, a microscope, six insect cages, rags for packing, 20 pounds of tow, five quires of tissue paper, bottles for live snakes, gunpowder and small shot, percussion caps, 100 jars and stoppers, two boxes of poison, and – for her education was poor – an English dictionary.[5]

The feminine touch

Amalie, small and sturdy, was 42 when she sailed for Moreton Bay aboard *La Rochelle* in August 1863. She had left her daughter Charitas in the care of friends, but Charitas was to remain her mother's touchstone and correspondent throughout her eight years in the colony. At first, truly feminine, Amalie worried about her first consignments to Hamburg, 'they are sure to be a little anxious as to whether I am equal to the task'. But, with the competence of an experienced investigator, she revelled in the freedom of her work. Within eight months she had explored from Brisbane to Gladstone and Rockhampton and despatched 12 cases of botanical and zoological specimens to Hamburg. In the clammy subtropical heat of late summer in Rockhampton, she wrote her daughter, 'You can have no idea how things flourish here, and what a scramble there is for space. Ferns, amongst which I disappear entirely, grow under the giant trees, and I am often frightened when I have to force my way through the luxurious creepers, ferns and branches. Large orchids hang from the trees by almost invisible threads; they are so wonderfully formed, have such beautiful colour, and look at me so mysteriously, that I pick them with a certain awe.' Her keen eye noted the unconforming oddities of the land: 'The swans are black, some mammals have beaks, . . . and I noticed a water wagtail which moved its tail not up and down, but from side to side. There are trees the edges of whose leaves turn upward. Some trees shed their bark instead of their leaves, and a mournful impression is produced by the sight of these giants, chill and naked among the others.'[6]

If Australia offered a weird and lonely backdrop for this solitary woman, it also offered an invigorating freedom. Amalie delighted in it. In a colonial environment, her very foreignness and 'outsider' status provided her strength. 'No one,' she wrote, 'circumscribes my zeal. I stride across the wider plains, wander through virgin forests. I have trees felled in order to collect different kinds of wood.' (Her fifty specimens of different varieties won a gold medal at the Paris International Exhibition of 1867.) 'I cross rivers and lakes in a small canoe, visit islands and collect-collect-collect . . . It is just as if Herr Godeffroy had made me a present of this vast continent.'[7] Throughout her botanising and collecting, Dietrich did far more than pluck and pack the natural treasures that came to hand. She was rigorously accurate in her descriptions, skilful in her selection, undaunted by the range of specimens, and intellectually committed to her native land. She collected for Germany in all fields – botany, zoology, anthropology – killing and disembowelling a crocodile, starting a butterfly farm to grow specimens, and calmly packing up 13 Aboriginal skeletons and several skulls for her employer. She held in view the 'scholars who go to work on what I send' and through them she foresaw that she would gain recognition. Recognition was important to her.

Amalie Dietrich was a striking figure in Australian science. As an alien detached from the Australian community, she suffered none of the constraints that shackled colonial women in this 'manly' arena of endeavour. As a German, she remained as passionately committed as her more tragic compatriot Ludwig Leichhardt to pursuing the scientific mysteries of the fifth continent and returning diverse consignments of specimens for the study of scholars in Europe. Most remarkably, Amalie Dietrich won contemporary recognition from her peers. Leaving Brisbane in March 1871 now 'a little, grey-haired, bent lady wearing canvas shoes with slits in them for greater comfort', and accompanied by two tame eagles, she found her reputation had preceded her. She had been elected

The feminine touch

a Fellow of the Stettin Entomological Society in 1867 for her collection of Australian insect, and was rapidly employed on her return to Hamburg by the Godeffroy Museum. When the Museum's collections passed to the city of Hamburg in 1885, Amalie was appointed Curator of the Hamburg Botanical Museum where she remained for the rest of her life. A number of Australian insects and botanical species bear her surname, while the Australian skipper butterfly of Queensland *Cephrenes amalia*, flutters perennially in the regions she explored.

So intrepid and independent a woman investigator in the 19th century would have been outstanding in any land. In Australia, well-informed and able colonial women could traditionally serve, at best, as humble amanuenses of science. Two such, whose work attests their outstanding abilities, were the sisters Harriet and Helena Scott, of Ash Island, New South Wales. The daughters of Alexander Scott, a member of the New South Wales Legislative Assembly and later Legislative Council who settled on Ash Island, on the Upper Hunter near Newcastle, the two girls were reared in a home where the study of Australian natural history was pre-eminent. Scott, a naturalist, the President of the colony's Entomological Society and a Trustee of the Australian Museum, made detailed observations of the butterflies and insects of the colony from 1838 and published his *Australian Lepidoptera and Their Transformations* in 1864. The work was superbly illustrated with equal skill by his two daughters, who shared authorship with their father. When Alexander died in 1885, a second volume, edited and revised, was brought out under the daughters' joint married names, Harriet Morgan and Helena Forde in 1890. Their depictions from life were fresh, and executed with masterly verve.[8] Through their father, Harriet and Helena were thrust into a circle of colonial scientists who were eager to commission their work. W.S. Macleay used them, and the sisters executed all the drawings of venomous and non-venomous snakes in strikingly accurate and powerful presentations for Gerard Krefft's *Snakes of Australia* (1869). Yet despite their artistic gifts and keen observational powers, they were second-class citizens in science, although both were made honorary members of the Entomological Society of New South Wales, an unusual honour for women of their time. As Virginia Woolf wrote 40 years later, 'there was an enormous body of masculine opinion to the effect that nothing can be expected intellectually of a woman'.[9] The mood was reflected deeply in the drawing-rooms of the colonies. Moreover, feminine modesty and an eagerness to be of service added to their self-devaluation.

In 19th-century Australia, a considerable coterie of women collected specimens for leading scientists. Botany was their speciality, and Victoria's scientific bachelor, Ferdinand von Mueller, was one who owed much to their diligent care.[10] One or two Australian-born women found more public roles. Caroline Louisa Atkinson (1834–72), largely self-educated in New South Wales, developed a taste for botany and the study of birds and animals, and, self-directed, became a keen student of natural history and an accomplished botanical illustrator. She studied the writings of Australian explorers and built a sound knowledge of Australia's emerging botanical, zoological and geological science. Initially a writer of fiction, Louisa became a populariser of science and published a series of sketches on natural history entitled 'A Voice from the Country' in the *Sydney Morning Herald* from 1861–72, based on her rambles about the countryside. She identified new localities of known plant species, sketched ferns and plants, and built a considerable collection of her own. She furnished

Mueller with many species, while the friendship and professional interest she aroused in the scientific clergymen botanist William Woolls and geologist W.B. Clarke attest her competence as a perceptive scientific observer. Louisa married James Calvert, a member of Leichhardt's first overland expedition to Port Essington, and a keen botanist himself, in 1869. But she died in childbirth a short three years later at the age of 38.[11]

The beauty and distinctiveness of Australian wildflowers evoked a strong creative response from a number of Australian botanical artists, best described as the 'excursionists and illustrators'. They were not, strictly speaking, scientists; but they were acute and discerning observers of nature who studied the landscape of the country, wrote about it, published, and made accurate and ornamental studies of Australian flowers. One woman who exemplified this tradition to high degree was Louisa Anne Meredith, who came to Australia in 1839 as the bride of her cousin Charles Meredith, successively pastoralist, magistrate, MP and minister in the Tasmanian House of Assembly. When she arrived in the colonies, she was already well established in England as the author of several books on flowers and their seasons under her maiden name of Louisa Tramley. Flowers had become her passion and she was an accomplished miniaturist. Louisa quickly became well known in the colonies for her acerbic *Notes and Sketches of New South Wales* (1844) in which she noted the philistine character of colonial life and observed sharply that 'most gentlemen have their souls so felted up in wools, fleeces, flocks and stock, that I have often sat through a weary dinner . . . without hearing a syllable on any other subject'. Her descriptions of plants and flowers, however, were competent and exact. From various bases in Tasmania, where she moved with her husband in 1840, Louisa travelled extensively, a keen excursionist, and illustrated her works with depictions of landscape and flowers. Her major books included *My Home in Tasmania During a Residence of Nine Years* (1852), *Our Island Home: A Tasmanian Sketchbook* (1879), and *Tasmanian Friends and Foes, Feathered, Furred and Finned: A Family chronicle of Country Life, Natural History and Veritable Adventure* (1869). All were beautifully produced and illustrated with line drawings or colour plates.[12] She loved to paint the delicate, highly scented wildflowers of Tasmania, collecting most of the specimens herself; but rarer specimens were also provided by her friend, the Tasmanian botanist Dr Joseph Milligan. Her drawings and descriptions were regarded by as 'excellent source material' and 'faithful representations'. Bernard Smith categorises Louisa's interests as 'never quite those of the professional botanist and zoologist,[13] but the Tasmanian Government, in a mood of unprecedented recognition, granted her an annual pension of £100 in her widowhood for having 'by her writings and paintings rendered considerable services to the cause of Science, Literature and Art in Tasmania'.

There were others such as Mary Morton Allport (1805–1895), also of Tasmania, who belonged to this genre. Unquestionably the leader among them, at the end of the century, was the distinguished Victorian painter and botanical illustrator Marian Ellis Rowan (1848–1922). She also fits the tradition of the independent and determined field collector, which Amalie Dietrich had begun. Ellis Rowan was born in Melbourne, the daughter of Charles Ryan, in 1848. Her marriage to Frederick Rowan in 1873 took her to New Zealand where her husband's interests in botany encouraged her to paint wildflowers. Untrained as an artist, she had from childhood a singular gift for the observation of butterflies, birds and flowers and quickly revealed a talent for illustration that conveyed a notable lushness and richness in her work. She painted rapidly with a brush in watercolours 'with speed and concentration to capture the delicate plants that wither almost as soon as they are picked'.

In 1877 Ellis returned to Melbourne and, while her husband launched himself on a business career, embarked on her own professional journey, an excursion to Queensland that was to establish her as a noted botanical painter. In 1898 she published an account of her travels in *A Flower Hunter in Queenland and New Zealand*, in which she emerges as a highly intrepid, resourceful traveller, walking, or using every form of transport from horses, camels, bullock drays, ships or railway to search out her botanical specimens, and hauling herself up cliff faces to grasp at fugitive flowers. Like her German predecessor, she cut a swathe through Queensland, travelling alone from Mackay to Townsville, Hughenden, Cairns and Cooktown and on to Somerset Island. From there through rain forests and rugged arid country, she went on to Thursday Island, Mabuiag Island, Murray Island and the remote and diminutive Stephens, York and Darnley islands, sending off rare plants to Ferdinand von Mueller in Melbourne to describe and name the new species she discovered.[14]

Ellis Rowan left Australia for a decade on her husband's death in 1892, though she continued to paint both Australian and American plants in the United States. Her flower paintings, exhibited in London in 1905 with brief botanical descriptions supplied by Mueller, aroused considerable interest in the exotic flora of the Antipodes. Queen Victoria accepted three paintings for her private drawing room. Ellis Rowan herself was greatly delighted and amused by one newspaper review, which summed up her dauntless work in these words: 'Mrs Rowan set to work to paint, as they grew in their native haunts, the gorgeous flora of those comparatively unknown regions. She worked enthusiastically and with patience and skill, and the results are hundreds of paintings that are valuable to both artists and botanists, and a wondrous monument to a weak woman's activity.'

It is doubtful if any of the women described in this chapter were schooled in botanical theory or were alive to the debate on evolution versus fixity of species, which Hooker's important work on the Tasmanian flora stirred. Rather, they responded to the beauty of the buds of the strange native tamarind, the grey-green leaves of Australian foliage, to the ferns and the vivid desert flowers. They responded and painted the variety they saw.

Science, as Huxley once summed up, has need of many workers, 'of servants of various qualifications: of artistic constructors . . . of people to design her palaces and of others to see that the materials are sound'. Despite the cramped confines of their society, a small band of talented women took some lead in Australian natural history: Lady Franklin in Victoria as a patron of scientific life; Elizabeth Gould, a fragile but competent woman artist who poured her skills into her husband's important illustrated work; Georgiana Molloy, an early contributor to botanical science; and the remarkably able Scott sisters of New South Wales. There were, in addition, many other nameless contributors whose collecting skills expanded the suites of herbaria plants. Childbearing and the lack of a foothold in the scientific system kept these women in a minor role. By the end of the century, a small trickle of women students was penetrating the universities. Change would be slow. Amalie Dietrich, the self-tutored village girl, remained a singular, and unassimilated, example of

19th-century Australian feminist science. The rest, however, in their optimism and creativity, emerge as discerning observers and artistic constructors, contributing to a widening picture of the plants and fauna of a bright and savage land.

CHAPTER SEVEN

The conquest of the rocks

The great debate

By the third decade of the 18th century, geology and mineralogy had made such strides in England and Europe that its practitioners were eager for information on Australia to confirm and extend their understanding of the physical structure of the earth. Packets of rocks were sent back to England. George Bass (1771–1803), cruising along the southern coast in a whaleboat in 1797, reported the presence of coal at Coalcliff, New South Wales. Six years later, Adolarious Humphrey (1782–1829), 'His Majesty's Mineralogist', sailed with David Collins to found a settlement at Port Phillip. Humphrey explored for minerals in New South Wales and Van Diemen's Land and sent iron ore samples to Sir Joseph Banks in London before resigning his isolated post in 1812. The *Investigator* expedition and the geologically well equipped Baudin expedition gathered rocks and fossil specimens and conveyed them for the scrutiny of geologists in Britain and Europe. In addition, the explorer-surveyors King, Oxley, Sturt and Mitchell collected geological specimens that found their way to experts abroad.

But this work was fragmentary, and for nearly 50 years after settlement no one had turned a trained eye on the physical structure of the colonies or attempted to assess Australia's position within the framework of evolving stratigraphical knowledge abroad. The questions posed were fundamental. Would Australia prove, as some suspected, to be a geologically 'recent' country in the history of the world? Would the classification of strata being worked out in England and Europe find counterparts on the other side of the world? Or would this Antipodean land mass reveal singular differences in its geological life, as it had in its zoological life?

The first resident geologist to attempt to find answers to these questions was the Anglican clergyman and spare-time geologist Reverend William Branwhite Clarke. Clarke trained for holy orders at Cambridge and was initiated into the study of geology by attending the lectures of the new Woodwardian Professor of Geology, the Reverend Adam Sedgwick, who became his lifelong friend. In 1826, after wielding his geological hammer on several continental excursions, Clarke became a fellow of the Geological Society of London, and for the next 13 years, from rural parishes in Suffolk and Dorset, contributed papers on English and European geology to the journals of British science. In 1839, he accepted a chaplaincy in New South Wales, and with a library enriched by the most up-to-date publications of geological science, he arrived in Sydney exhorted by his British geological colleagues to make the age of the colony's coal deposits the object of his first research.

Economically, resources of coal were important to the young colony; but geologically the position and relationship of the coal beds could furnish fundamental clues to the complex stratigraphy of the little known land. Clarke wasted no time in committing his leisure hours to exploring outside

Sydney, making large collections of rocks and fossils (consignments of which he sent to the Woodwardian Museum at Cambridge) and communicating his discoveries to the geological journals at home. From his early investigations of the coalfields of the Hunter River and the Illawarra, he postulated that there was a perfect conformity between the upper botanical fossil beds, the coal seams themselves and the marine fossil beds underlying the coal, and that all belonged to one continuous and uninterrupted series, which he believed was considerably older than the coal deposits of England and India and belonged to a Palaeozoic age. His verdict brought him into conflict with Frederick McCoy who, first as Sedgwick's palaeontologist examining Clarke's specimens at Cambridge and later as the influential incumbent of Melbourne University's Natural History chair, contended on the palaeontological evidence of the fossils that a vast interval of time separated the Carboniferous marine fossil beneath the coal, the coal seams, and the botanical fossil beds above, the last of which he assigned to the Oolitic age contemporaneous with the coalfields of India and Europe.[1] The debate, hammered out in private correspondence and scientific journals, smouldered between the two scientists for 30 years.

Judged from this century, the quarrel seems unreasonably cantankerous and prolonged. Yet there were several factors involved. Geology in Australia was influenced inevitably by concepts of stratigraphy that originated in the northern hemisphere and were transported sometimes uncritically to the new land being explored. There were problems of juxtaposition of strata and relationships that were puzzling in respect of the known strata of rock formations of Europe and England. But the debate was a critical test case. Importantly, it bore on the matter, crucial to geologists in all countries, whether the palaeontological evidence of fossils examined in isolation outweighed the conclusion drawn from their stratigraphical position in the field. McCoy, refusing to leave his study to inspect the controversial sections or to collaborate with Clarke on the work, held fast to the palaeontology. Clarke, tracing and retracing the coal beds around Maitland and despatching specimens to his adversary as the only palaeontologist in the colony, insisted on the stratigraphy and continued to publish his arguments in papers in the colonies and abroad.[2]

Eventually, other researchers were drawn into the debate. James Dwight Dana, the United States Exploring Expedition geologist who had poked with Clarke among the Illawarra coal beds and inspected the Hunter River formations during his visit in 1840, adduced supporting evidence on the conformity and continuity of the coal series in his report on New South Wales geology in 1849.[3] Joseph Jukes, naturalist to HMS *Fly* on its maritime survey of the Great Barrier Reef and north Australian waters from 1842–5, who had also examined the New South Wales coal beds and published in 1850 a broad outline of the country's geology (A *Sketch of the Physical Structure of Australia*) based on his observations on two circumnavigations of the continent, backed Clarke from his own field work. 'I think the notion of asserting that a widely spread formation in Australia is Oolitic on the authority of a few plants which may, or may not be identical with some that are found in Oolitic formations elsewhere, unaccompanied by a single Oolitic fossil of any description,' he wrote his friend from Dublin, 'is an insult to the common sense of geologists. All I ever saw in Australia convinced me that the rocks were palaeozoic, covered in the interior plains with tertiary, some probably of very recent age. Are we to believe,' he asked, 'in the faith of a very few doubtful & rare plants . . . that these widely separated Palaeozoic localities each received small local deposits during the middle of the Mesozoic period containing nothing but plants & deposited without any trace of unconformability or discordance? The idea is preposterous & McCoy might stand on his head and swear it until his brain sprouted out at his boots before I would believe it.'[4]

Controversy is the life-blood of science; but the Clarke-McCoy battle, generating much heat between protagonists, threatened to transcend the bounds of even scientific 'good taste'. The President of the Victorian Royal Society, Sir Henry Barkly, drawn in as an adjudicator, judged the tone 'rather warm even for scientific controversy', and felt bound to warn the godly geologist that some of his remarks about McCoy were 'not very complimentary.'[5]

Yet despite bile, slowness and some muddle, Clarke, basically, was right. Through the 1850s and 1860s, the young geologists who joined the colonial geological surveys took up the question in their colonies and conveyed lively reinforcement in letters to their father figure, Clarke. Charles Gould, John Gould's geological son, appointed to head the Geological Survey of Tasmania, wrote him from the coal deposits of Fingal, Tasmania, in September 1860: 'I am glad to see that your views of the age of our coal measures agree with my own experience: wherever I have seen them yet, they appear to overlay the Carboniferous limestone in a perfectly conformable manner, and at no great distance from it. The Oolitic facies of the flora associated with it ought not surely to be allowed as an argument of superior weight to this important relation.'[6] C. D'Oyly Aplin, a British recruit to the Victorian Geological Survey, pinpointed the broader problem of 'establishing a direct parallelism between some of the more important rocksystems in Australia & those in Europe & N. America' and the special difficulties attaching to the coal seams. 'Your Govt. is illiberal in the extreme,' he declared to Clarke, 'in not furnishing you with the means of making measured sections & something in the nature of a proper Survey. New South Wales has the materials for determining the true classification of these rocks in a development of them to which, as far as we know, Victoria can offer no parallel; & yet the work is left to the zeal & love of Science of an individual to accomplish at his own expense.'[7]

Later geologists working in Australia would feel free to determine stratigraphical classification more independently of direct correlation with stratigraphical systems overseas. McCoy, however, emerged as the arch exponent of Australian palaeontological parrallelism with the coal measures 'at home'. Clarke, over various vacations from parish duties, diligently pursued the subject in the field, and when, in 1869, the Director of the Victorian Geological Survey, A.R.C. Selwyn, capitulated to Clarke's side, it meant that one of McCoy's most formidable allies had changed camps.[8]

Clarke's findings were eventually corroborated by the European palaeontologists de Koninck and Feistmantel, to whom he consigned his large collections of specimens for classification. In his last years, Clarke's own detailed researches on the age of the coal formations, with other identifications of the tertiary, secondary and Palaeozoic systems of New South Wales, were published in his *Remarks on the Sedimentary Formations of New South Wales* (4th ed. 1878). Clarke was elected Fellow of the Royal Society in 1876, awarded the Murchison Medal of the Geological Society of London in 1877, and nominated 'father of Australian geology' for establishing the Palaeozoic (Permian) stratigraphy of the coal deposits of New South Wales. Dogged field work had triumphed over dogmatic theorising. Though many geologists were heartily tired of the geological squabble before it was finally set at rest, the great coal debate in Australia gave vital proof to the concept – which geologists now consider axiomatic – of the wisdom of relating evaluations of the palaeontology to the structural geometry of the country.

McCoy, for his part, declined to concede defeat. Despite his estimable work on the *Prodromus of the Palaeontology of Victoria*, his undeviating attitude and his exclusive hold on palaeontological determinations provided an obstacle to geological classification in Australia and served to illustrate the dangers and delay caused by a stubborn 'loner' in a pioneering field.

Geological surveys

For a long period, geological investigation remained a private matter in the colonies. Apart from Adolarius Humphrey's unusual appointment at the beginning of the century, and the brief employment by the South Australian Company in 1836–8 of Johann Menge as their geologist to search for minerals, pioneering geological description of the country initially came from visiting geologists, from the freelance Clarke, and from two Europeans who spent some time in the colonies, P.E. de Strzelecki and John Lhotsky. The last of these yielded substantial information and maps on the physical structure of parts of eastern Australia – Strzelecki's *Physical Description of New South Wales and Van Diemen's Land* (London 1845) was based on field work during which the author zigzagged across the eastern colonies in the early 1840s, ascended Australia's highest mountain peak and named it for the Polish democratic leader Tadeusz Koscuisko. Lhotsky's more modest *Journey from Sydney to the Australian Alps* (published in parts in Sydney 1834–5), brought the Snowy River and the Monaro region before the attention of colonists. In Western Australia, geological enquiry was spurred by the explorer brothers Augustus and Charles Gregory, who found coal at the Irwin River in 1846, while two years later, the Western Australian Government gained a base of physical and mineralogical data through the appointment of Dr F. von Sommer as their mineralogist from 1848–9.[9]

The search for metals was the stick that prodded governments into action. By the mid-century, the New South Wales government responded to pressure for a geological surveyor and, early in 1850, unable to lure the experienced Jukes, appointed Samuel Stutchbury (1797–1859) to the post. A shy retiring Englishman who had been serving as curator of the Bristol Museum, Stutchbury began his researches at Carcoar in February 1851. But unfortunately for him, Edward Hargraves' discovery of gold in the nearby ranges at Ophir in May that year put paid to any prospect of orderly survey in the colony. Having confirmed the discovery of gold, Stutchbury spent the next five years largely ignored and neglected by government, pursuing a geological and mineralogical examination from Bathurst to Port Curtis, in present-day Queensland. His sense of neglect and isolation, however, were acute. 'I may take this opportunity here,' he wrote in his private diary in May 1852, 'of recording my feelings of disappointment and pain at the general treatment I have met with from the Colonial Government from the first moment of entering upon the duties of my survey until the present time. Arrived, a stranger in the country, unacquainted with the peculiar requisites for a lengthened sojourn in the Australian "bush" – a never-ending journey, alone from township to township, but not infrequently beyond the boundaries of settlement and civilization – I was left almost entirely to my own resources and did not receive that aid and assistance I think I was entitled to look for and expect.'[10]

Yet despite his unhappiness, and private expense, Stutchbury diligently examined a large sweep of territory and submitted 16 detailed reports to the government. His work was supplemented in the south and east of the colony by the appointment from September 1851 to July 1853 of W.B. Clarke as a geological surveyor and auriferous adviser to the government. With only a horse and one servant to assist him, Clarke covered a large region stretching from Marulan in New South Wales to Omeo in Victoria and north-west from Twofold Bay to the Darling Downs, and he preached as he went of God's eternal riches as he searched the earth for evidence of gold. Shrewder than his British colleague, Clarke also published his southern findings as *Researches in the Southern Goldfields of New South Wales* (1860) while Stutchbury's reports gathered dust on departmental shelves. Stutchbury left the colony, largely a forgotten geological pioneer, in December 1855.

In one sense, the advent of geological and mineralogical surveys instanced a major government commitment to science funding in Australia. New South Wales set the ball rolling in 1850; Benjamin Babbage arrived in 1851 to make a geological survey for the South Australian Government; Victoria launched its Geological Survey in 1852; Tasmania followed with the appointment of a single geological surveyor, Charles Gould, in 1859, while the Queensland government set up two geological surveyors, Richard Daintree in northern Queensland and Christopher Aplin in southern Queensland,

Ferdinand Bauer's watercolour of *Eucalyptus pruinosa* marks the scientific precision of his botanical drawings.

Joseph Banks, from a mezzotint by Benjamin West. In addition to his role as ship's botanist and naturalist, Banks was responsible for the *Endeavour*'s water, the provision of sea birds for food, trawling for microscopic marine organisms, and for recording the customs and language of the natives.

Sydney Parkinson's *Banksia serrata*, gathered at Botany Bay in 1770. The first artist to land on the continent, he made 243 drawings of Australian plants during the *Endeavour*'s voyage.

Charles Alexandre Lesueur described these birds as casoar from Kangaroo Island, New Holland, but they may be mainland emu or the now extinct species from Kangaroo or King Islands.

Nicolas Martin Petit's drawing of a native of Maria Island, Van Diemen's Land. Data gathered by the French concerned the physical and social anthropology of the Tasmanian Aborigines.

Overseas scientists thought the platypus, *Ornithorhynchus anatinus*, might have been a skilful scientific hoax.

Convict artist T.R. Browne's black and white cockatoos reflected the strangeness of the new land.

Western Australia's black swan caused a considerable stir. For centuries such a bird had been considered an impossibility.

John Lewin's watercolour of a koala, described by writer George Perry as 'torpid, senseless creatures'.

The wombat, 'a newly discovered animal from Botany Bay', was first portrayed in George Perry's *Arcana*, 1811.

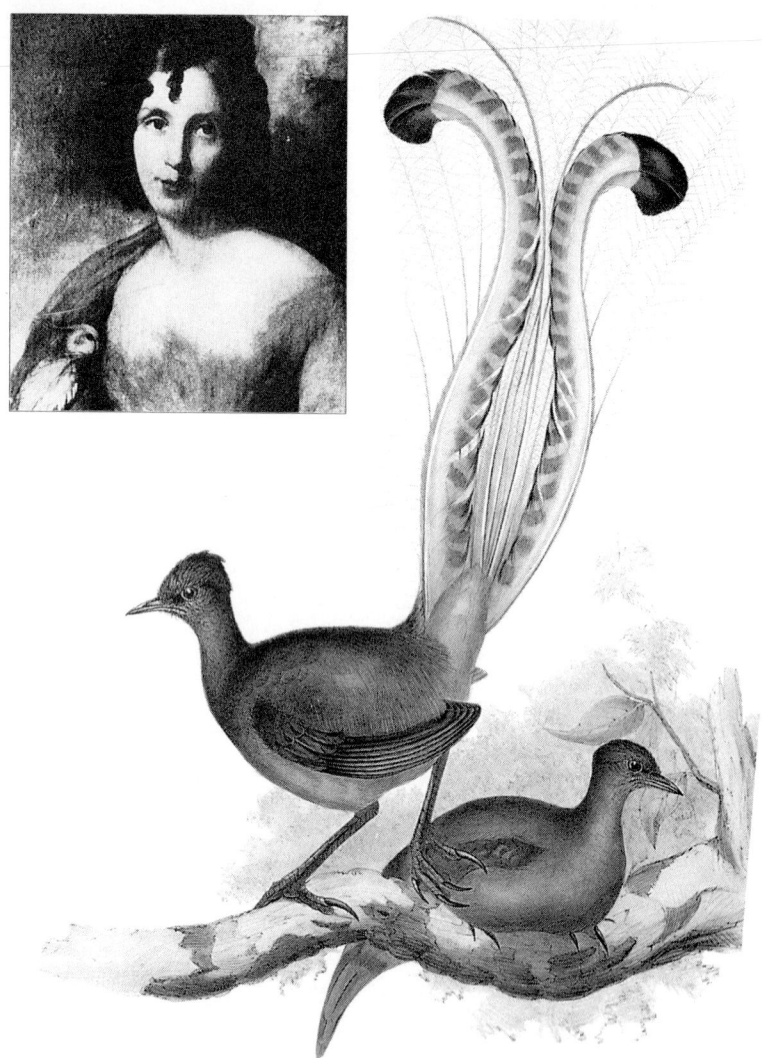

Lyrebirds, *Menura superba*. John Gould's drawings were accompanied by precise descriptions of habits, formation, folklore and environment of the birds.

Elizabeth Gould (top), natural history artist, completed 600 drawings of birds during her time in the colonies.

The boobook owl, *Athene boobook*. Its note resembled the English cuckoo. By 1845, John Gould noted, it had been seen in all the Australian colonies.

The black-gloved wallaby. Gould's careful observations shed considerable light on the habits of the species.

George French Angas's portrait of a native encampment at Portland Bay on a cold morning.

Joseph Selleny's pencil drawing of the naturalist's cabin on board the *Navara*, 1858, showing its phials, nets, instruments, hammers, microscope and books.

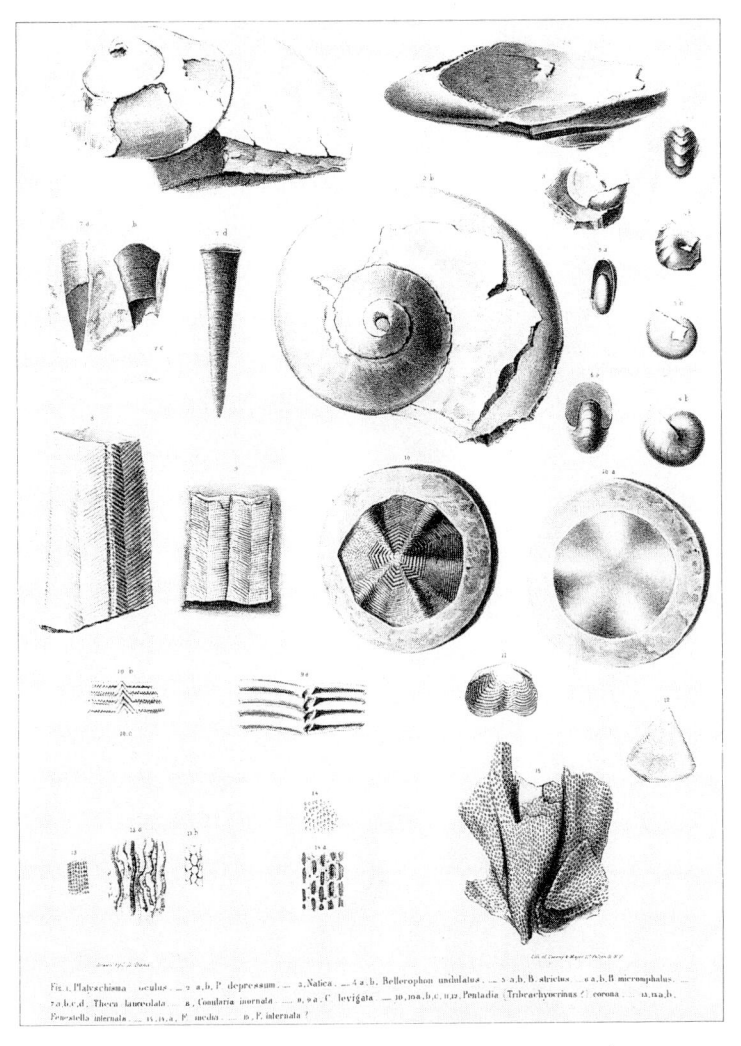

Crinoid fossils from the coal measures collected by American geologist James Dwight Dana from his excursions in the Hunter Valley and Illawarra districts of New South Wales. His findings contributed to the debate on the age of coal deposits in the colony.

The 1880 Melbourne Exhibition was full of machinery and scientific displays to attract both children and adults.

Lady Jane Franklin took an eager interest in all aspects of botanical and natural science and was Australia's first 'patroness' of science.

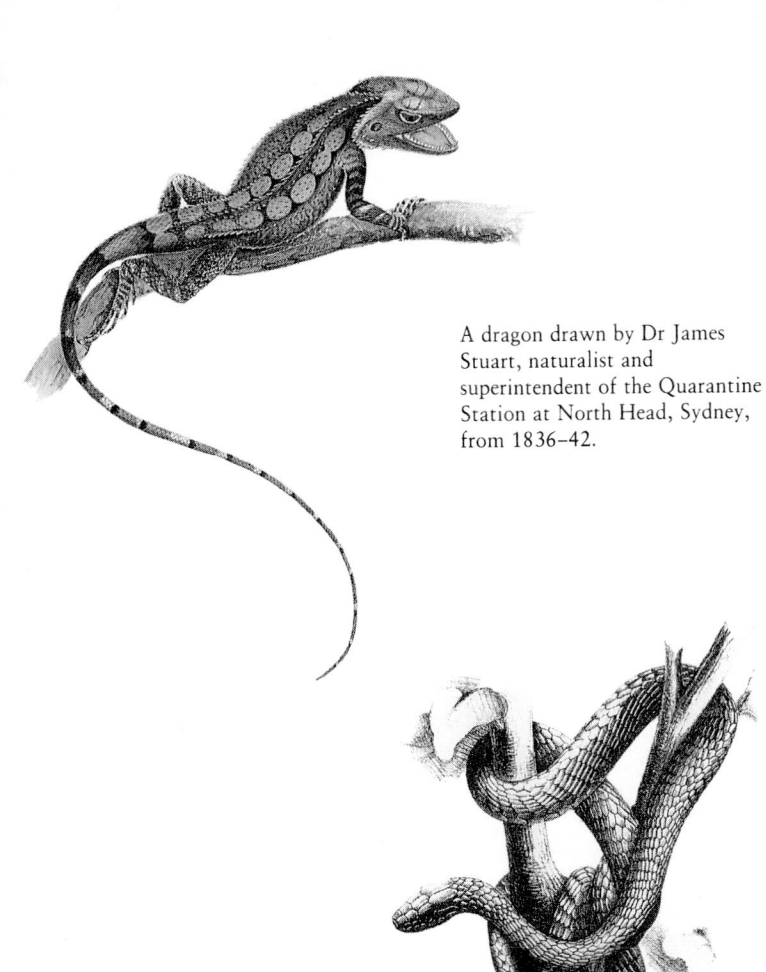

A dragon drawn by Dr James Stuart, naturalist and superintendent of the Quarantine Station at North Head, Sydney, from 1836–42.

The venomous diamond snake, *Morelia spitotes*, drawn by Helena Scott Forde, from Gerard Krefft's *Snakes of Australia: Illustrated and Descriptive Catalogue of all the Known Species*, 1869.

Harriet Scott's *Antheroea eucalypti*, 1864, from the family publication *Australian Lepidoptera*, illustrated by the Scott sisters and written by their father, entomologist Alexander Scott.

Richard Daintree (1831–1878), appointed geological surveyor in North Queensland in 1868, gave his name to the famous Daintree Rainforest.

Daintree applied photography to his geological work; an important transition from the sketchbook.

Transit telescope at Melbourne Observatory; a more reliable instrument than the Great Melbourne Telescope, imported from England to focus on southern skies.

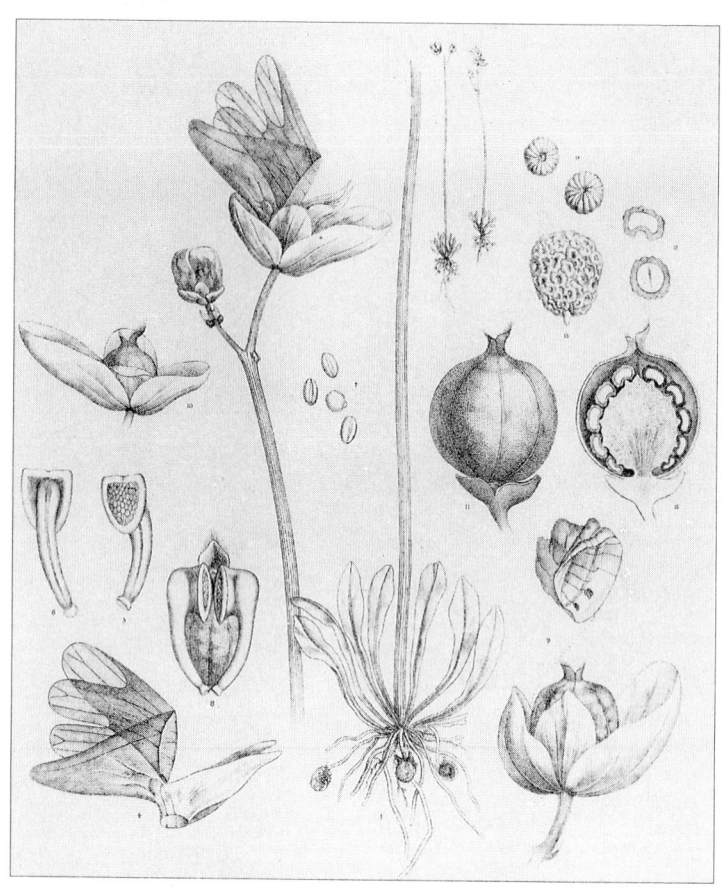

Polypompholyx exigna, from Ferdinand von Mueller's *Plants Indigenous to the Colony of Victoria*, exemplifies his meticulous style.

Ferdinand von Mueller, first government botanist of Victoria, gathered more honours than any other 19th-century colonial scientist.

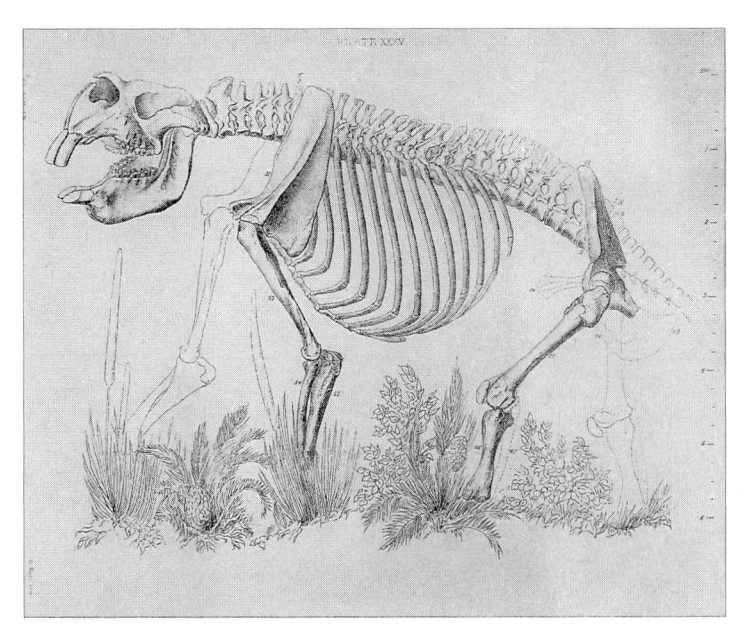

A skeletal reconstruction of *Diprotodon Australis* roaming among the flowers, from Richard Owen's *Fossil Mammals of Australia*.

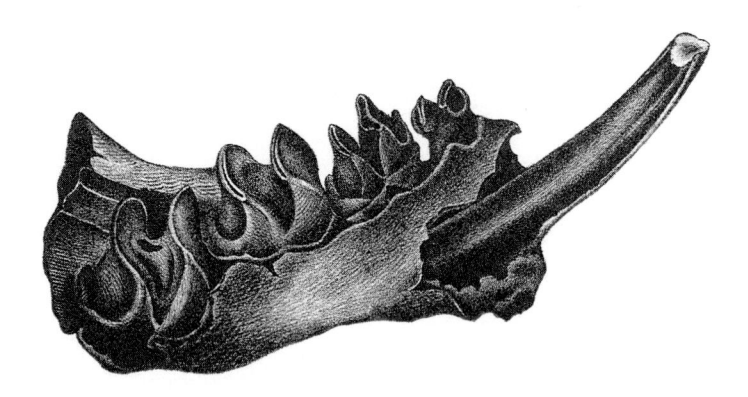

A fossil tooth of *Diprotodon Australis* from which Richard Owen recreated and described the herbivore marsupial.

From the 1890s Sydney University nourished a circle of brilliant researchers in the physiological and embryological development of marsupial species under Professor J.T. Wilson (left), seen here with his associates Charles Martin and the youthful J.P. Hill.

in 1868. With the exception of the outstanding Victorian Geological Survey developed under A.R.C. Selwyn, the growth and fluctuations of these surveys shared similarities in the colonies. At first colonial governments, dominated by pastoralists and producers, cared little for the scientific aspects of survey and spent public money only when practical objectives could be clearly seen. The colonial geological surveys hence focused strongly on mineral search.

Not surprisingly, geologists handpicked from the British Geological Survey to man the colonial posts resented this strictly pragmatic emphasis and sought to fuse scientific concepts of survey with their basic mineralogical work. The conflict between administrators and geologists was often overt. Selwyn, appointed to head the Victorian Geological Survey in 1852, fought a sustained battle with a demanding and dominant Secretary for Mines, the 'half-mad bureaucrat' Robert Brough Smyth.[11] Selwyn, however, enjoyed a greater freedom and flexibility than his colleagues in the other colonies. Funded by a Government made prosperous by gold, he managed to add nearly a dozen field and assistant geologists to his survey between 1854 and its abrupt disbandment in 1869, and to establish a firm scientific base in his survey's work. A hard taskmaster, Selwyn brought a special rigour to the study of Australian geology, and despite Government pressure for the discovery of metals, his team established systematic mapping in Victoria, producing 50 district map sheets, a geological map of Victoria in eight sheets, and numerous reports on the geology of the colony. Selwyn also contributed to auriferous theory – then under debate in Europe[12] – and his conclusions were important for deep mining in Australia. His survey also established the Cambrian/Lower Silurian system in Australia.[13]

Importantly for Australian geology, Selwyn's teams were to fertilise the whole landscape of colonial geology when the Victorian Survey was disbanded for lack of funds in 1869. Selwyn himself moved on to become the distinguished director of Canada's Geological Survey but left a generation of geologists – Daintree and Aplin in Queensland; C.S. Wilkinson and R.F. Pitman in New South Wales; H.Y.L. Brown in South and later Western Australia; R.A. Murray and E.J. Dunn in Victoria and R. Etheridge Jnr as a leading palaeontologist in the later New South Wales geological survey – to consolidate a strong geological professionalism in Australia.

Despite government pragmatism, all the early surveys managed to produce systematic geological, mineralogical and topographical mapping, to make stratigraphical determinations, and amass collections of rocks and fossils for economic and palaeological examination. All this despite the cries from field geologists echoed by Aplin in Queensland that 'I am only a *Govt. prospector* & not Govt. Geologist at all.'[14] Charles Gould, whose one-man survey in Tasmania was also abolished in 1869, wrote Clarke with equal grievance: 'Geologically speaking the results of my last year are absolutely *nil* . . . the Government hampered me with a large party . . . avowedly and solely for the purpose of getting gold. I was so much disgusted at having my geological work knocked upon the head, that I made an express stipulation with the Ministry that I was never afterwards to be requested to take part in Gold expeditions.'[15]

All the geological surveyors endured enforced prospecting work as gold and other precious metals glittered seductively at governments. In time, too, all the early colonial surveys were truncated by legislative vote. In an egalitarian society, governments cut spending on geological survey but gave handsome rewards to prospectors who stumbled on gold. Edward Hargreaves (1816–81), the man who promoted the discovery of gold near Bathurst in 1851, procured rewards totalling more than £10,000 from the Government of New South Wales and the Victorian Gold Committee, while the two discoverers of Ballarat and Bendigo and others received smaller sums. Colonists and the press clearly preferred miners and gold diggers to 'scientific gentlemen'. It was, as Governor Sir William Denison summed up a prevailing mood, extremely difficult 'to persuade either individuals or Governments, that it is both cheaper and better to do a thing well at once, than to act upon the principle that everything is good enough for the infancy and early life of the Colony.'[16]

Yet ultimately, the geologists' work formed the groundwork for the permanent geological surveys founded in each colony as the last quarter of the century advanced. Charles Wilkinson (1843–1891) headed the New South Wales Geological Survey in 1874; a Geological Survey was instituted in Queensland under Robert Logan Jack (1845–1921) in 1878; Henry Y.L. Brown (1844–1928) became Geological Surveyor in South Australia in 1882; a Victorian Geological Survey was permanently reactivated under J. Stirling (1852–1905) in 1887, and, after a succession of short appointments, a Tasmanian Geological Survey was set up under W.H. Twelvetrees in 1899. Finally, Andrew Gibb Maitland launched the Western Australian Geological Survey in 1899. While these surveys were still geared to a mineralogical search, they would become increasingly designed for the systematic development of related geological, petrographic and palaeontological research.

Through private vigour, the importation of excellent young geologists from Britain's Geological Survey, and the resourcefulness of field staff in resisting restrictive Government bounds, geological science was planted soundly in Australia. Selwyn had the satisfaction of knowing his Victorian Survey won the reputation (with that of the United States Geological Survey) of being 'the best in the world': a Chair of Geology was established under the youthful A.M. Thomson (1841–1871) at Sydney University in 1869 (and inherited by Archibald Liversidge on Thomson's death): the Elder Chair of Natural History, including Geology, was created and assumed by Professor Ralph Tate (1840–1901) at Adelaide University in 1875; while Australia's highly creative geologist, T.W. Edgeworth David, having served on the New South Wales Geological Survey, took up the Chair of Geology at Sydney University in 1891. A new period of high geological endeavour was set in train.

CHAPTER EIGHT

The weather & the sky

The rise of meteorology

Until at least the third decade of the 19th century, the study of meteorology was in its infancy. Centuries of scattered observations had failed to give the subject the dimensions of a science and, as one leading practitioner noted in 1831, the medley of information assembled on the world's atmospheric conditions represented 'an appalling mass of heterogeneous and uncoordinated facts'.[1]

Australia, with its insular position and vast hinterland, was destined to yield important findings for meteorological science. The earliest records were gathered by navigators and explorers around the coast.[2] Sir Thomas Brisbane entered the meteorological lists by establishing a sprinkling of weather stations dispersed around New South Wales, while the Rossbank Magnetic Observatory, set up in Hobart Town in 1840, furnished climatic and meteorological data and linked Australia's magnetic records with those of stations overseas.[3] Much early meteorological investigation, however, remained in private hands. Explorers and surveyors kept meteorological journals; Oxley, Sturt, Strzelecki and Mitchell provided magnetic and climatic data from inland points. P.P. King (who had made excellent climatological observations on his circumnavigation of the Australian continent in 1817–22) maintained a private observatory at Port Stephens and published his deductions in colonial journals and on his printing press; while the ubiquitous Reverend William Clarke, an amateur of meteorology while still in England, set up weather registers in his country parishes, kept thrice-daily readings of wind and weather, and supplemented his observations on geological tours. Clarke, who saw the need for coordinated weather records in Australia, kept in touch with government observers and coastal mariners, published 20 meteorological articles in the *Sydney Morning Herald* early in 1842, and used his role as scientific correspondent of the Sydney press to urge 'gentlemen' to collect meteorological information to help establish the country's scientific laws.

Clarke's mind was preoccupied with vortices and storms. He early advanced the rotary or gyratory action of southern hemisphere winds and adduced evidence that gales blew off the eastern coast, moved from left to right, while the southerly gales blew from the north. One view he hammered concerned the hot winds of Sydney, which he believed originated near the Equator as a prolongation of the trade winds arriving from the north-west to rotate and follow a true curvilinear course back to equatorial zones. His opinion roused sharp comment from Ludwig Leichhardt, a discerning meteorologist himself, who was also applying theories worked out in Europe to the Antipodes, in reverse.

In May 1842, Leichhardt wrote to the German Professor Heinrich Dove, whose law of veering was a starting point for meteorological research in both hemispheres:

Here in Sydney I reconsidered your theory of winds, and

found, that here too it applies, but as expected, only in reverse. At the entrance to the beautiful, indented Port Jackson they have been recording meteorological observations for quite a long time. Judging from such of the weekly observations as I was able to verify, they are carefully made, and are of the greatest value. An Anglican clergyman, Mr. Clarke, has been making similar observations on the meteorology of New Holland and has also been contributing a series of articles on the subject to the Sydney Herald, *based, in part, on the comparison of several registers. He has been trying to prove that all thunderstorms move around from the S through WNE, but the regular change of wind is really from S through ENW. Furthermore, he wanted to demonstrate that the Southeast winds were the incipient Trade Winds. The observations made at South Head show, however, that the Northeasterlies are the prevailing winds, not the Southeasterlies . . . [Clarke] does not believe that central Australia is arid, because the hot winds are so heavily charged with electriciy that they even affect the magnetic needle, and because gases and water vapour are always produced over water basins or over plains covered with vegetation, and this generation of gases is the only source of atmospheric electriciy. He therefore assumes the existence either of a great salt lake or of surfaces clad with vegetation. Nevertheless, the extraordinary dryness of these winds, which so quickly dry everything up, is evidence against the belief that the air masses originate over an inland lake; and their effect on the magnetic needle is easily explained as the effect of the passage of steadily streaming, warm air.*

If it be true that the remarkable, hot Northwesterly winds are masses of air which have been heated and have risen over the tropical part of New Holland, their astonishing dryness would be decisive indication of a desert in the interior of the country.[4]

Leichhardt was right. Tracking inland on his last expedition, in 1848, he would prove the point with his life.

One of the most distinguished, if unexpected, contributors to early Australian meteorology was the British economist and philosopher William Stanley Jevons (1835-82), who arrived in Sydney as a young man in 1854, as assayer to the Sydney Mint. Jevons was 'pretty hard on meteorology' on his Journey to Australia and was soon providing regular weekly meteorological reports to the *Empire* newspaper in Sydney. 'My duties [self-imposed] of meteorological reporter,' he wrote his sisters, 'I find quite onerous, and I am now, I believe, the sole acting meteorologist in Sydney . . . It is a most complicated subject, requiring a knowledge more or less of light, heat, chemistry, electricity etc; and is, therefore, a sort of difficult *scientific exercise* rather than a science.'[5] Jevons collected a battery of instruments and in 1859 published an elaborate paper on the 'Climatology of Australia' based on an historical overview of available weather data in which he offered perceptive generalisation of Australia's climatic phenomena, including cyclones.[6]

By the mid-1850s, meteorological work was consolidated on an official basis in the colonies. In 1853, the Victorian Government built an observatory at Williamstown and recorded data on climate. Three years later, the arrival of Dr Georg Balthasar von Neumayer (1826-1909) brought a highly qualified German physicist, oceanographer and meteorologist to the colonies. Neumayer was, academically, probably the best qualified scientist to come to Australia. A PhD of Munich University, he held a Chair of Physics at Hamburg and had helped carry out a magnetic survey of Bavaria under the direction of King Maximillian. Trained in navigation, he had also sailed to South America to pursue oceanographic studies, and in 1852, he set out as ship's mate to Sydney, from where he left to see the Victorian gold-diggings at Bendigo. Two years later, after some brief research at Hobart's Magnetic Observatory, Neumayer returned to Germany convinced of the valuable opportunities for research in his fields in the colonies and determined to drum up some financial support. Fortunately, he was backed by the geographer Alexander von Humboldt and won the support of the King of Bavaria for his plan to set up a physical observatory at Melbourne for the study of terrestrial magnetism and related phenomena. Other support came from the Royal Society of London and the British Association, and, with £2000 worth of instruments supplied by the altruistic Maximillian, Neumayer arrived back in Melbourne in January 1857.[7] By early 1858, he had established a magnetic and meteorological observatory at Flagstaff Hill joined, with Victorian Government support, by the old observatory from Williamstown.

Neumayer himself became the colony's meteorologist and director of the Victorian Magnetic Survey. During his following seven years in the colony he made sophisticated contributions to meteorological science, including a major paper, a 'Climatological Outline of the Colony of Victoria', and papers on the application of Dove's law of veering to Australian winds, drawing systematic data from the many weather stations he set up throughout the colony. His most signal work was the magnetic survey of Victoria he conducted almost single-handed between 1858–64. Neumayer travelled some 18,000 kilometres on foot or by pack-horse and established over 230 field stations for magnetic survey, which laid the foundation of continuing magnetic survey work in the colony. The report on this survey was published in 1869. On Neumayer's return to Germany early in 1864, Flagstaff observatory was absorbed into the new Melbourne Observatory.

In New South Wales, astronomical and meteorological work begun under Brisbane's regime and carried on officially by Rümker and Dunlop[8] gradually fell into decline. James Dunlop suffered severely from his isolation despite the private encouragement of Clarke and King, and gradually gave up all attempts to reduce and publish observations made on the new transit instrument installed at the Parramatta Observatory in 1835. When Captain Ross of HMS *Erebus* called to check the ship's chronometer in 1841, he found Australia's first small observatory much run down and, on his recommendation and a report from P.P. King, the Parrramatta Observatory was closed by the British Government in 1848, the year following Dunlop's retirement. Eight years elapsed before the establishment of Sydney Observatory and the arrival in 1856 of the Reverend William Scott (1825–1917) as government astronomer, bringing with him the newest meteorological instruments from London, which he deployed in 12 weather stations about the colony.

In South Australia the energetic and innovative Charles Todd (1826–1910), trained at Greenwich Observatory by the astronomer royal, George Airy, filled the dual posts of astronomer and superintendent of posts and telegraphs from 1855. Mindful of the need for a knowledge of rainfall and climate in a predominantly agricultural land, Todd used his positions to place weather stations in the hands of country postmasters and outlying telegraphists with precise instructions to gather information on climate, rain and winds. As

The weather & the sky

time went on he imported improved instruments, extended his stations to the Northern Territory, and used the Overland Telegraph Line, which he installed between 1870–72, to report immediate news of storms and weather.[9] By 1874, all Overland Telegraph repeater stations provided meteorological observations which were coordinated widely, as the 1870s progressed, by the astronomers in other colonies. The dot dash of Morse code spelt out daily weather information across a vast continent. Todd's techniques, indeed, launched a system of weather reporting that boasted 1600 weather stations in New South Wales, and a thousand in Victoria by the century's end, and were linked with meteorological establishments in Western Australia (1876), Tasmania (1882) and Queensland (1887).

H.C. Russell, government astronomer in New South Wales, and Robert Ellery, who succeeded Neumayer in Victoria, were key figures in the extension of colonial meteorology. Vast distances, wide-flung contacts, and the sometimes daunting inexpertise of helpers had first to be conquered before a scientific meteorological network could function effectively. H.C. Russell's blunt communication to his scattered helpers underlines the point. Each observatory issued a manual of instructions and supplied instruments so that a heterogeneous army could aid the process of gathering facts. It was not always easy. H.C. Russell wrote tersely to one observer in the far west of New South Wales:

1 *Did you receive a copy of 'Instructions' about the same time as you received the Meteorological Instruments?*
2 *If so: Did you read them?*
3 *If not: Why not?*
4 *Are you aware who imposed the Observations upon you?*

> *Your Return for January is almost* worthless *because you have not been guided by your Instructions.*[10]

But the astronomers' patience and perseverance paid dividends. Meteorological analysis and theory matured on the basis of daily weather records amassed from strategically located points. Geodetic, seismological and magnetic studies proceeded in the wake of the consolidation of meteorological science, while the separate state meteorological services were integrated and developed under the Commonwealth Bureau of Meteorology founded in 1907.

Astronomical pioneers

When the Parramatta observatory was closed down by government edict in 1848, few citizens could have anticipated the immense progress in astronomical and astrophysical researches that would distinguish their country in the next hundred years. Rather, in a settlement with growing maritime and agricultural interests, the event seemed to foreshadow the end of a number of important undertakings in geophysics as well as the eclipse of astronomical science. One editorialist reflected: 'The stars come out at night, comets traverse the solar system, and one mighty comet, in the course of 1848 will startle, or otherwise pass unnoticed before our vision, and there is no one here endowed with sufficient skill . . . or authority to register these heavenly tokens. Ships come and go . . . destined to circumnavigate the globe; and there is no one spot to which their commanders can refer for the adjustment of their chronometers, or for the exact point of time.'[11]

Yet the elements of Australia's recovery lay both in her unrivalled physical conditions for astronomical survey and in the advent of men of sufficient scientific vision and influence to advance the building of observatories and telescopes in defiance of the perennial colonial preference for constructing railways and roads. Where these two elements fused, the colonies produced two active centres of southern astronomy in Sydney and Melbourne in the next two decades.

Eight years after the abandonment of Parramatta, the appointment of Sir William Denison FRS, soldier, astronomical observer and engineer,[12] as Governor of New South Wales, led to the decision to appoint a government astronomer in 1856 and the following year work on the construction of Sydney Observatory began at Flagstaff Hill. The new astronomer, the Reverend William Scott, Cambridge wrangler and lecturer in mathematics from Sydney Sussex College, Cambridge, supervised the erection of the observatory, brought in the meteorological instruments for new weather stations, began meridian observations on the position of certain stars and, during 1861, acquired an equatorial telescope of $7\frac{1}{4}$-inch aperture on which he began observations of comets.

The most creative astronomer of the period, however, was not, as Scott himself realised, the government astronomer, but the 'local boy' John Tebbutt (1834–1916), of Windsor, New South Wales. Born in the colony and educated at parish and private schools, Tebbutt early developed an interest in mechanical objects and celestial mechanisms and began his explorations of the southern heavens from his home at Windsor using an ordinary ship's telescope and sextant, at the age of 20. In May 1861 he had the grand experience of discovering 'the great comet' of 1861 – 'one of the finest comets on record' – on his marine telescope and of making his own reputation and enlarging that of Australian astronomical science. Scott had recognised Tebbutt's qualities over a year before. 'I cannot resist the inclination,' he wrote the young man from Sydney Observatory in April 1860, 'to remark what a pity (I may almost say what a shame) it is for you to waste your energies as you seem likely to do. With your enthusiastic love of Astronomy, mathematical ability and industry you might become one of the distinguished Astronomers of the age, in fact Australia's first Astronomer; but if you remain where you are without instruments you may amuse yourself by rough observations and calculations, but cannot add one particle to the real treasures of science.'[13] Scott was both wrong, and right. Tebbutt's name spun in astronomical circles; but he himself saw the need to upgrade his equipment and, during 1862, acquired a 3¼-inch refracting telescope, and this same year made the acquaintance of Encke's Comet (first seen in Australia by the Parramatta astronomers 40 years before). In 1863 Tebbutt built his own small wooden observatory at Windsor.

Scott had marked this 'gentleman astronomer' as his successor as government astronomer of New South Wales. But Tebbutt declined. He assisted Scott in computing occultations and eclipses, but continued with his own work at the Windsor Observatory, maintaining a remarkable series of patient and accurate observations on comets, occultations of stars by the moon, eclipses, transits of Jupiter's satellites, variable stars and double stars, and the position of minor planets, all of which were invaluable to world astronomers. In 1881, exactly 20 years after his first major sighting, Tebbutt discovered his second 'great comet' known as the 'Great Comet of 1881', or 'Tebbutt's Comet'. He first saw this striking celestial visitor with the naked eye on 22 May, 'a few degrees', he later reported, 'above the place where I discovered the Great Comet of 1861'. His instruments had been updated the previous year,

The weather & the sky

and during 1879 he had erected a substantial observatory of brick near the original wooden structure. Tebbutt's instruments now included a 4½-inch equatorial refractor, his marine telescope, a sextant, an eight-day clock, and a box chronometer. With his 4½-inch telescope he could now observe the broad tail of the new comet, and he confirmed its first recorded existence on 23 May in the Sydney press. The event, and other sightings, caused much stir and jubilation among residents of New South Wales. 'You from your watch tower, the sentinel of our southern heavens, the first to challenge the celestial stranger', extolled one excited citizen in congratulation; while there was passing clamour that other residents might have seen it first. Tebbutt's accomplishment in tracking and recording the 1881 comet is not, however, in doubt. Across 13 nights, he made 58 positional measurements of the comet and later completed the onerous orbital calculations. He observed it last on 14 June 1881, disappearing from the Windsor skies, although Tebbutt's Comet became a magnificent northern hemisphere object visible to the naked eye for three months and was last observed by telescope on 14 February 1882, some 555 million kilometres from earth; one of the major cometary discoveries of the second half of the 19th century.[14]

Tebbutt's remarkable span of work proved what could still be done in the late 19th century by a professional amateur. He published 300 papers in scientific journals; wrote *On the Progress and Present State of Astronomical Science in New South Wales* (Sydney 1871); made extensive meteorological observations across 30 years from 1863 to 1896, reviewing some in *Meteorological Observations made at the Private Observatory of John Tebbutt Jnr* in 1868; and, a comet seeker first and foremost, reported his cometary observations in no less than 61 research papers, which brought him high prestige abroad.[15] He was awarded the Royal Astronomical Society's Medal in 1905.

Like Tebbutt, Sydney's other distinguished astronomer, Henry Chamberlain Russell FRS (1836–1907), combined original work in astronomy with significant investigations in geophysical science. Another Australian-born scientist, Russell was one of Sydney University's early graduates. In 1858, with a BA behind him, he joined Sydney Observatory as a computer. Eleven years later, he became government astronomer on the death of Scott's successor, G.R. Smalley, and held the post until 1905. It was Russell who, as a talented designer of self-recording instruments, equipped a vast number of meteorological stations in New South Wales and based his many important pioneering papers on weather and the cyclic behaviour of Australian climate on the mass of evidence he accumulated from these scattered posts. In astronomy, two undertakings brought his small observatory international fame: his organisation of Australia's observations of the transit of Venus in December 1874, and his sustained participation in the International Astrographic Catalogue projected at the Paris conference in 1887, which Russell attended and in which Sydney Observatory was assigned the zone of south declension 54° to 62°. Russell developed his work of stellar and lunar photography to a high degree of excellence. His photographs of the transit of Venus were pronounced 'the best and most complete' and he reproduced remarkable early photographs of the Milky Way and Magellanic Clouds. His photographs of large stars for the Astrographic Catalogue won unqualified praise from his international colleagues. Russell became the first graduate of Sydney University to become a fellow of the Royal Society of London.

The weather & the sky

Melbourne's heyday as a centre of astronomical activity dates from the acquisition of the Great Melbourne Telescope in 1869. As early as 1852, the Royal Society of London discussed the plan for erecting a powerful reflecting telescope in the southern hemisphere to extend the work performed by Sir John Herschel on southern stars and nebulae at the Cape of Good Hope. While much advice was taken on its ideal location, the bid made by Victoria's scientifically minded governor, Sir Henry Barkly, and the Professor of Mathematics at Melbourne University, William Parkinson Wilson netted the prestigious instrument for that colony. In 1862, the Victorian Legislature voted £5,000 for the construction of the largest equatorially mounted reflector in the world, and the new Melbourne Observatory to receive it was established under the government astronomer, Robert Ellery (1827–1908) in 1863. Five years later, the giant telescope, designed and mounted by Thomas Grubb in Dublin, and comprising a 48-inch cassegrain reflector with speculum metal mirror and focal length of 160 feet, was shipped to Melbourne in the care of the British astronomer, A. Le Sueur.[16]

The Victorian Government astronomer, Robert Ellery, expressed his joy. 'The telescope has at length arrived,' he wrote British astronomer Sir Edward Sabine enthusiastically, 'and we are now very busy getting it erected, for nothing could be done towards it till the great machine came to hand. It will be nearly two months before it can be fairly tried, when a spacious rectangular building and its travelling roof will be completed . . . The Government, with hard economy in all other directions, have still acted very liberally about this work, and I only trust the telescope itself will turn out all that is expected of it.'[17]

Alas, it was not to be. Despite the scope and promise of

this enterprise, the great leviathan ran into difficulties. Innumerable problems plagued the installation: news of the problems spread around the world, and Le Sueur himself returned to England immediately after the telescope was ready for working in August 1869. Thereafter, responsibility for using the instrument passed to Wilson, who readily abandoned his mathematical researches for astronomical work. But the Great Telescope proved a failure of instrumentation. The surface of the speculum, which was coated in shellac to protect it during transportation, never recovered its pristine state. While investigations with it resulted in a series of drawings of southern nebulae, stellar photography and daily photographs of the sun, none rivalled Russell's contribution on more modest equipment in New South Wales. The imaginative Victorian project never equalled its planners' hopes. With the eventual closure of Melbourne Observatory in 1944, the great telescope was transferred to the Commonwealth Observatory at Mount Stromlo, Canberra, where it was modernised and adapted for light collection on a large scale for spectroscopic and photometric work.[18] In the event the thrust of 20th-century observational astronomy in Australia passed from the state observatories to Mount Stromlo, which was linked to the Australian National University in 1946.

CHAPTER NINE

Evolution in Australia

Living fossils

Australia as the most recently discovered continent, was to fill a distinctive place in the evidence and discussion of evolutionary theory that spilled across 19th-century discussion and challenged scientific and religious thought. In itself, the remote landmass offered an unprecedented opportunity for investigating the unique and undisturbed fauna of a major biological subdivision of the globe. Long before Cook and his scientists landed, Dutch observers had carried back scattered information on the 'unnatural monsters' seen around the West Australian coast. Francois Pelsaert, wrecked off that coast at Houtman's Abrolhos in 1629, recorded the first description of Australian marsupials, which he called 'dogs', and was the first to air the false, though long-held, opinion that the baby wallaby was born on the nipple of its mother.[1] The discovery and naming of the strange animal *Ornithorhynchus anatinus*, the platypus, confirmed that all things in the Antipodes were 'queer and opposite', and, as one thoughtful observer summed up, 'that the Australian section of the garden of creation appeared to be planned on principles not easily reconciled with the idea of a chain of universal being'.[2] Charles Darwin, whose theory of the evolution of species by natural selection would later startle the world, arrived in Australia in 1836 and was himself moved to write, 'An unbeliever in anything beyond his reason might exclaim "Surely two Creators have been at work".'[3]

Ideas coined in the Antipodes would fertilise some of the earliest writings on evolution. Naturalist Captain John Hunter, sketching and observing the Australian wildlife for his *Journal of the Transactions at Port Jackson*, which he published in London in 1793 affirmed that 'a promiscuous intercourse between the different sexes of all these different animals' in Australia might account for their unlikely forms. The idea found favour with Charles Darwin's grandfather, the lively Dr Erasmus Darwin, who took over the concept of random promiscuity and Hunter's exposition to underpin his early theory of evolutionary development from a single form, which he published in his *Zoonomia* the following year.[4]

From the outset, Australian biological evidence gave rise to singular difficulties of classification. Both plants and fauna posed novel and perplexing questions that challenged accepted systems of taxonomy and raised doubts about established notions of the natural world. The Australian marsupials, and their most eccentric kin the monotremes,[5] instantly engaged the attention of naturalists. Banks had moved early on the subject,[6] and his surmise had not been wrong. In the new theatre of the Antipodes however, the furred platypus and the spiny anteater would play tricky and elusive roles.

Two scientists, at opposite ends of the world, who would devote much skill and research to the unravelling of the anatomy, habits, and reproductive processes of these players were Dr George Bennett (1804–1893) in Australia, and the British comparative anatomist Richard (later Sir Richard)

Owen FRS (1804–1892). Bennett had trained at the Royal College of Surgeons, London when Owen was Assistant Curator of the College Museum. In 1828 Bennett set out for the Pacific where he travelled extensively, visiting Australia in 1829 and again in 1832–33. He filled numerous bottles and boxes with zoological specimens for the College, which Owen used at the outset of his research career. Owen's classical study *Memoir on the Pearly Nautilus*, which won him election to the Royal Society of London in 1834, derived from a specimen Bennett collected for him in the Pacific, and for the next half century, Bennett was to serve the influential British scientist as an expert collector in the field.

Bennett was himself a discerning naturalist. After his Australian visit of 1832–33, he published *Wanderings in New South Wales . . . the Journal of a Naturalist* (1834), and from 1836 he settled in Sydney, working as a physician and doubling as Curator of the newly constituted Australian Museum. His own house bristled with live and stuffed fauna collected on his trips, and he published a number of descriptive papers and a second volume, *Gatherings of a Naturalist in Australasia*, in 1860. Across his long career, he kept in close touch with his friend and colleague Richard Owen, to whom he sent consignments of Australian faunal skeletons, organs and fossil bones. His despatch of a foetal kangaroo in uterus to Owen in 1833 was to disprove the entrenched claim of pastoralists and bushmen that the embryonic kangaroo found attached to the mother's nipple was conceived in the pouch, although the larger question of how the infant reached the pouch and teat after birth would remain unsettled for many years.[7]

The problem of the classification and generation of the monotremes formed a central question of Australian natural science. Were they, like birds and reptiles, oviparous (producing their young by means of eggs expelled from the body before being hatched), or were they ovoviviparous (hatching their young from eggs within their bodies before the process of birth)? The difficulty in determining the question lay in bridging the gap between specimens gathered in various stages of impregnation and the advent of the young found, in the case of the platypus, in the burrows, and of the echidna, in the pouch.

For many years, these strange creatures kept their secret. Bennett tried strenuously but unsuccessfully to observe their habits by domesticating them in his home. 'I procured from the burrows four living specimens,' he wrote Owen while travelling in the colony in 1833, 'one escaped during the journey to Sydney, one died on the road (both females) and two (male and female) nearly full grown species, I brought safe (carrying them on horseback upward of 200 miles) to Sydney; they became much thinner lately than when I first had them, although they appeared to feed well on the bread and water and chopped meat which I gave them (their usual food is very small shellfish and river insects). One, the female, died a few days since from the effects of a fall (for they run about my room), the male is living, lively and seems to be regaining flesh, it is a most interesting harmless animal, but restless and difficult to keep quiet when once awake; but they sleep much during the day and also night, only coming out of their berth a short time to feed and play about the room.'[8] Together with this remarkable tale, Bennett also sent off a preparation of several uteri of the female *Ornithorhynchus* 'showing an egg in the left uterus' and two smaller eggs in a second uterus.

Other collectors were pressed into service. Owen particularly sought the assistance of Surveyor-General Sir Thomas Mitchell to gather specimens on his inland surveys 'to enable me', as Owen put it, 'to solve some of the most puzzling enigmas of Physiology'.[9] Collection was needed on a large scale. 'A female (*Ornithorhynchus*) should be shot and pickled every week during the months of September, October and November,' Owen instructed from London. 'Nothing short of this will enable us to determine the exact nature of the peculiarities of her reproductive economy. A hole should be cut in the belly, and spirit thrown in, and then she should be placed in spirits bodily.' The same treatment was to be accorded 'the equally paradoxical *Echidna*', of which, Owen confessed, he knew much less than of the *Ornithorhynchus*. 'The only chance of success is to get specimens in all seasons, pickle them and send them over: 100 would not be too many; if we could only thereby settle the long disputed question, oviparous, ovoviviparous, or viviparous and how the young suck.'[10]

Such substantial 'sacrifice' of these fauna appeared the more essential when zoological determination of their anatomy and their subsequent classification was being determined overseas. Charles Darwin showed insight when, after his party killed a platypus on his journey to Bathurst in 1836, he wrote P.P. King, 'I consider it a great feat to be in at the death of so wonderful an animal.'[11]

Bennett, however, would take prime responsibility for the long-term field work in locating specimens, and his regular consignments to Owen contained every form and organ of monotreme and marsupial, and other curiosities as well. Working on the contents of these consignments, between 1833 and 1868 Owen published 25 papers and monographs on the structure, generation and development of living Australian monotremes and marsupials. On the evidence of the specimens and his careful dissections, both he and Bennett increasingly subscribed to the verdict that monotreme generation was ovoviviparous and that both female platypus and echidna brought forth their young in a living state. It was a viewpoint the Aborigines tended to endorse. 'The Yas[s] natives,' Bennett reported early, 'at first asserted that the animals lay eggs but very shortly after contradicted themselves. In the Tumat [Tumut] country . . . the result was the same: "Tambreet (the platypus) no make egg; pickaninny tumble down".'[12]

In the event it fell to a young visiting zoologist, William Hay Caldwell (1859–1941) on a research grant from Cambridge University, to settle the matter in 1884. In late August that year, while doing field work on the Burnett River, Queensland, Caldwell shot a platypus that had laid one egg and held a second, partially dilated egg containing an embryo ready for laying inside. Caldwell wrote a message, which he left at a neighbouring station to be picked up by the local postman and relayed by telegraph to his friend Professor Archibald Liversidge in Sydney. His splendidly terse telegram, dated 29 August, read: 'Monotremes oviparous, ovum meroblastic.'[13] (It meant monotremes egg-laying: the egg has an undivided yolk as with birds.) Acting on Caldwell's request, Liversidge at once flashed the news by cable to the British Association for the Advancement of Science meeting in Montreal. The secret was out. Across the continent, in one of those coincidences that mark discovery in science, Dr William Haacke (1855–1922), curator of the South Australian Museum, exhibited an eggshell he had found in the pouch of an echidna before the Royal Society of South Australia;[14] this was on 2 September 1881, the very day that

Caldwell's news was read to scientists in Montreal. Caldwell, too, in this string of felicitous findings, also found an echidna on the Burnett River, which, held upside down, dropped an egg from its pouch. The Englishman used the telegraph again – this time to George Bennett in Sydney – to confirm that he had 'obtained all stages development Monotremata oviparous Meroblastic'. Beaten to the post, Bennett showed generosity. 'We must now wait with patience,' he at once wrote Owen, 'for Mr Caldwell's able development of the mystery and it will be of the greatest interest . . . but none more than to ourselves that the problem of the Monotremes will be solved during our lifetime.'[15]

Science needs many workers to check and challenge its inductions, and for some years these were lacking in Australian zoological science. Owen's acceptance of the ovoviviparous generation of the monotremes provided one example of how research could stabilise around an inaccurate concept until the advent of other well-qualified researchers gave it fresh review. Certainly, Owen's reputation as a leading comparative anatomist served to underwrite and strengthen what proved to be a faulty view. For Caldwell, however, fortune favoured the prepared mind and opened up the study of monotremes to new research directions in Australia.[16]

Despite the lack of one elusive answer, Owen's contribution to Australian zoology was large. Working across an immense spectrum – South African, European, South American, Australian and New Zealand living and extinct species – his researches on morphology and classification served to fill vast gaps in the existing knowledge of the changing nature of species, their adaptation and variation under differing geographical conditions, and their place in the fragmented yet emerging picture of organic life. On the Australian front, his work on the osteology and morphology of the Australian marsupials enabled him to make generalisations on distinctive geographical developments and to explain the significance of adaptive forms.

I have always connected with the long droughts in Australia [he wrote Bennett] – *with the extensive tracts where there are no waters – with the difficuly of obtaining that necessary element of life, the singular peculiarity of organisation which prevails among the Mammalian quadrupeds of Australia. No matter what their diet, whatever their powers of locomotion and spheres of action – whether they burrow like the Wombat, climb like the Phalanger, jump like the Kangaroo, trot like the Bandicoot, or fly like the Petaurist – all these creatures are marsupial, . . . creatures having the power of carrying their delicate prematurely born young with them wherever they go. They have this condition, viz. a soft, warm, well-lined portable nursery-pocket or 'perambulator'. In order that quadrupeds should be fitted to exist in a great continent like Australia . . . those quadrupeds must possess an organisation suited to such peculiar climatic conditions . . . And since we find that marsupial animals have lived in Australia from a very remote period, so we must infer that its peculiar climate had prevailed during a vast lapse of time.*[17]

On the evolution of these adaptive mechanisms, however, Owen had less to say, and a 'creationist' in his ideological thinking, he attributed the anatomical development of the pouched marsupial to the 'irrefragable evidence of Creative foresight' and of 'Final cause'.[18] His ideas of the origin and adaption of species found wide adherence in Australia, and his judgment and researches carried the support and admiration of the many naturalists in the colonies. Considerably less congenial, and far in advance of most scientific thinking, were the concepts espoused by a former 'scientific visitor' to the colonies, Charles Darwin.

The impact of Darwinian ideas

Back from his voyage on the *Beagle*, Charles Darwin settled down to working on his journal and notebooks and piecing together the immense array of facts and correlations he had assembled from observations around the world.[19] From a number of books and papers, he quickly established a name as a percipient observer and in 1844 he began to set down his ideas on the selection and adaptation of species, which he was to extend and authenticate in the next 12 years. It was not until 1856 that Darwin commenced to prepare his controversial concepts on the origin of species for print, a process unexpectedly precipitated by the arrival two years later of a short unpublished paper from the British naturalist Alfred Wallace enunciating views on natural selection similar to Darwin's own.[20] Prodded by friends, Darwin published an outline of his own and Wallace's theory in the Linnean Society *Journal* of August 1858; a year later, his influential book *The Origin of Species* was launched.

Darwin's thesis of spontaneous mutation and evolution of species by selection threw the intellectual community into embattled camps. With the exception of the triumvirate of Darwin's intimate friends, Huxley, Lyell and Joseph Hooker, and one or two others as the idea gained ground, the great majority of British scientists rejected the ideas of adaptation and renounced natural selection as inimical to their religious beliefs. Richard Owen led the attack with a hostile review of *The Origin* in the *Edinburgh Review*, and the battle was aired publicly at the famous Oxford meeting of the British Association in 1860 when Huxley replied to Bishop Wilberforce's sneer about his presumed ancestry, that he would rather have an ape for a grandfather than a man who used his superior talents to denigrate scientific debate; Darwin's former captain, Robert FitzRoy, prominently displayed a Bible shouting 'The Book, the Book!'. Across the Channel in the home of Lamarckian evolution, Darwin's supporters were few while in the new world the influential palaeontologist Louis Agassiz led the creationist defence and condemned *The Origin* as mischievous and unscientific.

In the Australian colonies, the climate of scientific opinion was equally unfavourable to Darwinian thought. Some notions of an evolutionary process were already in circulation in Australia when Darwin's opus reached Sydney in 1860. Lamarck's progressive development and Charles Lyell's advocacy of the appearance and extinction of species over infinitely changing eras, formed part of the intellectual background of scientifically minded colonists as they did of their colleagues overseas. But the majority of colonial scientists accepted separate creation, the fixity of species and the 'Genesis' account of Creation as crucial explanations of the origins of the physical world.

The Origin of Species took colonial scientists by storm. Despite the part played by Australian evidence, Darwin was not in correspondence with Australian scientists and none were privy to the formulation of his far-reaching views. Their reaction was unequivocal: they admired Darwin as a scientist, but detested the implication of his evolutionary ideas. W.S. Macleay, whose early participation in the debate on species qualified him to take a scientific stand, saw the issue primarily in theological terms and wholly misinterpreted Darwin's thesis of natural selection, confusing it with the evolutionary theory of Lamarck. When a copy of *The Origin of Species* reached Sydney in 1860, Macleay dashed off a long letter to an English friend:

The question is no less 'What am I' 'What is man?', a creature being under the direct government of his Creator, or only an accidental sprout of some primordial type that was the common progenitor of both animals and vegetables. . . The naturalist finds himself on the horns of a dilemma. For, either from the facts he observes, he must believe in a special creation of organised species, which creation has been progressive and is now in full operation, or he must adopt some such view as that of Darwin, viz. that the primordial material cell of life has been constantly sprouting forth of itself by 'natural selection' into all the various forms of animals and vegetables. As for his two kinds of 'selection' by which he accounts for all the species of animals and vegetables – viz. sexual selection and natural selection, I find them quite impossible to digest. . .

The theory is almost a materialistic one – nay, even so far atheistic that, if it allows of a deity at all, He has been ever since the institution of the primordial type of life fast asleep. I am myself so far a Pantheist that I see God in eveything; but then I believe in His special Providence, and that He is the constant and active sole Creator and all-wise Administrator of the Universe. . . It is far easier for me to believe in the direct and constant Government of the Creation of God, than that He should have created the world and then left it to manage itself, which is Darwin's theory in a few words.

Nonetheless, Charles Darwin is an old friend of mine and I feel grateful to him for his work. I hope it will make people attend to such matters, and to be no longer prevented by the first chapter of Genesis from asking for themselves what the Book of Nature says on the subject of Creation.[21]

Victoria's two leading scientists, Ferdinand von Mueller and Frederick McCoy, lent their strong expressions of opposition and professed their belief in the permanence of species and in a universe of order and design. Writing to Owen in August 1861, Mueller acknowledged Darwin's influence upon him in his boyhood in giving his life its direction and plan, but he sought now, he said, 'to endeavour to strengthen the opinion, so powerfully upheld by you on zoological and geological grounds that nature created species by design'. Mueller based his testimony on his own field work and affirmed that, 'during scarcely less than 22 years of observing of the forms of vegetable life in free nature, I had never cause to entertain any doubt, that we are surrounded by species clearly defined in nature, all perfect in their organisation, all destined to fulfil by unalterable laws those designs for which the power of our creating God called them into existence.'[22] McCoy went further. In two public lectures in Melbourne, he asserted the immutability of species and declared that his own palaeontological researches in the colonies confirmed the sudden appearance and cataclysmic disappearance of species and clearly suggested a 'separate creation' for Australian mammals.[23]

One scientist who gave *The Origin of Species* an open-minded reception was the New South Wales geologist the Reverend W.B. Clarke. Clarke was greatly impressed with the array of evidence Darwin had marshalled, and sent off his early congratulations in a letter to 'Down'. Clarke's interest was chiefly geological. He did not enlarge on the theory of organic selection, but, confident about the fate of the Scriptures, assisted Darwin with his experiments and supplied him with new evidence from his own geological work. Later, as vice-president of the Royal Society of New South Wales, Clarke took the lead in urging his fellow members to an unbiased investigation of Darwin's scientific views.[24] In turn, Darwin absorbed Clarke's notes and corrections in later editions of *The Origin*, corresponded with him on experimental subjects, and acted as a powerful sponsor for Clarke's selection to a fellowship of the Royal Society in 1876.

Darwin's most eloquent advocate in the colonies, however, was Gerard Krefft. Krefft (1830-81), a German emigrant who developed his interest in natural history in Australia and became a recognised authority on Australian snakes and vertebrates, was for 13 years curator of the Australian Museum. He corresponded with Darwin, proselytised his theory in Sydney newspapers, and sent him much corroborative data, sometimes of a trivial nature, on the behaviour and emotions of animals. Darwin thought well of Krefft, knew his writings, and gave him encouragement in his running battle with Richard Owen on the classification of extinct Australian forms. In Sydney, Robert D. Fitzgerald (1830-92), a government surveyor whose side-line study of orchids derived much from Darwin's own, also carried on a correspondence with his scientific mentor and dedicated his completed *Australian Orchids* to Darwin on its final publication in 1882. In South Australia, the Chief Justice, Richard Hanson, gave the most explicit and cogent contemporary examination of the Darwinian thesis in Four Papers read before the Philosophical Society of Adelaide in 1864.[25]

These men were exceptions. At best they contributed peripherally to Darwinian themes, though their interest provided a platform for the dissemination of evolutionary ideas. For a quarter of a century they were not conspicuous in the Australian universities. McCoy and Halford at Melbourne,[26] and John Smith at Sydney,[27] were openly hostile to evolutionary thought, though Edward Hearn, Professor of History and Political Economy at Melbourne, propounded a theory of social evolution in industrial society in his remarkable work *Plutology* published in 1864. The churches in Australia set the tone for the strong rejection of evolutionary opinion and radical intellectual thought. Bishop Perry, Anglican Bishop of Melbourne, defended the Bible against all current evolutionary literature in a public address on 'Science and the Bible' in Melbourne in September 1869 and though he clearly found *The Origin of Species* a curiously absorbing book, he roundly declared that not one of Darwin's illustrations of natural selection 'nor the whole of them together, in the slightest degree corroborates his theory'. The Roman Catholic priest and geologist the Reverend Julian Tenison Woods, whose pastoral duties enabled him to engage in palaeontological studies in South Australia, Tasmania, Queensland and New South Wales, also offered solid evidence to support the counter-revolutionary cause. He wrote: 'During more than twenty years of researches in Australian tertiary geology I have carefully sought for any reasonable evidence in favour of evolution or clues to its mode of operation, but have found none – none whatever. I must add that Australian geology, whether reluctantly or not, must admit that she can urge nothing in favour of that theory being true – the true explanation of Nature as we find it.'[28]

It fell to Sir William Macleay, president of the new Linnean Society of New South Wales, to sum up this negative tenor of Australian opinion in his address of 1876, in which he asserted 'that the Scottish version of "not proven" would be the best way of meeting all these barren theories . . . It seems really as if we had at this point reached the utmost range of the human intellect.'[29]

Modes of thinking changed slowly in the colonies. Sixteen years after *The Origin of Species* had broken on the scientific world, a considerable percentage of British scientists had accepted some form of progressive evolution for the origin of species excepting man. In Australia, however, this process was delayed. Although Darwin was made an honorary member of the Royal Society of New South Wales in 1879, and both Huxley and Joseph Hooker were awarded the society's first scientific honour, the Clarke Medal, in 1881 and 1885, acceptance of their major intellectual contributions did not come for another 20 years. In the event, the transformations that affected biology, physiology and biochemistry as a result of the Darwinian breakthrough could not be ignored and found expression in the last decade of the century in the new departments of biology and physiology that emerged in the universities of Sydney and Melbourne. Here evolutionary thought took root through the investigations carried out by researchers like William Haswell, J.T. Wilson and Charles Martin at Sydney, Baldwin Spencer at Melbourne and in the talented young workers they gathered to their schools.[30]

CHAPTER TEN

Colonial scientists versus the 'experts'

During the 1850s, two trends marked a changing cultural climate in the colonies; first, a sense of political nationalism and independence that stimulated self-government in the eastern colonies and the creation of a separate Victoria and Queensland in 1852 and 1859; and second, an upsurge of self-awareness that found expression in a spirit of optimism and equality and in a growing sense of self-motivation and responsibility in the country's intellectual life. In science these sensations were keenly felt. The new observatories, museums, and universities established through the 1850s became the signposts of institutional growth, while governments assumed increasing authority for fostering science. In Victoria, the richest legislature in the land went so far as to appoint a Board of Science composed of university and public service scientists to advise them on science and technology policy matters in 1858. This 'reality of newness and freedom' irradiated the individual scientist at work and moved him to cast off the old sense of unquestioning deference to expertise overseas.

Flora Australiensis

One field where this was demonstrated explicitly was botanical science, an area of the longest 'metropolitan' dominance and one in which, in the more recent years, the direction provided by leaders like Sir William and Joseph Hooker at Kew, had shaped a benevolent but specific British hegemony over Australian affairs. In the late 1850s, spurred in part by the Victorian Government's readiness to commit £1000 to the publication of a book on the flora of Australia, conflict reared, the first manifestation of tension between the rising self-confidence of experienced Australian researchers and the traditional overlordship of British science. The conflict was painful and far-reaching. Colonial experts, familiar with a distinctive environment and achieving a growing mastery over their own data, became anxious to put their knowledge to systematic and deductive use and were increasingly less willing to serve as the amanuenses of British science. In botany, the conflict crystallised around the figure of Dr Ferdinand von Mueller (1825–1896), government botanist of the colony of Victoria.

Mueller was the first of the professionally trained resident botanists in Australia.[1] Born in Rostock, Germany, of Danish parents, he was educated in Germany, became interested in botany at an early age, and took his doctorate in pharmacy at Kiel University with a thesis on the common shepherd's purse. Excited by all Dr Preiss told him of the unique vegetation of Western Australia, Mueller emigrated to South Australia in 1847 for reasons of botany and health. He took employment with an Adelaide pharmacist and scoured the surrounding countryside for specimens of plants. His resulting paper on the diagnosis and description of new Australian plants published by the Linnean Society of London in 1852 brought him to the attention of Sir William Hooker and, on Hooker's recommendation, he was appointed first government botanist of Victoria in 1853.

With Teutonic thoroughness, Mueller at once applied himself to enlarging his knowledge of Australian plants. Between 1853–5, he made three expeditions on horseback around Victoria and its mountains to Mount Buffalo and the Ovens River, reaching the summit of Mount Buller and the mouth of the Snowy River and collecting the truly Australian alpine plants. On these excursions Mueller observed the remarkable range of the genus *Eucalyptus*, a topic that was to form a central part of his work, and he developed an interest in the medicinal value of some plants and in the economic importance of eucalyptus oil. With a fellow emigrant, the British pharmacist Joseph Bosisto (1822–1898), Mueller began distilling oil from eucalyptus leaves in 1854, and Bosisto carried this phytochemical work forward throughout the century, commercially exporting eucalyptus oil. For his part, Mueller published his great work on the genus, *Eucalyptographia: A Descriptive Atlas of Eucalyptus of Australia*, from 1879–84. His collections of plants from these journeys were immense, and he formed a scheme to publish a series of volumes on the flora of Victoria. In 1856 Mueller interrupted the plan to join the North Australian Exploring Expedition on its intrepid journey from the Victoria River to Moreton Bay which brought him in touch with very different tropical fauna and launched him on his other vast project, a work in Latin on all new Australian plants.[2]

In all these ventures, Mueller sent off his best specimens to Kew. There, working across world botany, the Hookers, father and son, carried out identifications, classified plants for Mueller's papers, and kept up a steady flow of correspondence.

Colonial scientists versus the 'experts'

Mueller's design for a Victorian botany escalated into further plans for a botany of tropical Australia. Joseph Hooker, completing his own volume, the *Flora of Tasmania*, warned him off, and cautioned him about his rather 'provisional' way of publishing species in his papers. 'It is from no desire of fault-finding that I remark this,' wrote Hooker, 'but in justice to myself – that I observe that the consultation & reference to your fragments have cost Mr Black and myself more labour than the work of any other Botanist whatever.' His letter to Mueller of 3 June 1857 shed considerable light on the British side of botanic collaboration with colonial scientists; and the arduous task the Hookers faced.

I have often felt [Hooker wrote] *that the best I can do towards comparing your specimens before publication, correcting the proofs etc etc is infinitely far short of all you deserve & all I would be glad to do – & as it is I feel it is infinitely less than you must normally expect, for I know that not one half or one quarter of the queries you address to us are answered; nor half the descriptions fully compared. You have no idea of the length of time such comparisons take in this count, owing to the size of our Herbaria, the number of books to consult; & the variable nature of specimens; the imperfection of published descriptions, the number of already instituted bad genera and species . . . Every Botanist who has come to Kew to work, however experienced, has confessed that so large a Herbarium puts his materials & labors on a very different point of view from what he expected.*[3]

It was Mueller's intention to follow his specimens to England. Hooker urged him on. In his view, it was essential for Mueller to refrain from publishing his Victorian flora until he had compared his plants in England. Both Hookers, moreover, were campaigning ardently for a series of colonial floras, financed jointly by the British and Colonial governments, and based on the collections at Kew. Mueller, with his continental field work behind him, and parts of his *Flora of Victoria* coming off the press, undoubtedly expected to undertake the Australian work. When his projected visit to England failed to mature, however, the authorship of the *Flora Australiensis* was entrusted instead to the eminent British botanist George Bentham FRS (1800–1884), who had acquired a considerable reputation for his penetrating systematic work.[4]

The argument for British authorship was sound enough. Hooker's letter expressed the hazards of nominating new species far from the essential research tools. Any systematic study of Australian flora must take into account the collections and descriptions of the early botanic investigators Banks, Solander, Brown and Cunningham – all of which were deposited in the British Museum or at Kew. Mueller, however, struggling to the high point of his scientific career when priority and recognition were important to him, did not agree. His knowledge and familarity with the living species, and the essential part he would play in gathering and describing new data, qualified him, he believed, for the major task. With the Colonial Government's financial backing for the important botanic work, Mueller sought a compromise in joint authorship with Bentham. Bentham, however, declined.

I am perfectly aware of the indefatigable zeal and industry [he wrote Mueller] *you have shown in the investigation of the vegetable productions of Australia, of the high scientific ability you have shown in the varied and numerous botanical papers you have published; and that, could you come over to this country for the purpose, no one could nearly so well as yourself prepare the general flora that is so much wanted. Yet... I feel also that to be satisfactory to the Botanical world, it must be done in this country, for nowhere else can the old species published ... be verified ...*

The offer to undertake the task having been made to me, and accepted by me, I feel loth to give it up.[5]

Mueller's position was unenviable, and his own sense of achievement and importance added to his distress. He had published volume one of *The Plants Indigenous to the Colony of Victoria* in 1860[6] and was elected a Fellow of the Royal Society of London the following year. He had also built up significant suites of Australian specimens in the herbarium of the Victorian Botanic Gardens and an extensive botanic library. But he could not withstand the strong forces arraigned against him at Kew. A final agreement whereby the Australian botanist's assistance in the collection and description of data was fully recorded on the title page, under George Bentham's title as author, oiled the wheels of the collaborative venture, but did not mitigate Mueller's sense of grievance and hurt.

In addition to Mueller's bruised feelings, his close collaboration with Bentham was further complicated by the two men's differing attitudes to taxonomic work. With the publication of *The Origin of Species* (1859), the whole question of the definition of species was then in critical debate before the scientific world. Bentham, a former disciple of de Candolle, originally held that species had fixed limits but accepted the need for some modification in the light of Darwin's carefully marshalled facts. Bentham, indeed, with Joseph Hooker, was in the van of British botanists in conceding the weight of natural selection and, throughout the writing of *Flora Australiensis*, moved steadily into the evolutionist's camp. Mueller, conversely, rejected the concept of trasmutation and applied sharp criticism to any tendency by Bentham to extend the limit of species. Much of their correspondence, as they worked together, must have been written with pursed lips. 'His Excellency Sir Henry Barkly,' Mueller wrote on one occasion, 'did me the honour while referring to Banks as the father of Australian Botany to designate me its Guardian. Allow me then to exercise the Guardianship on this occasion & say that your Rhamnaceae must be overrated in species.' 'I wish it was possible for me to conduct you for only one walk around some parts of our "bush" and you would fully concur in the limits I have generally assigned to our species.'[7] It was a rough trail. 'I regret very much,' Bentham replied with equal phlegm, 'that you should have found reason to be so thoroughly dissatisfied with the execution of my second volume, that you find my genera miserable, my declination of species often ridiculous and my diagnosis unavailable for practical use. I do my best . . . I trust that notwithstanding my failure you will continue to give me your valuable assistance.'[8]

Despite friction, the *Flora*, completed in seven parts, was published between 1863–78. Mueller himself went on to publish over 800 papers and numerous volumes of Australian botany and to build a botanical empire of his own. His collectors stretched from Kangaroo Island to New Guinea, providing him with specimens and descriptions from every corner of the continent and consolidating a unique national collection of Australian plants. His research herbarium at the Melbourne Botanic Gardens, of which he was made director in 1857, equalled, at least by the 1880s, the standards and resources of major herbaria abroad. Mueller was often arrogant and unbending in his views, and his 'stiff garden of science' did not appeal to the citizens of Melbourne. To his great chagrin, he was deposed as director of the gardens in 1873 though he retained his post as government botanist. But he had established an international reputation for colonial botany. Scientific honours continued to crowd upon him, including a German baronetcy and a British CMG and KCMG, and he was awarded the Royal Medal of the Royal Society of London for his botanic researches in 1888.

Significantly, the *Flora Australiensis* was the last of the major systematic works carried out by extraterritorial experts on Australian botanical science. A decade later, with authoritative Australian publications firmly behind him, Mueller might have triumphed over the resistance from Kew. In the event, his show of independence marked a turning point in colonial science. Australian botanists would continue to pursue fruitful collaboration with colleagues overseas, but the days of their deferential dependence on British leadership were over.

Bones of contention

Similar conflicts began to emerge in other sciences. Possibly no science generated so intense a public interest in Australia as that of palaeontology. The discovery of the fossilised bones of huge extinct marsupials, creatures of a distinct geological age when lush flora covered the now arid tracts of inland Australia, excited community interest in the colonies, and, as bones were sent in, drew large crowds to view the reconstructions of these strange fauna in the local museums. For scientists, the discoveries were dynamic and provided evidence of a continuous and distinctive line of faunal development in Australia that was different from other countries and continents, and linked the living marsupial species with extinct ancestral forms.

The first recorded discoveries of these extinct marsupials were to have a stimulating influence on key scientists in Britain. It was the surveyor-general, Thomas Mitchell, who announced the discovery of a large cache of fossil bones in the Breccia Caves of Wellington, New South Wales, on one of his inland expeditions, and who sent specimens to London's Hunterian Museum. There, both the young comparative anatomist Richard Owen, and the Museum Curator, William Clift, examined the bones and identified both living and extinct species of wombats, koalas, and kangaroos. Owen, who would name the 'dinosaurs' from the Greek words 'deinos' meaning 'fearful' and 'sauros' meaning 'lizard', was already working on specimens of living Australian marsupials. He identified the large extinct kangaroos *Macropus atlas* and *Macropus titan*, and defined two distinct new genera of extinct herbivorous marsupials which he named *Diprotodontia* and *Nototherium* and which he said were of 'portentous' size.[10] News of these interesting findings reached the geologist Lyell, who referred to the discoveries in his *Principles of Geology* (1833). 'These facts are full of interest,' wrote Lyell, 'for they prove that the peculiar type of organisation that now characterises the marsupial tribes has prevailed from a remote period in Australia.' Lyell's work in turn affected Darwin, and, reinforced by his own observations in the Galapagos Islands and South America, Darwin enunciated his crucial 'law of the succession of types' in specific regions in his *Journal of Researches* in 1839. The early evidence from the colonies of extinct marsupials thus left their imprint on the first important stirrings of Darwin's evolutionary thought.

It was Richard Owen, however, who would make this

corner of palaeontological history his special domain and who, during the next 40 years, working from a tooth here, a fragmented jaw or thigh bone there, furnished the unique reconstructions of extinct marsupials that remain a cornerstone of Australian palaeontology today. Throughout the century, resident Australian scientists were eager to contribute to this dramatic retrieval work. Leichhardt brought him some diprotodon bones from the Darling Downs in southern Queensland in 1844, and some of a young animal of 'the gigantic Pachyderm. . . which once lived in and near the swamps and lagoons which must have covered these rich plains'.[9] The geologists Clarke and Stutchbury also found such fossils on their northern geological surveys from along the creeks of the Darling Downs, while pastoralists sinking wells in Queensland would dig out fossilised teeth and femurs and send them to the Australian Museum in Sydney. W.S. Macleay brooded long and hard over one extraordinary specimen brought together in cast form from a collection of fossils bones and skull from Queensland. He gave it the name *Zygomaturus* and sent it for identification to Owen.

Owen's own concentration on Australian fossil mammals intensified in 1857 with his appointment as Superintendent of the Natural History Department of the British Museum. The following year, he issued the first of his ten-part 'Fossil Mammals of Australia' (published in volume form in 1877). With this important research in view, in 1867 Owen was instrumental in persuading the Government of New South Wales to sponsor an intensive re-exploration of that original, rich fossil site, the Wellington Caves. The project, funded by the Colonial Government, was carried out in September 1869, led by Gerard Krefft, Curator of the Australian Museum, accompanied by the youthful Dr Alexander Thomson, Reader in Geology at Sydney University. With one assistant, they sank shafts in the inner chamber of the caves, sifted through enormous quantities of loose deposits, and emerged triumphant with 'many valuable and rare specimens . . . consisting of the remains of mammals, birds and reptiles', Krefft reported, 'some quite new to science'.[10]

Unfortunately, the experience labouring in the damp caverns cost the delicate Thomson his life (he died in 1871 from a pulmonary disease contracted on the expedition), but the returns for the British scientist were rich. Specimens from the genera *Diprotodon, Nototherium, Zygomaturus* and *Thylacoleo* were extracted from the debris and found their way, either as original pieces, casts, or in complete sets of plates, to that brilliant reconstituter of ancient species Richard Owen.

Meanwhile, in Australia, Gerard Krefft was extending and deepening his own researches on extinct and living mammals, as well as publishing papers and monographs on birds, snakes, fish and whales, which brought him considerable recognition from scientists abroad. A rugged individualist and evolutionist who did not shrink from outspoken comment when he had confidence in his view, Krefft came into conflict with the venerated British authority, Richard Owen.

The matter involved the identification of the extinct marsupialian, *Thylacoleo carnifex*, the marsupial lion, a significant collection of whose fossilised teeth emerged from the excursion to the Wellington Caves. Unlike the giant kangaroos and wombats found in the Breccia Caves, this bizarre early extinct Australian creature did not fall clearly into any recognisable modern mould. Several of its long, ridge-like teeth had been sent to Owen for determination with the early fossils that Thomas Mitchell found. He illustrated these for his Appendix to Mitchell's work, named it a flesh-eating lion, but gave no classification. With the material he received from the caves at a later date, Owen declared it to be 'one of the fellest and most destructive of predatory beasts in the forest'. Krefft begged to differ. On indications from the animal's dentition, he pronounced it a vegetable-eating phalanger somewhere in the evolutionary scale between the wombat and the koala 'bear'. Krefft pursued the argument in reviews of Owen's classifications, in books and papers, and in some trenchant comments to the great man himself. In a review article of Owen's work published in the *Sydney Mail* in 1872, Krefft asked the question, 'If these teeth did not strike Professor Owen in 1836 as uncommon, why are they considered valuable evidence of carnivority in 1858 or 1859? In that year . . . the first attempt was made to fit some fragments of a *Thylacoleo's* skull into such a shape as to produce a cat-like head.'

To his friend W.B. Clarke, who was also deeply interested in the old bone business, Krefft wrote more frankly. 'I know the tooth well that Owen describes as 'furrower', he alludes to the premolar or as he will call it the *carnassial* tooth . . . Owen will make a lion of his *Thylacoleo* after all the discussion we have had about it & one of his plates showing the head (palate) of the great *Carnivore* looks very formidable, but had evidently been drawn *on order* "lionlike". But I will never believe the *Thylacoleo* to be quite as savage as he looks & prove him quite a different sort of animal.'[11]

Owen also used the clerical geologist as a sounding board in the debate. But secure in his judgment and in his considered reconstruction of what he called 'the old monsters which it has pleased God to blot out of his Creation', he allowed himself only an occasional lunge at the dissenting Krefft. 'As to that unfortunate man who seems to have tried to smash all evidence of *Thylacoleo* in the Cave exploration,' he wrote Clarke, 'a compassionate silence is one's best return.'[12]

Krefft's stand was spirited. Owen, despite his great reputation, had made mistakes and Krefft was ready to allude to them. He was, moreover, an evolutionist who felt that Owen's creationist viewpoint sometimes contributed distorting effects. He took the conflict to Darwin who responded sympathetically. To British naturalists, Owen appeared brilliant but flawed. A man of rare scientific ability in his knowledge of anatomical structure, he was wrathful in opposition and philosophically confined. As Huxley put it writing to Macleay, 'he can only work in the concrete from bone to bone.'[13] Darwin encouraged Krefft: 'It is lamentable [he wrote] that Professor Owen should show so little consideration for the judgment of other naturalists, and should adhere in so bigoted a manner to whatever he has said. This is a great evil as it makes one doubtful on other points about which he has written.'

Yet for many of his colonial correspondents, Owen had great charm. Cosiness and humour were mixed with his firm interpretations of the pieces of fossilised fauna that they sent. To the Reverend W.B. Clarke, who continued to send bundles of particularly small, fragmented bones to Owen, which caused the distinguished anatomist to exclaim 'Timeo Clarkeii et fosiles mittentem!' (I fear Clarke and the fossils he sends!), Owen wrote engagingly in December 1876:

I was sitting by my fireside this winter's evening, playing a bit of backgammon with my old sister, when the postman came & the maid brought in your letter from the Antipodes dated 11 October 1876. 'What a wonderful institution!' I exclaimed, 'is this postal blessing! Here I get news not two months old from a friendly correspondent & colabourer dated 'Northshore' & telling me of exciting fossil discovered 'not far from Mudgee on the road to Gulgong'. 'Where in the world are Mudgee & Gulgong?' asks my sister. 'Why, they are as familiar Molly to the doctor as "Barnes" is to us at Mortlake: only we spread ourselves & make all the globe our neighbours.' I don't know whether I shall find the box at the B.M. [British Museum] tomorrow with the bones marked 'red & blue' but I shall trot off in hopes, & in as cheerfully excited mood of mind as some of my grandiose neighbours who go by the same train to the city Counting houses to turn over £1000 or two.

Now, as to the big wingless bird, the only bone yielding information testified against Moa-ship. Your later pelvic fragment, in the Photo, does not speak decisively pro or con. This gossiping commencement will keep till I receive your kindly transmitted box, when its contents will have my best attention & the results will be annexed . . .

Gerard Krefft, however, was not drawn in. He held to his view that 'the great Richard' displayed a cavalier attitude to some of the palaeontological evidence and bent his philosophical concepts to extremes. Krefft and Owen's squabble over the proper classification of *Thylacoleo* was not resolved by them. It would agitate palaeontologists for decades more. Yet the dispute illuminated other questions. Despite his generous help with Owen's researches, Krefft represented the new breed of colonial scientists who were no longer satisfied to bow uncritically to the experts' deductions, arrived at on the other side of the world from the site of research. Owen, tenaciously jealous of his reputation and ambitious for honour and prestige, was better served by colonial naturalists like George Bennett than by independent workers such as Krefft. Additionally, the dispute focused attention on home-grown needs and skills. As Krefft wrote Henry Parkes, Premier of New South Wales in 1873, a thorough history of Australian animals could only be written in Australia where collections such as those of his own Australian Museum, in Sydney, held unrivalled suites of specimens for the work. His letter summed up the incongruity of perpetuating a ministering subservience to British science. 'There is no Museum in the World,' he informed the Premier, 'which has the Australian Collections we have and not one Professor can command such a series of skulls & skeletons & the young in all stages of growth as I brought together . . . for the last 13 years . . . I had to supply Professor Owen with some of the most important skeletons which he had *not got* & how can a man write a proper & correct History without these first & most essential means?'[14] His judgment won support. Richard Owen's *Researches on the Fossil Mammals of Australia*, like George Bentham's *Flora*, marked the end of the practice of Colonial Government funding of classificatory volumes where preference was given to Britain's senior scientific men. Australian science was coming of age.

Owen, however, was right. The palaeontological riddle grew clearer when the first postcranial skeletal material of *Thylacoleo carnifex* was unearthed in South Australia in the 1950s and later in New South Wales, and was finally solved when two men working on a construction project in Queensland meticulously unearthed a full skeleton of *Thylacoleo* with young. With its big cat-like shape, its shearing teeth, and a pronounced thumb claw by which it could hang in a tree and pounce on prey, the skeleton confirmed it as an incontrovertible carnivore marsupial lion.

CHAPTER ELEVEN

Science in colonial universities

There has long been a belief that until after World War II, scientific tertiary education in Australia was oriented to teaching, scientific research was negligible, and imported and indigenous talent was drained away from the Australian universities to more illustrious centres overseas. It is a picture of university science as isolated, parochial, 'outside Europe', where the colonial endeavour was a poor substitute for men of ability 'except as an interlude in a career open to talent'. This picture is misleading; it ignores specific development, dismisses trends that produced distinctive patterns of growth, and underestimates the role of a number of British and colonial scientists who made their Australian university experience the sound basis for distinguished careers.

From their very beginnings, the Australian universities leaned conspicuously in the direction of science. Sydney University, constituted as the first full university in the British Empire in 1852, and the University of Melbourne, established in the prosperous colony of Victoria in 1855, took as their model not the classically dominated ancient universities of Oxford and Cambridge, but the new University of London

(1826) which, opening up a new spirit in education, had appointed 17 chairs in medicine, science and engineering in its first ten years. The founders of Sydney University, in touch with development abroad, projected no less than four scientific chairs in their original blueprint of 1849; in mathematics, natural history, anatomy, physiology and medicine; and chemistry and experimental physics. But in the contraction that followed the initial planning, they settled for mathematics and a combined chair of chemistry and experimental physics. It was a decision that lost them T.H. Huxley, an eager candidate for the proposed natural history chair, and brought them John Smith MD (1821–1885), lecturer in chemistry from Aberdeen University, a substitution of steadiness for genius which has frequently characterised Australian university life.

One consequence of Sydney's change of plan was that the professionalisation of natural science passed to the foundation professor at Melbourne University, Frederick McCoy. McCoy held no degree but arrived in the colonies with several academic posts and publications to his credit and with testimonials from Britain's leading scientists which indicated, perhaps with too much fervour, that he was indeed God's gift to the Australian colonies. McCoy was appointed initially to teach botany, zoology, geology and chemistry, a load he carried for 20 years. Curiously, it was not until 1867, with the appointment of Dr Alexander Thomson as reader in mineralogy and geology, that the natural sciences reached Sydney University, and passed, with Thomson's early death in 1871, to the highly capable Professor Archibald Liversidge. Three years later, in 1874, the colonies' third university was founded at Adelaide where Professor Ralph Tate (1840–1901), a geologist and botanist from Britain, was appointed to the first Elder chair of natural science. A country whose amateur, public service, and visiting scientists were steeped in natural history was now turning out students in the bachelor of arts degree with some grounding in the natural sciences.

The new biology

In the event, at least in the last two decades of the century, the major developments in biology, physiology, biochemistry and microscopy which Darwin's findings set in train, increasingly broke down the old concept of natural history as a general omnibus for the study of organic and inorganic life, and these changes were reflected in the colonies' academic life. The appointment of Walter Baldwin Spencer as professor of biology in 1887 at Melbourne marked the trend. A product of the red-brick Owens College in Manchester, Baldwin Spencer would infuse new life into the teaching of natural science; relieve McCoy of his outdated tuition in zoology and botany (he had, it was noted, 'been delivering the same lectures for 37 years past'); and secure the construction of modern laboratories for the new department of biology. His advent would also introduce Darwinian concepts, long resisted by McCoy, into biological instruction at Melbourne. A ranging researcher in biology, ethnology and anthropology, Baldwin Spencer would enhance both research and teaching and bring international lustre during his reign at the university from 1887–1919.[1]

It was in organic chemistry and the newly shaping disciplines of physiology and biology that the most notable advances in Australian research and tertiary education were made. With limited openings in England, the colonial universities were well placed to attract first-rate graduates

Science in colonial universities

from Britain and to produce, in time, promising researchers of their own. In chemistry, David Orme Masson (1858–1937) at Melbourne and Edward Henry Rennie (1853–1927) at Adelaide were two exemplars. Masson, a graduate and research fellow of Edinburgh University, assumed the Melbourne chair of chemistry in 1886 and at once set out to establish a close-knit association between teaching and research. In his inaugural address to the University in 1887, he outlined a blueprint for chemical education that envisaged effective laboratories, vocational training, a close interaction between the universities and the growing fraternity of professional chemists, and essentially original research.

'We in the Universities,' said Masson, 'have other aims besides the technical education of professional men and manufacturers. These are important duties and must not be perfunctorily performed, but neither must we be content to do these things and no other ... Science must grow, new knowledge must be made ... There is no reason why we should not have here a small band of students devoting the bulk of their time for a few years to the study of chemistry in the University. It is to these, as well as to the teachers, that the institution must look to maintain and increase its reputation with the world as a school of original work.'[2]

True to his aims, Masson himself carried out fundamental research (notably on the constitution of atoms and the theory of dissociation of electrolytes in water for which he won an FRS), built a major centre of research and teaching, and helped to found the Chemical Society of Victoria and the Australian Chemical Society during his 37 years in the Melbourne chair. At Adelaide, Rennie, an Australian-born graduate of Sydney University (1871) with a doctoral degree in organic chemistry from London University, held the first professorship of chemistry from 1885–1927, and founded an influential school of organic chemistry, which retains its research prominence in the field today.

This explicit concern to link research and teaching characterised the Australian universities in the 1880s. Masson and Spencer, with Thomas Lyle, Professor of Natural Philosophy, were all influential in securing a program for the doctoral degree in science at Melbourne University in 1887. From differing British backgrounds (Lyle came from Trinity College, Dublin), all brought high intellectual standards. They saw the need for innovative approaches, and geared their disciplines to modern lines. Importantly, the biological and physiological sciences developed distinctively oriented schools. The original school of anatomy and physiology founded by Professor George Halford (1824–1910) at Melbourne University in 1863 – the first such school established in the southern hemisphere – served the needs of all Australian medical students for 20 years and attained standards of organisation and teaching that equalled, if not rivalled, those of medical schools overseas. As a result, the Melbourne Medical School became the first within the British Empire to receive formal recognition for its medical and surgical degrees, a grant of autonomy that Professor Harry Brookes Allen accepted on behalf of the University in 1891.

While Melbourne led the field in medical teaching, the Medical School established at Sydney University 20 years later would attain a prominent reputation in the last decade of the century for its penetrating physiological and anatomical studies of marsupial life. (Sir) Thomas Anderson Stuart (1856–1920) assumed the foundation chair of anatomy and physiology in 1883. Four years later, James Thomas Wilson (1861–1945), a graduate of Edinburgh University, arrived in

Science in colonial universities

Sydney as demonstrator in anatomy and rose rapidly, to hold a separate chair in that discipline in 1890. Wilson would transform the study of zoology in Australia. No field was of greater interest to the new breed of biologists that Wilson represented than the physiological and embryological development of the marsupial species who had carved out an ecological niche in Australia and bypassed the normal developments of mammals in other lands. Wilson quickly earned a reputation from several papers on the anatomy and homology of marsupials. He attracted two gifted young British physiologists, Charles J. Martin (1866–1955) and J.P. Hill (1873–1954), to Sydney and stimulated the original researches of one of the department's own graduates, Grafton Elliot Smith (1873–1954).

Both separately and in collaboration with Professor of Biology W.A. Haswell (1854–1925),[3] this distinguished trio carried out some fundamental studies on the morphology, neurology and evolutionary physiology of Australian marsupials and monotremes, work that represented clinical advances on Richard Owen's research and earned a high measure of acclaim abroad. Martin's period in Australia was seminal to his later work. From 1891 he served as demonstrator in Wilson's group and moved in 1897 to become lecturer in physiology in Melbourne and professor in 1901. He returned to London to become director of the Lister Institute in 1903, a post he held for 27 years. But he kept his links with Australia firm. Sir Charles Martin FRS returned as professor of biochemistry and general physiology at Adelaide University and chief of the Division of Animal Nutrition, CSIR, from 1931–3. James Hill, like Wilson and Elliot Smith, won an FRS. Moving between Sydney and Melbourne Universities as demonstrator in biology from 1892–4, and lecturer in embryology in Melbourne University from 1894–6, Hill did far-reaching work on the reproduction and embryology of marsupials and monotremes and became Jodrell professor of zoology and comparative anatomy at London University in 1906 taking with him a large collection of preserved organs of these animals which he worked on all his life. Elliot Smith, a researcher whose fame spread widely overseas, also began by studying the brain and evolutionary physiology of Australian monotremes, and left for Britain in 1896. He subsequently became a physical anthropologist and anatomist, was appointed professor of anatomy at the Government Medical School, Cairo, in 1900 and held the chair of anatomy at University College, Manchester from 1909–36.

Reared in research in Sydney, these men won high rewards. Their careers underlined the potent influence of Australian university research. For Wilson himself, Australia continued to represent a sustaining environment for his work. He remained in the mainstream of anatomical research, corresponded critically with eminent colleagues, applied the theory of natural selection to Australian species, projected important developments in Australian physiology and embryology, and built a thriving school of teaching and research. He accepted the chair of anatomy at Cambridge University in 1920. Fundamentally, he was an advanced and constructive theorist who applied physico-chemical concepts to investigating organic phenomena and tied work to seminal advances in scientific thought.

Patterns in physical science

While chemistry, with its roots in medicine and agriculture, found a natural impetus in Australia towards original research, the mathematical sciences suffered in their isolation

Science in colonial universities

from the centres of theoretical work. At Sydney and Melbourne universities, research in mathematics was negligible throughout the century, despite the selection of brilliant men. The first professor of mathematics at Sydney University, Morris Birkbeck Pell (1827-1879), and his successor in 1876, Thomas Gurney, were both senior wranglers in their Cambridge years, as was the first professor of mathematics at Melbourne University, William P. Wilson. Appointment committees for these colonial placements, themselves made up of leading British scientists, were required to seek only 'first-rate men'. All three taught the compulsory three-year core courses in mathematics in the BA degree, but Gurney was no researcher, and Pell and Wilson found their stimulus elsewhere; Pell in actuarial work, while Wilson turned his skills to astronomical research and helped secure the Great Melbourne Telescope for Victoria.

By contrast, the University of Adelaide nourished two researchers of great distinction. Horace Lamb (1849-1934), a lecturer from Trinity College, Cambridge, was appointed to the first chair of mathematics from 1875-85. Lamb is sometimes taken as the exemplar of the 'colonial interlude' theme. Yet in the new and remote university in South Australia, Lamb launched a decade of brilliant research in hydrodynamics, not noticeably daunted by his isolation. There he published 18 papers on statics and hydrodynamics and *A Treatise on the Motion of Fluids* (1879), which formed the core of his famous *Hydrodynamics*, and was elected to a fellowship of the Royal Society of London before he returned to England to become professor of mathematics at Owens College, Manchester, in 1885.[4] His successor was William Bragg (1862-1942), who held the combined professorship of physics and mathematics from 1886-1908, and who was chosen by a selection committee that included Horace Lamb.

Bragg is also cited as a pertinent illustration of the cramping effects of colonial academic life. He gained distinction, it is said, after a full 18 years in the Adelaide chair, and five years later, earned his passage 'home'.[5] In fact, Bragg's creativity, which won him an FRS, the Nobel Prize and an Order of Merit, was the direct product of his colonial post. Like so many of his professorial colleagues in the Australian universities, he was very young at the time of his appointment (he was 24 when he arrived in Adelaide) and surprised to get the post. Yet, trained exclusively in mathematics at Cambridge, he taught himself physics at Adelaide and became an ingenious and inventive experimentalist (setting up the first x-ray tube in Australia), and began his seminal investigation of radioactive substances while preparing his paper for his presidential address to the Australasian Association for the Advancement of Science in January 1904. Bragg's major experimental work on the properties of x-rays and the electron would take place in Adelaide over the next four years. In 1908 he returned to England to become Cavendish professor of mathematics at Leeds University and to carry forward his work on x-ray analysis of crystal structure, for which he received the Nobel Prize with Lawrence Bragg, his son.

His formative work in Adelaide, however, was crucial to his development. It also sheds light on the cluster of research scientists who were forming stimulating networks in Australia. At Sydney, Richard Threlfall took up the chair of physics in 1886, four months after Bragg arrived in Adelaide. Threlfall was the most experienced of the Australian science professors. He had won first class honours in the natural sciences tripos in 1884 and had spent two years as demonstrator in the Cavendish Laboratory in Cambridge. There he was on close terms of friendship with its distinguished director, J.J. Thomson, who described the young Threlfall as 'one of the best experimenters I have ever met'.[6] Positive and determined, Threlfall blew a brisk wind of action through Sydney University. Within a week of his arrival, he presented the senate with an account of £2400 for laboratory and workshop equipment, which he had prudently ordered before starting for Australia, and his plans for a new physics laboratory. Within 18 months his new laboratory was operative, funded by the New South Wales Government. Bragg learnt much from Threlfall, used him as a sounding board for his tentative ideas, and gained increasing intellectual confidence from their exchanges. 'Thanks for correcting my mistake about the coefficients of self induction,' he wrote Threlfall in 1891. 'I might have gone on bothering about that point for ever so long.' The traffic was not all one way. 'I don't think you are quite right [he added in the same letter] in saying there isn't a solution, or rather that there is no problem: there must be, I believe, if Maxwell's theory [James Clerk Maxwell, a Scottish scientist who in 1845 predicted the existence of radio waves] is correct.'[7]

Threlfall became Bragg's mentor and his friend. His own 12-year stay in Sydney was productive. He wrote *On Laboratory Arts* and carried out electrochemical research. He was one talented recruit to the colonies, however, who freely admitted his error. 'I made the greatest mistake of my life,' he declared. 'I went to Sydney to a Professorship. If I had stayed in Cambridge, I should have been in with J.J. Thomson in the discovery of the electron.'[8] Threlfall returned to England in 1898 to become director of the London firm Alright and Wilson. But in Adelaide, using the network of contacts which the now active federal scientific body, the Australasian

Association for the Advancement of Science made available, Bragg, alternatively, was en route to his career of high achievement. There was now a handful of scientific colleagues who removed intellectual isolation from his career. One was his father-in-law, the innovative government astronomer and director of posts and telegraph of South Australia, Sir Charles Todd, with whom Bragg conducted the first public demonstration of the working of wireless telegraphy in Australia in September 1897, using Marconi apparatus constructed at the university.'[9]

Another vital contact was the highly original researcher in physics, Willliam Sutherland (1859-1911). Born in England, Sutherland graduated from Melbourne University, undertook postgraduate training in experimental physics at University College, London, held brief lectureships in physics at Melbourne University in 1888-9 and again in 1897, but published most of his 69 papers on physico-chemical subjects from his Melbourne home. His most famous paper derived an equation giving the dependence of viscosity on temperature in gas involving the well-known 'Sutherland constant'. Sutherland, however, belonged to the disappearing breed of 19th-century freelance workers who remained largely outside academia, though such aloofness was becoming unfashionable even then.

What, then, was the sum of university research and teaching in Australian 19th-century science? Some of it was pragmatic, empirical and fitted to vocational needs. Australia needed its cadre of trained scientific men. The early graduates, and the staff who equipped them, added significantly to the ranks of professional science. But in addition there was a clear contemporary respect at Sydney, Melbourne and Adelaide universities for scientific research. It was a trend that would be reflected again when the University of Tasmania was founded with three science lectureships in 1893, when Queensland University was established in 1901, and when the University of Western Australia was founded in 1913. From the outset, the teaching of science was built into tertiary curricula in the colonies. A faculty of science was created at Sydney University in 1885, and a few years later at the University of Melbourne. The establishment of a doctoral degree in science at Melbourne in 1887 also compared favourably with universities around the world. Despite pockets of mediocrity, an impressive number of Australian scientists won Britain's coveted accolade, the FRS, and there was a respectable output in the three major universities of theoretical and applied research. Importantly, new researchers were being trained in the colonies. Traditionally, the best research students gravitated to England for their postgraduate work – the 1851 exhibition scholarship established in 1891 sharpened this trend – but there was also local emphasis on learning and research. Bragg, Rennie, Lyle and Masson reared a cluster of research disciplines in Australia.

Distance and isolation played their part in the contours of colonial academic science. Viewed, however, against the strongly 'science shop' orientation that characterised university science departments in Australia in this century until 1946, the standards of scholarship set by 19th-century professors of both the physical and the biological sciences were not excelled or matched in Australia until the upsurge of research and experimentation that followed government investment in university research after World War II.

CHAPTER TWELVE

Experimenters & inventors

When governor Arthur Phillip landed with the First Fleet in Australia, no country, as he wrote the British authorities, 'offers less assistance to the first settlers than this does'. Faced with the unknown, four millstones were landed in the first weeks, along with 40 iron handmills and other rudimentary pieces of equipment for the colony's survival – the first life-saving import of technology into Australia. But it was not until Governor John Hunter arrived in 1795 that the working parts of a windmill and a model to guide installation reached the struggling settlement. The first windmill, installed at Miller's Point, caught the useful breezes and began operation in January 1797. In a major thrust, Governor Macquarie opened the first steam-driven mill in 1815.[1]

As a predominantly agricultural and pastoral country, Australia depended heavily on imported technology and imported ideas. The food supply of the expanding colonies relied, for a long period, on materials brought from overseas. The application of science and the encouragement of indigenous technologies made slow headway at the Antipodes. In land use, the very practice of squatting and the vast areas available for cultivation militated against technological improvements that sprang from population pressures on land in Britain and Europe. Fencing proved one major early development adopted in the colonies to relieve the shortage of men in the pastoral industry through 'manmade' control of flocks. It was not until depression hit the eastern colonies in the 1840s, however, that the tallow industry took shape, while a farm labour shortage and the dry climatic conditions of South Australia fostered an important agricultural innovation in John Ridley's stripper machine for harvesting ripe grain, launched in 1843. The stripper, made up of a horizontal projecting comb and revolving wooden beater powered by belts, was an enormous labour-saver and enabled four men to do in one day what had previously taken two labourers a whole harvesting season to complete. Such rapid harvesting proved a great boon in regions where hot dry winds brought the grain to ripeness too quickly for ready manpower to harvest it, and its manufacture led to the extensive development in the 1850s of the South Australian and Victorian wheat belts.

It was in agriculture that the most significant innovations tended to be made. In 1876, another South Australian farmer, R.B. Smith, invented the stump jump plough, a singularly Australian invention that eliminated the expense of grubbing out the stumps of the deep-rooted eucalypts; a land-clearing mechanism caused the plough to rise vertically on meeting a stump and resume its work after leapfrogging onto land the other side. Eighteen years later, H.V. McKay invented and began production in Victoria of a harvester that combined the functions of stripper and winnower.

Lines of innovation there were. Australia was not without technological pioneers, though the move from invention to viable development proved difficult. Nonetheless, there was considerable adaption from crude resources, and many improvements were made by colonials on imported models. Australians gained a reputation as 'tinkerers and adapters'. They were also quick to take up major technologies pioneered abroad. Railways were laid down and telegraph lines, strung across hostile environments and the arid interior, brought Australia early recognition for the longest line telecommunications in the world. Inventive pioneers surfaced in many fields. Both James Dunlop and H.C. Russell were ingenious instrument makers whose skills contributed to the country's early astronomical and meteorological work. In Victoria, Henry Sutton (1856–1912), the son of a gold-miner who established a music warehouse at Ballarat showed a youthful interest in science and engineering. He absorbed the contents of engineering journals from the well-stocked Mechanics Institute at Ballarat, designed an ingenious assortment of electric motors, vacuum pumps, and 20 telephone instruments, all working on different principles. J.E. Edwards, an English emigrant to Victoria, also designed his own telephones and set up a flourishing business for their sale in Melbourne from 1878–1885.[2] William Bland (1789–1868), the Sydney physician and educator, invented several schemes for transport and shipping, including one for the suppression of spontaneous combustion in wool ships by the free circulation of carbonic gas through the ship's hold (exhibited in London and patented in 1851), and a second for reducing travel time between England and Australia by means of a propeller driven 'atomic' ship, which he exhibited at the International Exhibition in London in 1854. In the same decade, Sir Thomas Mitchell, that versatile contributor to Australian science, applied the principle of the boomerang to ships' propellers, an invention tested successfully in Sydney Harbour but rejected by the Admiralty in 1854. Twenty years later, an Irish immigrant, Louis Brennan designed a dirigible torpedo and sold the patent to the War Office.[3]

In a country isolated by distance, it was not surprising that inventive approaches turned on transport, conveyance, communication and technologies that would bring the colonies and their produce into connection with the larger world. After many ventures, much capital, two path-finding papers delivered in 1875 by Thomas Mort and the engineer Eugene Dominique Nicolle to the Agricultural Society of New South Wales 'On the Preservation of Food by Freezing, and the Bearing it Will Have on the Pastoral and Agricultural Interests of Australia', the refrigeration of meat was mastered successfully in the colonies, the first cargo being despatched on SS *Strathleven* on 29 November 1879. Its arrival in London in early February 1880 and the success of the shipment notched up an important lead in Australian technology and proved the feasibility of a crucial new industry.[4] By 1881, three Orient vessels were fitted for refrigeration and the export of meat to Britain on a significant scale was proceeding.

The majority of these innovators enjoyed the advantages of British and European education and engineering skills. The educational system of the colonies was not fashioned to foster great technical expertise. The Mechanics Institutes, offering lectures in the natural and physical sciences, aimed to provide some practical and cultural tuition for working men. But these efforts were at best spasmodic and poorly planned. Even more so than in England, there was little official impulse in Australia to attend to the training of that important army which T.H. Huxley called 'the footsoldiers of science'. The 1870s and 1880s saw the beginnings of this educational change. In Victoria in 1870, the industrial chemist James Cosmo Newbery (1843–1895) was appointed scientific superintendent of Melbourne's new Industrial and Technological Museum and, within a year, courses were being offered in chemistry, metallurgy, geology, astronomy and telegraphy. Pharmacy was added in 1876. In New South Wales, Archibald Liversidge and H.C. Russell were active promoters of the new trend. Liversidge's investigation of industrial and technical instruction in Europe during 1878 led to the formation of a Board of Technical Education in Sydney and to the establishment of the Sydney Technological Museum. Increased industrialisation and urbanisation promoted the formation of technical education and technological museums in most capital cities. Chairs of engineering were also introduced at Sydney and Melbourne Universities in the 1880s. W.C. Kernot gained the first certificate in engineering at Melbourne University in 1866 and became the first professor of engineering in 1883. At Sydney, one year later, Professor W.H. Warren founded an engineering school.[5] Education in agriculture, hitherto non-existent, also experienced a forward thrust. Agricultural colleges were built at Roseworthy, South Australia (1884), Dookie, Victoria (1885), Hawkesbury, New South Wales (1888), Longeronong, Victoria (1889) and Gatton, Queensland (1895), although the first chair of agriculture – at Sydney University – was not created until 1910.

Government funds moved slowly in the colonies into fruitful experimentation or applied research. Yet, fittingly, in a country that, across the 19th century, derived so much of its scientific impetus from private research, two episodes in applied science and technology, in the disparate fields of agricultural and aeronautical science, serve to exemplify the

William Farrer

William Farrer (1845-1906) was the pioneer of scientific wheat breeding in Australia. He graduated from Cambridge as a mathematical wrangler and came to Australia in poor health in 1870, intending to become a sheep farmer. Instead, he took a post as tutor to a pastoral family in the Monaro District and in 1875 became a licensed surveyor in the New South Wales Department of Lands. Travelling about the country on his official affairs, Farrer soon became deeply interested in the experimental aspect of breeding wheat. In 1885 he left the government service to marry the daughter of a Tharwa pastoralist, Nina de Salis, and shortly afterwards set up his own experimental farm at Lambrigg near Queanbeyan, New South Wales.

Despite the availability of large areas of land suitable for wheat cultivation in Australia and the areas that the new agricultural innovations had opened up, the industry had suffered from its inception from haphazard and unscientific methods of production. Wheat was raised from unadapted strains brought from England and Europe, and problems of rust, bunt, weak milling, soil exhaustion and poor baking quality seriously restricted output and confined production to domestic needs. Farrer's interest lay in developing a hardy, disease-resistant strain of wheat, adapted to local conditions and capable of yielding a significantly superior crop. As early as 1882, he entered a controversy in the *Australasian* newspaper in which he first put forward his views of systematic crossing for rust-resistance. Settled in the gentle countryside near Queanbeyan, he began his own practical experiments in 1886. Though his purpose was practical, Farrer saw the problem in scientific terms. Importantly, Farrer was a convinced Darwinian who accepted that the mechanism of natural or artificial selection could perpetuate better adapted mutant forms. He also believed strongly in public advocacy of his evolving view.

'The first suggestion I ever ventured to make on the subject,' he wrote an American colleague, 'was one which has since yielded excellent results: it was that farmers who had rusty crops should make search for individual plants that were free from the parasite; and save the seed from such plants . . . By doing this they might become possessed of strains of existing varieties which possessed superior power of resisting the parasite.'[6] This reasonable suggestion Farrer reported in the *Sydney Mail* in words that brought Darwinian principles before the Australian wheat breeding public.

In order to be able to improve a plant in any given direction, it is only necessary that it should possess a tendency to vary in that direction. Variability being given by means of selection & by expedients in breeding, man can work wonders (These are almost Darwin's own words) . . . It is by selection, either natural or intentional or both, that we have become possessed of our blight-proof or blight-resistant apples, of varieties of the grape which are not affected by ordium, which resist mildew, which possess roots that the phylloxera cannot injure: & what is to stand in the way of our taking advantage of the variability as regards the amount of resistance they offer to rust, that our wheats exhibit? . . . In effecting this improvement we have everything on our side, since wheat is a plant which reproduces itself at an early age & at short intervals; since a single individual produces a large number of offspring at a time; since our chances of selection are much enlarged by our being able to grow a large number of individual plants to select from; & since the chances of spontaneous crossing between different individuals are remote & little likely to interfere with us in our work of hybridisation & selection, we have also on our side to help us the general principle that a quality, which is being cultivated or secured through its variability tends to go on varying in the direction in which it has already varied.[7]

Thus, without prior knowledge of the far-reaching experiments in plant hybridisation carried out by Gregor Mendel in Europe several decades before,[8] Farrer was applying Mendelian principles of inheritance in determining the constancy of certain strains or units in his experiments in stabilising varieties of Australian wheat. It was a preknowledge and perception that the Australian experimenter was ready to confirm when Mendel's genetic work was resurrected by cytologists early in the new century. 'It seems to me,' Farrer reflected with satisfaction, 'that the consideration I gave to the matter of fixing variables, led me to adopt a system which, for all practical purposes, Mendel's theory indicates as being the best.'

Farrer was well in the van of the Government research scientists in his scientific assault on rust. Dr Nathan Cobb (1859–1932), plant pathologist and wheat experimenter to the New South Wales Department of Agriculture and Dr Daniel McAlpine (1849–1932), plant pathologist to the Victorian Government, both drew upon his insights and research. Farrer also proved a central figure when, during 1889 the combination of an abnormally wet spring followed by a warm humid period during the flowering of the wheat created a spread of rust that threatened the very existence of the wheat industry and prompted the annual Rust-in-Wheat Conferences called annually by the Government from 1890–96. Both inside and outside the conferences, Farrer's influence was widely felt. He was also active in communicating detailed reports of his experimental methods, with seeds from successful crossings, to university and governmental agricultural researchers in the United States. His was no narrow or competitive field of endeavour, and the painstaking and meticulous method that he spelt out in detail to his American correspondents contributed notably to raising the standards of wheat experimentation abroad.

In accordance with a promise made in a letter written to you about a week ago, [he addressed Professor B. T. Galloway, Chief of the Division of Vegetable Pathology at the United States Department of Agriculture, later Assistant Secretary of Agriculture, who worked on the control of plant diseases] *I am sending you . . . the Canadian bags containing small samples of some unfixed cross-bred wheats made by myself by artificial impregnation & of named varieties which . . . have exhibited in my hands superior powers of resisting rust-fungi . . . In some cases I have sent you wheats which are distinctly rust-liable: wherever I have done this, it has been for special reasons & I have in every case stated the fact of rust-liability on the seed-envelope. I must apologise to you for sending the samples in old seed-envelopes. The fact is it would have taken some time to have procured new seed-envelopes from Sydney & to have transferred the samples from their old envelopes. The writing on the envelopes which is intended for your use is in red ink. Some of the samples sent are very small: in such cases they are generally residues of packets from which I have made my own plantings.*[9]

Care, concern and a dedication free from pretentious formality were hallmarks of Farrer's work. His own precious forceps used in the mid-1890s for his hybridisation tasks also found their way, on loan, across the Pacific to another American colleague, to enable him to get its pattern and style. Throughout the 1890s, Farrer enlarged his objects and worked to produce earlier maturing, drought resistant and hard milling varieties of wheat. In 1901 he established the strain 'Federation', which dominated Australian wheat production for 30 years. During 1898 he accepted the post of 'wheat experimenter' to the New South Wales Government, in succession to Cobb, but, frustrated by the lack of researchers capable of carrying out experimental work, he left to continue with his independent investigations until his death. Fundamentally, Farrer was aware of the solitariness of research commitment before he put himself into government harness in 1898. Writing to McAlpine in Victoria three years earlier, he observed, 'To tell the truth, my work has become almost too much for me although I can & do give it all my time. From this you will see how impossible it must be for you with all the other work you have to do, to do anything like justice to the work. I have come, in fact, to see that I must depend upon myself & not look to the Governments to do what I had hoped they would have been able to do.'[10] He had also come to see that his cross-selection work was representative enough to serve all the Australian colonies.

Farrer's persistent commitment brought returns. By 1906, by continued selection, he succeeded in supplying the wheat industry with varieties of higher yielding, earlier maturing, more drought- and rust-resistant strains and of greatly enlarging the capacities of Australian wheat production. His application of scientific method to agricultural research provided a much needed lever to government interest and promoted plans that led eventually to the creation of the Council for Scientific and Industrial Research.

Lawrence Hargrave

A feature that several key colonial experimenters had in common was their belief that their findings 'should benefit fellow workers in science'. The point was plainly made by Farrer; Henry Sutton espoused it to his cost in Ballarat – 16 of his unpatented telephone designs were patented by others overseas; while the store set on open communication by Lawrence Hargrave was to ensure that his ideas fertilised other men's successful efforts in powered flight. The very uncompetitiveness of the Australian environment doubtless contributed to this mood. Many ideas were patented, as colonial listings show. But isolation, distance and the drive to spread knowledge from singular outposts in the colonies acted as potent factors among highly creative, men.

Lawrence Hargrave (1850–1915) was an important contributor to the technology of powered flight. Born and educated in England, Hargrave emigrated to Sydney in 1865 to join his father John Fletcher Hargrave, a puisne judge of the Supreme Court of New South Wales. In the following years he worked as a member of the drawing office of the Australian Steam Navigation Company and later as assistant astronomical observer to H.C. Russell at Sydney Observatory from 1879–83. Earlier in the 1870s, however, Hargrave became a member of four exploratory expeditions to New Guinea, including Sir William Macleay's *Chevert* Expedition of 1874, and it was on these adventurous travels that Hargrave had occasion to observe the power and movement of ocean waves. Allying this with a boyhood interest in the movement of insects, fish and birds, he began experiments on the theory of flapping flight. He was able to give up work in 1883 as the result of a small inheritance, and he devoted himself to research into human flight. During 1884, Hargrave presented his first paper to the Royal Society of New South Wales on 'The Trocoided Plane', launching a series of 23 such papers on aeronautical theory delivered before the society, which would propel him to the forefront of aeronautical research.

Hargrave made his first free flight with a machine operated by flappers powered by two rubber bands in tension in December 1884. As it happened, he was not the first. The credit of being the first successfully to fly a model ornithopter in Australia belongs to the prolific Henry Sutton, in 1870.[11] But Sutton was eclectic; Hargrave was dedicated to flight. Over the four years from 1884–8, he constructed no less than 19 India rubber powered models of aircraft for flapping flight, the most successful of which, incorporating 48 rubber bands with flapper propulsion, flew over 90 metres in level flight. Hargrave obtained more power from rubber bands than any other inventor, but the technique had obvious limitations, and he turned to experimenting on the propelling effects of compressed air. He built 14 engines on this principle and used ten to power flying machines, storing the compressed air in a long cylinder of sheet tin which formed the body of the machine. The most successful, which was flapper operated, attained a free flight of 112 metres. During 1889, he developed the radial rotary airscrew engine regarded as his most significant work. Two years later, he began his long-term research on the problem of supporting surfaces as a solution to techniques of soaring flight.

Throughout these arduous years of trial and error, Hargrave worked as an isolated researcher, drumming up materials, refashioning and adapting engines and improvising new methods and techniques. His engine designs ran the gamut of pure jet, jet propeller, turbine, spring recoil, rotary and semi-rotary, single cylinder and horizontally opposed types. It was a relentless performance for one man. He also experimented widely with petrol vapour, steam, carbonic acid, petrol and kerosene. But Australia's manufacturing environment offered him scant technological support. Mechanical help was hard to come by, fuel scarce and expensive, and Hargrave was obliged to make most of the parts himself. More insidiously obstructive was that obstacle familiar to colonial researchers in the lack of encouragement and appreciation for one's work. Neither the Royal Society, where Hargrave read his many papers, nor the government or citizenry of the colony, believed in the credibility of powered flight. 'The people of Sydney who can speak of my work without a smile,' Hargrave wrote in 1892, 'are very scarce.' Yet among them were the most skilled and perceptive scientists, the astronomer H.C. Russell, Professor Threlfall and his demonstrator at Sydney University's Department of Physics J.A. Pollock, who gave Hargrave their facilities and help.

Despite struggle and the persistent application of different styles, Hargrave never faltered in his desire to communicate both his progress and failures to all those with an interest in powered flight. As a Social Darwinian, he resisted any notion of restriction on invention and emphasised the link between innovation and cultural and national needs. He saw the inventor as the evolutionary link in the chain. He set down his ideas in a Memorandum on Patents in June 1888, 'I simply wish to sow the seed.' But he hammered certain points which provide an interesting blueprint for invention and patenting where broad limits could be struck.

Experimenters & inventors

1 *The inventor wishes to see his idea generally adopted.*
2 *The speculator seeks to acquire the sole right to make and sell the idea of the inventor by beating him down to the lowest figure he can.*
3 *The public will adopt any time or labour saving appliances more readily if they are not taxed with the speculator's exorbitant demands.*
4 *The country that has no patent law and does not protect the inventions of any other country becomes the resort of inventors, manufacturers & labourers, who bring with them prosperity.*
5 *The inventor should be rewarded by the country, when his invention has been generally adopted.*
6 *The reward should be a sum equal to the cost of producing or selling (say) 100 of his inventions.*
7 *The date of deposit of models & drawings, or publication of them should determine who is the inventor.*
8 *The deposit of models & drawings of an improvement to an invention necessary prove by their adoption, that the originator of an invention has forfeited his right to reward by his lack of inventiveness or haste.*
9 *If less than 100 (say) of the inventions are produced & sold the inventor may claim at any time one per cent of their cost as his reward; this is final should the demand for the invention afterwards become larger.*
10 *Inferior copies of an invention do injure the sales of the invention but advertise it.*
11 *Our patent laws benefit the speculator and not the inventor or the country.*
12 *The inventor is rarely able to successfully negotiate a business transaction & he therefore readily becomes the pigeon of the speculator.*

13 *Inventors cannot help producing novelties, and will do so wherever there are men who use tools and compete with one another.*[12]

Such ideas were emancipated and fresh, but Hargrave's view of patents struck his contemporaries as naive and he himself was obliged to admit that he did not have a friend he could trust as a business partner.

Throughout the 1890s his work centred on the evolution of the cellular box kite. In the early 1890s, he moved his family to a house south of Sydney, where broad beaches and high cliffs gave him spaces from which to launch his delicate machines, the largest of which measured 10 feet (3 metres) long, 5 feet (1.5 metres) high, had a cell span of 11½ feet (3.5 metres) and weighed 25 pounds (11 kilograms). Hargrave constructed 50 cellular kites, four of which were used to lift him off the ground in 1894.

Hargrave's most influential and supportive colleague was the American engineer and aerial navigator Octave Chanute (1832–1910), based in Chicago. Author of *Progress in Flying Machines* (1894) and a host of papers on heavier than air flight, Chanute came upon Hargrave's published papers, became his sincere admirer, and corresponded, offering critical and helpful comments and, importantly, relaying news of Hargrave's progress to the growing circle of aeronautical experimentalists abroad.

'I congratulate you upon the production of a steam engine which, as I understand it,' Chanute wrote the Australian in 1892, 'weighs with its boiler a little less than 20 lbs per horse power. This certainly is a very remarkable achievement, for the small scale on which is it accomplished . . . I shall be glad to receive anything which may be printed concerning your

Experimenters & inventors

experiments, the accounts of which I find tantalisingly brief.'[13]

'It will be some time,' Hargrave replied,[14] 'before there is anything to report, I am very busy with my boiler; there are not any insuperable difficulties about the whole machine and I feel confident that [in] time (I shall hew the thing out of the solid if I cannot get the material otherwise) the machine will be aloft with me on it. Of course I will let you know as soon as I have anything that will help others who are working on the same job, but I wish we heard more of them and less of the balloonists.' The first soaring machine, Hargrave went on to predict, would not be a 'birdlike structure'; 'It must be stable initially, & not kept stable by the action of the man & mechanism on it: it must therefore assume the form of some of my kites.' 'Curved wings when arranged as birds have them,' he told the American, are extremely unstable and the feat of making a flying or soaring machine steady with one pair of curved wings is about as difficult as making a dead man stand on his feet . . .'[15]

To the English aeronauticist P.S. Pilcher, a specialist in gliding, Hargrave pressed the virtue of his kites, 'quasi-flying machines' he called them, which was where their valuable stability came in. 'In working a flying machine,' he wrote Pilcher, 'the fewer things a fellow has to think about the more chance he will have of being successful. Now, if your system of aeroplanes is neutral as you call it, the element of balancing has been eliminated, and the operator has only to attend to deflecting the system . . . to alter his course. He is confident the machine will go straight if he lets go the tiller. This is what you have in a cellular flying machine . . . On a cellular flying machine you would only lose way due to the vertical surfaces. But I can only conceive that a sudden turn to right or left is to avoid collision: and in flying machines you will have the choice of up and down as well as right and left.'[16] Pilcher carried his own convictions to finality; he was killed in a gliding accident in 1899.

Hargrave's experiments with curved surfaces and soaring machines gathered pace from 1897, and the following year he visited England in the hope of obtaining financial and engineering backing for his work. He took with him six cellular kites and soaring kites, which were given to the Aeronautical Society so that, as he put it with his usual generosity, 'they have some original work to start from if any one in England wishes to help the cause'. No one, however, helped him and he returned to Sydney a few months later, disappointed but keen to get on. Chanute put his finger on the perseverance and loneliness of the independent researcher. 'I infer from your letter,' he wrote his friend in August 1899, '. . . that you did not receive in England that recognition and appreciation to which your labours and discoveries entitle you. This is, to be sure, the usual fate of those who are far in advance of their fellows, and it is not pleasant at the time. The important thing, to my mind, is that you should not be discouraged by it . . . I shall be very glad to hear from you at any time.'[17]

In the event the prize for the first controlled heavier than air machine went to the American brothers Wilbur and Orville Wright for their launching of a plane weighing 750 pounds (340 kilograms) in Ohio in December 1903. Hargrave was quick to congratulate them. His own achievements were exceptional in any terms. In the technological isolation, they were a remarkable record of undaunted inventiveness and perseverence.

From 1884 until his death in 1915, his ingenious mind

spawned a steady stream of models and designs: his total output numbered 70 powered models worked by India rubber, compressed air and clockwork, 91 cellular kites and soaring machines, and 52 engine designs, 33 of which were built. In terms of successful experimentation, he was probably only surpassed by the Wrights, the German Otto Lilienthal and Professor Samuel Langley, the Smithsonian Institution's secretary, generally regarded as the leading aeronautical researcher of the time. Hargrave was the first to give special attention to the question of lighter fuels to offset the problem of weight.

Despite isolation and the lack of any infrastructure of support, Hargrave's inventions passed into the language of flight. His radial rotary engine played a major part in the development of European aviation. The French radial rotary internal combustion engine, used to power Europe's first aeroplanes from 1909, was based on an idea originating in Australia. His box kite design also formed the basis of European models and was adopted by the United States Department of Meteorology. His curved surfaces cropped up, though unacknowledged, in the wing of the Wright brothers' successful plane. Hargrave's failure to achieve ultimate success in his own powered-flight experiments stemmed from the diversification and range of his efforts and the restricted technological environment in which he worked. His exhaustive approach and the challenge of the materials reduced the concentration of his thrust. As he wrote in 1908, 'Want of elementary knowledge of oil machines baulks me and causes much misdirected effort, I . . . feel like a fireman trying to hew out a donkey pump.' Yet Government and establishment indifference were significant stumbling blocks. 'It is the Australians that walked, rode, drove bullock drays, buggies and motor cars that are really interested in the evolution of the flying machine and who will see the thing through and keep it up to date,' Hargrave summed up. 'But with politicans and squatters I do not see how I can ever be anything but a circumstance.' Nonetheless, as Octave Chanute wrote towards the end of the 19th century, 'If there is one man more than any other who deserves to fly through the air, that man is Lawrence Hargrave of Sydney, NSW.'

Both Farrer and Hargrave were true representatives of individually motivated research. Both focused a strong light of international recognition on Australia. The new century would bring significant changes in the organisation, sponsorship and goals of science. An age of individual pioneering achievement was departing: a century of consolidation and extension was about to begin.

Endnotes

CHAPTER ONE
The Great South Land

1 The Spaniards, Torres and de Prado, threaded the straits between Australia and New Guinea in 1606 and dropped anchor along these shores: the Dutchmen, Jansz, Pelsaert, Hartog, Nuijts, Tasman, de Vlamingh and others, touched the mainland and the outer island of 'New Holland' throughout the 17th century, Tasman giving the name Anthoonij van Diemens to the 'first land in the South Seas that is met by us' in 1642. The British buccaneer William Dampier landed at Shark's Bay, Western Australia in 1688 and made the first observations on the Australian Aborigines. By the middle of the 17th century, Dutch navigators had charted the Australian coastline from Cape York west to the eastern end of the Great Australian Bight, and the southern coast of Tasmania. For details of their scientific observations see Gilbert P. Whitley, *Early History of Australian Zoology*, Royal Zoological Society of New South Wales, 1970, pp. 2–30.

2 J.C. Beaglehole, *The Life of Captain James Cook*, Adam & Charles Black, 1974, p. 278.

3 Spöring was trained in medicine. The servants chosen for the long journey were two countrymen whom Banks selected from his Lincolnshire estate, plus two negroes. The dogs were greyhounds.
4 Letter from John Ellis to Linnaeus, quoted by Sir Joseph D. Hooker (ed.), *Journal of the Right Hon. Sir Joseph Banks*, Macmillan, 1896, p. xxxix.
5 Beaglehole, *Cook*, pp. 227–8.
6 J.C. Beaglehole (ed.), *Endeavour Journal of Joseph Banks 1768–1771*, Public Library of NSW and Angus & Robertson, 1962, vol. 2, 25 April 1770, p. 51.
7 *Captain Cook's journal during his first voyage round the world made on H.M. Bark 'Endeavour' 1767–71*, A literal translation of the original MS edited by Captain W.J.L. Wharton, Hydrographer of the Admiralty, Elliot Stock, 1893, p. 243.
8 Beaglehole, *Banks Endeavour Journal*, vol. 2, May 1770, p.58.
9 These instructions were prepared by the President of the Royal Society, the Earl of Morton, principally for Cook, Banks and Solander. They recommended that they 'exercise the utmost patience and forebearance with respect to the Natives of the several Lands where the Ship may touch. To check the petulance of the Sailors, and restrain the wanton use of Fire Arms . . . shedding the blood of these people is a crime of the highest nature . . . They are the natural, and in the strictest sense of the word, the legal possessors of the several Regions they inhabit . . .', quoted Beaglehole, *Cook*, p. 150.
10 Sydney Parkinson, *A Journal of a Voyage to the South Seas . . .* , London, 1773, pp. 134–6.
11 Quoted Beaglehole, *Banks Endeavour Journal*, vol. 2, 29 May 1770, p. 71.
12 Quoted Beaglehole, *Cook*, p. 246.
13 Published as *Banks Florilegium*, Alecto Historical Editions in association with the British Museum (Natural History), 1983.

14 12 October 1800, Banks Papers, Brabourne Collection, vol. 8, Mitchell Library, Sydney.

15 Banks to Caley, 8 April 1803, *ibid*. Caley returned to England in 1808 and, still under Banks' patronage, became superintendent of the Botanic Gardens at Mauritius from 1816-22.

16 See Chapter 9, pp. 131-8.

17 Quoted Bernard Smith, *European Vision and the South Pacific: 1768-1850*, London, 1960, p. 6. Sir James Edward Smith was a leading naturalist and botanist whose collections founded the Linnean Society of London.

18 W.T. Stearn, Robert Brown, *Dictionary of Scientific Biography*, Scribner, 1970, vol. 2, pp. 516-22.

19 Banks to Brown, 8 April 1803, Sir Joseph Banks Correspondence, British Museum (Natural History), vol. XIV, pp. 43-5 (copy).

20 Brown managed to sell only 23 copies from an edition of 240, a result so discouraging to him that it curbed further intended publication.

21 Cunningham to Banks, 27 June 1819, Banks Papers, Nan Kivell Collection, National Library.

22 Ernest Scott, *Terre Napoleon, A History of French Exploration and Projects in Australia*, Methuen & Co., London, 1910, p. 26.

23 The sciences were not at war or, rather, scientific collaboration transcended war in this period, with the unfortunate exception of Matthew Flinders' incarceration at Mauritius for several years. Sir Joseph Banks made a practice of returning parcels of specimens gathered by French scientists – La Billardière's collection sent by the Dutch from Java was a case in point, while Benjamin Franklin, as United States representative in France after the American Revolution, also pressed for an unmolested passage for Captain Cook then embarking on his third expedition of scientific discovery.

24 Robert Brown to Banks, 30 May 1802, Sir Joseph Banks

Correspondence, vol. XII, pp. 141-6, British Museum (Natural History) reproduced in Ann Mozley Moyal, *Scientists in Nineteenth Century Australia: A Documentary History*, Cassell, Australia, 1976, p. 24.

25 F. Péron and L. Freycinet, *Voyage de découvertes aux Terres Australes . . . sur les corvettes Géographe, Le Naturaliste et la goélette Casuarina, pendant les années 1800, 1801, 1802, 1803 et 1804*, vol. 1-2, Paris, 1807-1816.

26 N.J.B. Plomley, *The Baudin Expedition and the Tasmanian Aborigines 1802*, Blubber Head Press, 1983, chapter 10.

27 C.M. Finney, *To Sail Beyond the Sunset, Natural History in Australia, 1699-1829*, Rigby, Adelaide, 1984, pp. 155, 158; and see L. Freycinet, *Voyage autour de monde. . . executé sur les corvettes S.M. L'Uranie et La Physicienne pendant les années 1817, 1818, 1819 et 1820 . . . Historique 1-2*, Paris, 1825.

CHAPTER TWO
Under a virgin sky

1 P.P. King, *Narrative of a Survey of the Intertropical Waters and Western Coasts of Australia performed between the years 1818-1822*, vol. 2.

2 Quoted George Perry, *Arcana or The Museum of Natural History*, George Smeston, London, 1811, p. 84.

3 Brisbane to Mr Bruce, 28 March 1822, Brisbane Papers, National Library of Australia, Canberra.

4 Rümker published a bitter pamphlet on his dismissal, 'On the Most Effectual Means of Encouraging Scientific Undertakings', in Hamburg, 1831.

5 *The Catalogue of 7,385 Stars from Observations made at the Observatory at Parramatta* was published finally in 1838 from

reductions prepared by William Richardson at Greenwich Observatory.

6 Brown to Banks, 30 May 1802, Sir Joseph Banks Correspondence, British Museum (Natural History), vol. XIII, pp. 141–6.

7 William Hooker's chief works at Kew, built on an earlier output of 14 volumes on British and exotic botany, included *Genera Filicum* (1842), *A Century of Orchideae* (1846), *Species Filicum* (5 vols, 1846–64), *A Century of Ferns* (1854), *Filices Exoticae* (1857–59) and *British Ferns* (1861–62). Among the periodicals he brought out were the *Botanical Magazine* (1822–65), the *Journal of Botany* (1834–42) and the *Journal of Botany and Kew Gardens Miscellany* (1849–57).

8 See Ann Mozley Moyal, *Scientists*, pp. 43–51, and T.E. Burns & J.R. Skemp (eds), Van Diemen's Land Correspondents 1827–49, Records of Queen Victoria Museum, 1961.

9 August and Alphonse de Candolle, father and son, popularised the natural system with their respective works *Elementary Theory of Botany* (1813) and *Prodromus systematis naturales* (16 vols, 1824–70).

10 Joseph Hooker to Gunn, October 1844, Gunn Papers, Mitchell Library, Sydney. See also Chapter 4, p. 65.

11 Joseph Hooker became assistant director of Kew Gardens in 1855 and succeeded his father as director on his death in 1865.

12 See Chapter 10.

CHAPTER THREE
Entrepreneurs & explorers

1 18 October 1838, quoted in A.H. Chisholm, *The Story of Elizabeth Gould*, Hawthorne Press, Melbourne, 1944, p. 33.

2 3 September 1839, Gilbert Letters, G.M. Mathews Collection, Australian National Library, Canberra.

3 *ibid.*, 4 May 1840.
4 24 August 1844, Gould Letters, Australian National Library, Canberra.
5 *ibid.*, 16 November 1840.
6 John Gilbert's Diary of the Leichhardt Expedition to Port Essington, 18 September 1844–28 June 1845, Mitchell Library, Sydney.
7 Five volumes produced by R. Bowdler Sharpe.
8 These included works on the birds of Asia, Britain, North America, humming birds and Paradisidae, and totalled 41 volumes and 3,000 plates.
9 John James Audubon (1785–1851), author of *Birds of America* (1828–38) and *Synopsis of the Birds of North America* (1839), supervised the production of these striking illustrated works in Edinburgh and Europe.
10 Letter to Ronald Gunn, April 1851.
11 See Chapter 9, pp. 134–5.
12 Letter to Gaetano Durando, 20 May 1846, Leichhardt Letters, Mitchell Library, Sydney.
13 *Fragmenta Phytographiae Australiae*, published from 1856–68.
14 See Chapter 4, p. 64.
15 D.J. Mulvaney & J.H. Calaby, *So Much That is New: Baldwin Spencer 1860–1929*, Melbourne University Press, 1985.
16 Quoted *ibid.*, p. 126 from Baldwin Spencer's Preface to *The Arunta*.

CHAPTER FOUR
Navigators & ship's naturalists

1 Sir William Parry commanded the earliest polar expedition in 1818; Captain John Franklin followed in 1819 and again from 1824–8, searching for the Northwest Passage that would link the Pacific and Atlantic oceans, in the interests of trade; while

Rear-Admiral Sir John Ross discovered the north magnetic pole at the end of his attempt to find the Northwest Passage, 1829–33.

2 John Lort Stokes, *Discoveries in Australia, with an account of the coasts and rivers explored and surveyed during a voyage of H.M.S. Beagle, 1837–43*, London, 1846, 2 vols.

3 28 January 1836, F. Burkhardt, Sydney Smith *et al.* (eds), *The Correspondence of Charles Darwin*, vol. 1, 1821–1836, Cambridge University Press, 1985, p. 482.

4 Charles Darwin, *The Voyage of the Beagle*, Everyman Library, 1959, Chapter XIX.

5 See Chapter 6.

6 J.B. Jukes, *Narrative of the Surveying Voyage of H.M.S. Fly*, T & W Boone, 1847, vol. 1, pp. 3 and 5.

7 *ibid.*

8 21 March 1848, Leonard Huxley (ed.), *Life and Letters of Thomas Henry Huxley*, New York, 1901, vol. 1, pp. 40–1.

9 Letter to the Royal Society of New South Wales, 12 November 1881, acknowledging the award of the Clarke Medal. Royal Society of New South Wales Letter Book, Sydney.

10 Huxley to Macleay 9 November 1851, *Life and Letters of T.H. Huxley*, New York, 1901, vol. 1, p. 100; also see Mozley Moyal, *Scientists*, pp. 98–100. The original prospectus for Sydney University in 1849 had included a natural history chair. By 1850 this had been changed to a combined chair of chemistry and experimental physics which lost the University T.H. Huxley but brought them John Smith MD, lecturer in chemistry from Aberdeen University.

11 *Life and Letters*, vol. 1, pp. 40–1.

12 J. McGillivray, *Narrative of the Voyage of H.M.S. Rattlesnake*, London 1852, vol. 2, 'Account of Mr E.B. Kennedy's Expedition for the Exploration of Cape York Peninsula in Tropical Australia. Narrative by Mr. Wm. Carron'; and *ADB*, vol. 2, 1788–1850,

pp. 43–4; and L. Gilbert, 'Carron, Botanist and Explorer, 1821–76', *Journal Royal Australian Historical Society*, 1961, vol. 47, pp. 292–311.

13 Marnie Bassett, *Behind the Picture, H.M.S. Rattlesnake's Australian and New Guinea Cruise 1846 to 1850*, Oxford University Press, 1966, pp. 98–9. (The cruise was cancelled and the *Rattlesnake* sailed directly for England under the command of Lieutenant York.)

14 Quoted A.J. Marshall, *Darwin and Huxley in Australia*, Hodder & Stoughton, London, 1970, p. 126.

15 See Chapter 2, pp. 36–9.

16 Withdrawal of Admiralty funds closed the Rossbank Observatory in 1853.

17 13 March 1841, *Sydney Morning Herald*, 10 February 1842.

18 Charles Wilkes, *Narrative of the United States Exploring Expedition During 1838, 1839, 1840, 1841, 1842*, Philadelphia, 1845, vol. 11, p. 175; also see William Stanton, *The Great United States Exploring Expedition of 1838–1842*, University of California Press, 1975.

19 Namely Charles Pickering and Titian Peale; J.D. Dana; William Rich; Joseph Couthouy; Horatio Hale; Joseph Drayton and A.T. Agate, and William Brackenridge.

20 For Dana's geological work in Australia see Chapter 7.

21 Dana to Clarke 3 February 1840, W.B. Clarke Papers, Mitchell Library, Sydney; and Moyal, *Scientists*, pp. 102–3.

22 Letters to Clarke 1854 and 1 September 1851, W.B. Clarke Papers, Mitchell Library, Sydney; also see Ann Mozley, 'James Dwight Dana in New South Wales, 1839–1840', *Journal & Proceedings, Royal Sociey of New South Wales*, 1964, vol. 97, pp. 185–191.

CHAPTER FIVE
Science, societies & the people

1 For the concept of 'metropolitan' and 'periphery' science see Roy M. McLeod, 'On Visiting the "Moving Metropolis": Reflections on the Architecture of Imperial Science', *Historical Records of Australian Science*, 1982, vol. 5, no. 3.

2 Founded by the Arctic explorer, Sir John Richardson, at the Royal Hospital, Haslar, the Museum gave encouragement to British naval officers visiting Australia and elsewhere to collect zoological specimens for its shelves.

3 The group consisted of James Bowman, principal surgeon of Sydney Hospital, Dr Henry Douglass, superintendent of the Parramatta General Hospital, Barron Field, judge of the Supreme Court of Civil Jurisdiction in New South Wales, Major Frederick Goulburn, colonial secretary, Captain Irvine, Edward Wollstonecraft, merchant, and John Oxley, surveyor-general.

4 Minutes of the Philosophical Society of Australasia, 27 June 1821, Mitchell Library, Sydney, quoted Mozley Moyal, *Scientists*, pp. 110-12.

5 Several were published in B.F. Field, *Geographical Memoirs*, London, 1825.

6 Michael Hoare, 'Science and Scientific Associations in Eastern Australia, 1820-1890', PhD thesis, Australian National University, 1974, p. 27.

7 *Sydney Monitor*, March 1833.

8 The short-lived *Australian Quarterly Magazine of Theology, Literature and Science* (1828-31), the *New South Wales Magazine* (1831-33), and the *Sydney Guardian, A Journal of Religious, Literary and Scientific Information* (1847-48) were cases in point. See also E. Newland, 'Forgotten Early Australian Journals of Science', *Journal Royal Australian Historical Society*, 1986.

9 See Chapter 4, pp. 65–7.

10 Letter to Herschel, 2 November 1838, John Herschel Correspondence, Royal Society of London; see also Chapter 2, pp. 30–1.

11 Clarke was for several years scientific correspondent of the *Sydney Morning Herald* and an occasional correspondent of *The Australasian*.

12 Quoted in Shar Jones, *Gentlemen Collectors in New South Wales 1826–1891*, Sydney, 1983, p. 8. See also J.S. Fletcher, 'The Society's Heritage from the Macleays', *Proceedings of the Linnean Sociey of New South Wales*, 1920, vol. 45, pp. 592–629.

13 John J. Tregenza, *George French Angas. Artist, Traveller, Naturalist 1822–1886*, Art Gallery Board of South Australia, 1980.

14 R. Strahan (ed.), *Rare and Curious Specimens: An Illustrated History of the Australian Museum 1827–1979*, pp. 29–37.

15 *ibid.*, quoted p. 44.

16 Michael Roe, *Quest for Authority in Eastern Australia*, Melbourne University Press in association with Australian National University, 1965, p. 9; and *Australian Heritage, A History in Pictures Since 1788*, Sunshine Books, 1982, p. 72.

17 Graeme Davison, 'Exhibitions', *Australian Cultural History*, 1982–3, no. 2, pp. 5–21; John Parris and A.G.L. Shaw, 'The Melbourne International Exhibition 1880–81', *Victorian Historical Magazine*, 1980, no. 4, pp. 237–53; John Allwood, *The Great Exhibitions*, London, 1977.

18 *Proceedings of the Philosophical Society of Adelaide*, vol. 1, 1877–8.

19 *Proceedings of Royal Society of New South Wales*, vol. 1, 1967.

20 Australasian Association for the Advancement of Science, *Report*, 1888, vol. 1, pp. 8–14.

21 The Australian Academy of Science was constituted by Royal Charter in 1954.

CHAPTER SIX
The feminine touch

1 Georgiana's letter to Mangles, begun in March 1837, was completed along with the gathering of seeds and flowers, in September 1838, quoted in Alexandra Hasluck, *Portrait with Background. A Life of Georgiana Molloy*, Melbourne University Press, 1955, pp. 154–8, 160–4, 165–70.
2 *ibid.*, p. 177.
3 *ibid.*, p. 178.
4 *ibid.*, p. 205.
5 F.M. Spoehr, 'White Falcon', *The House of Godeffroy and its Commercial and Scientific Role in the Pacific*, Pacific Books, 1965.
6 Charitas Bischoff, *The Hard Road: The life story of Amalie Dietrich, Naturalist*, 1821–1891. English translation by A. Liddell Geddie (London, Martin Hopkinson, 1931), letter 20 August 1863, pp. 234–6.
7 *ibid.*
8 *Australian Dictionary of Biography*, 1851–90, vol. 4, p. 73.
9 *A Room of One's Own*, Penguin, 1929.
10 Margaret Wills, *By Their Fruits. A Life of Ferdinand von Mueller*, Angus & Robertson, 1949
11 *Australian Dictionary of Biography*, vol. 3, pp. 59–60; and correspondence and press cuttings of Louisa Calvert; Mitchell Library, Sydney. Louisa Atkinson, *A Voice from the Country*, Mulina Press, Canberra, 1978.
12 Vivienne Rae Ellis, *Louisa Anne Meredith. A Tigress in Exile*, Blubber Head Press, 1979.
13 Bernard Smith (ed.), *Documents on Art and Taste in Australia. The Colonial Period, 1770–1914*, Melbourne University Press, 1975, p. 228.
14 Maie Casey, *An Australian Story*, Michael Joseph, 1962, p. 106

and M. Ellis Rowan, *A Flower Hunter in Queensland and New Zealand*, John Murray, 1898.

CHAPTER SEVEN
The conquest of the rocks

1 The Oolitic, now known as the Jurassic formation, belongs to the Secondary or Mesozoic era and represents some 135 million to 225 million years in the geological time scale. The Permian, Carboniferous, Devonian, Silurian and Cambrian rocks belong, in order of increasing antiquity, to the Palaeozoic or Primary era – from 225 million to 600 million years of geological time.
2 Notably in the *Geological Society Quarterly Journal*, the *Annals of Natural History*, *The Tasmanian Journal of Natural Science*, *Transactions of the Royal Society of Victoria* and several pamphlets and books.
3 *U.S. Exploring Expedition, Report Vol. X, Geology*; description of fossil shells of the collections of the exploring expedition under the command of Chas. Wilkes, USN, obtained in Australia from the lower layers of the coal formations, *American Journal of Science*, 1847, vol IV, pp. 151–60.
4 Jukes to W.B. Clarke, 22 March 1861, W.B. Clarke Papers, Mitchell Library, Sydney; and quoted Mozley Moyal, *Scientists*, p. 139.
5 Barkly to Clarke, 6 September 1860, *ibid.*, p. 137.
6 Gould to Clarke, 16 September 1860, *ibid.*, p. 137.
7 Aplin to Clarke, 20 February 1862, *ibid.*, pp. 137–8.
8 Letter from W.B. Clarke to A.M. Thomson, *ibid.*, pp. 39–40.
9 *Eight General Reports of the Colonial Land and Emigration Commissioners*, London HMSO, 1848, pp. 42–53; and 'A Sketch of the Geological and Physical Formation of Western Australia',

Quarterly Journal of the Geological Society of London, 1849, vol. 5, pp. 51–3.

10 S. Stutchbury, *Diary of a Geological and Mineralogical Survey of the Colony of New South Wales during the years 1850, 1851, 1852, 1853*, MS, Mitchell Library, Sydney; *Australian Dictionary of Biography*, vol. 4, 1851–90, pp. 216–17; Michael Crane, 'Samuel Stutchbury (1798–1859), Naturalist and Geologist', *Notes & Records Royal Society of London*, 1983, vol. 37, pt 2, pp. 189–200.

11 M.E. Hoare, 'The Half-Mad Bureaucrat, Robert Brough Smith (1830–1880)', *Records Australian Academy of Science*, 1973, vol. 2, no. 4, pp. 25–40.

12 For work on Sir Roderick Murchison's attempt to dominate theory in respect of Australian gold see E.A. Newland, 'Sir Roderick Murchison and Australia: A Case Study of British Influence on Australian Geological Science', MA hons thesis, University of New South Wales, 1983.

13 T.G. Vallance, 'Origins of Australian Geology', Presidential Address, *Proceedings of the Linnean Society of New South Wales*, 1975, vol. 100, pp. 13–43.

14 C.D. Aplin to W.B. Clarke, 9 September 1863, W.B. Clarke Papers, Mitchell Library, Sydney.

15 9 September 1863.

16 Letter to Sir Roderick Murchison, 1855, quoted in *Varieties of Vice-Regal Life*, 1870, vol. 1, p. 309.

CHAPTER EIGHT
The weather & the sky

1 James Forbes, 'Report upon the Recent Progress and Present State of Meteorology', British Association for Advancement of Science, Report, 1831.

2 J.B. Jukes, in his *Physical Structure of Australia*, also devotes space to the continent's meteorology.

3 See Chapter 1 and Chapter 4.

4 27 May 1842, published in M. Aurousseau (ed.), *The Letters of F. W. Ludwig Leichhardt*, 1968, vol. 2.

5 Letters of Jevons 4 January and 17 June 1857, *Letters and Journal of W. Stanley Jevons*, edited by his wife, London, 1886, p. 76.

6 Published in *Waugh's Australian Almanac*, Sydney, 1859.

7 *Australian Dictionary of Biography* 1851–1890, vol 5, pp. 329–31.

8 See Chapter 2, pp. 30–3.

9 Ann Moyal, *Clear Across Australia*, Thomas Nelson Australia, 1984.

10 Sydney Observatory Correspondence.

11 *Sydney Morning Herald*, 30 May 1848.

12 Denison had himself established an observatory when instructor in the Royal Engineers at Chatham in 1833 and later served as an observer at Greenwich Observatory.

13 Scott to Tebbutt, 16 April 1860, Tebbutt Correspondence, Mitchell Library, Sydney.

14 Four Great Comets were recorded in the period, the two discovered by Tebbutt in 1861 and 1881, the others in 1858 and 1882.

15 W. Orchiston, 'Illuminating Incidents in Antipodean Astronomy: John Tebbutt and the Great Comet of 1881', *Journal of the Astronomical Society of Victoria*, December 1981, vol. 34, no. 6; J. Tebbutt, *Australian Dictionary of Biography*, 1851–1890, vol. 6, pp. 251–2; Mozley Moyal, *Scientists*, pp. 163–8.

16 Le Sueur worked at Lord Rosse's private observatory at Parsonton. It was Rosse's detection late in the 1840s of changes in the northern nebulae that prompted Royal Society interest in erecting a powerful telescope in the southern hemisphere.

17 Ellery to Sabine, 4 January 1869, correspondence concerning the Great Melbourne Telescope 1852–70, Royal Society of London 1871, Parts II and III.

18 Mount Stromlo Observatory was first established in temporary quarters in Canberra in 1911 and given a permanent home in 1924.

CHAPTER NINE
Evolution in Australia

1 G.P. Whitley, *Early History of Australian Zoology*, Royal Society of New South Wales, 1970, pp. 10–11. This work contains an excellent chronological table of Australian fauna discovered between 1606–1777.

2 Bernard Smith, 'Evolution and Australian Nature', *Meanjin Quarterly*, April 1959, vol. 18, no. 1, pp. 83–6.

3 Quoted Gavin de Beer, *Charles Darwin*, New York, 1965, p. 107.

4 Smith, *op. cit.*; and E. Darwin, *Zoonomia*, London, 1818, vol. 1, p. 392.

5 Monotremes represent a sub-class of marsupials, notably the platypus and echidna, which use one aperture for both the reproductive and excretory functions; they became known colloquially as 'one holers'.

6 See Chapter 1, pp. 18–19.

7 The first eye-witness account of the unaided transference of an embryonic kangaroo to the pouch was in fact given by Alexander Collie, an anatomist and ship's surgeon, in a report published in the *Journal of the Zoological Society of London* in 1830. It was overlooked by Owen, who held that the embryo was transferred to the teat by the parent's lips, and despite other scattered observations of the process the true account was not widely accepted until this century. The first systematic observations of the

transferency of the infant kangaroo were published by C. Sharman and J. Calaby, *CSIRO Wildlife Research*, 1964, pp. 58–85.

8 George Bennett to Owen, 4 February 1833, Owen Archives, Royal College of Surgeons, London, (copy) Mitchell Library, Sydney.

9 Richard Owen to Sir Thomas Mitchell, 29 March 1840, Sir Thomas Mitchell Papers, Mitchell Library, Sydney.

10 Oviparous – producing young by means of eggs expelled from the body before being hatched; ovoviviparous – producing young by eggs hatched within the body; viviparous – bringing forth young in a living state.

11 Darwin to King, 21 January 1836, F. Burkhardt, Sydney Smith *et al.* (eds), *The Correspondence of Charles Darwin*, vol. 1, 1821–1836, Cambridge University Press, 1985, p. 481.

12 George Bennett, *Gatherings of a Naturalist in Australasia*, London, 1860, pp. 122–3.

13 W.H. Caldwell, 'The Embryology of Monotremata and Marsupials', *Philosophical Transactions Royal Society*, 1887, part 1.

14 *Transactions Royal Society of South Australia*, 1884. The echidna lays one egg directly into a temporary brood pouch of the abdomen. The baby leaves the pouch when covered with hair. The platypus alternatively lays from one to three eggs and incubates them curled around them.

15 Bennett to Owen, 10 September 1884, Owen Archives, and Mitchell Library, Sydney.

16 See Chapter 11, pp. 162–3 and 167–8.

17 Owen to Bennett, 1850, reproduced in Bennett, *Gatherings of a Naturalist*, p. 151.

18 *On the Classification and Distribution of the Mammalia*, 1859, pp. 28–30; See Ann Mozley Moyal, 'Sir Richard Owen and his influence on Australian Zoological and Palaeontological Science', *Records of Australian Academy of Science*, 1975, vol. 3, no. 2, pp. 41–56.

19 Four landmark works, his *Journal of Researches into the Geology and Natural History of the various countries visited by H.M.S. Beagle* (1839), *Structure and Distribution of Coral Reefs* (1842), *Geological Observations on Volcanic Islands* (1844), and *Geological Observations on South America* (1846) were published between 1838 and 1846.

20 Wallace (1823–1913), OM, FRS, naturalist and collector, had travelled widely on the Amazon and in the Rio Negro, 1848–52, and from 1854 worked on the zoology of the Malay Archipelago. He published *Essay on the Law which has regulated the Introduction of New Species* in 1855, but the idea of natural selection as the means of evolution did not strike him until 1858 when he communicated it at once to Darwin. Wallace's works included *The Malay Archipelago* (1869), *Contributions to the Theory of Natural Selection* (1870) and *The Geographical Distribution of Animals* (1876).

21 Macleay to Viscount Sherbrooke, May 1860, A. Patchett Martin, *Life and Letters of the Right Honorable Robert Lowe, Viscount Sherbrooke . . .*, 1893, vol. 2, pp. 204–7.

22 Mueller to Owen, 24 August 1861, Richard Owen Papers, vol. XIX, British Museum (Natural History), London.

23 Lecture by Professor McCoy delivered before the Early Closing Association, Melbourne, 1869–70, 1870, pp. 23–32, Australian National Library, Canberra.

24 *Royal Society of New South Wales Transactions*, 1867, vol. 1.

25 'Four papers . . . by Richard Davies Hanson', Adelaide, 1864, bound with *Proceedings of the Philosophical Society of Australia*, 1877–78, vol. 1.

26 George Britton Halford (1824–1910), professor of anatomy, physiology and pathology from 1862, was Owen's nominee for the post. He was a firm champion of Owen's anti-evolutionary views and after dissecting two monkeys soon after his arrival in Melbourne went to Owen's defense in his battle with Huxley over the descent of man in a treatise arrestingly entitled *Not Like Man, Bimanous and Biped, nor yet Quadrumanous, but Cheiropodous*, Melbourne, 1863. Halford also used his work on snake venom to illustrate God's omnipotent will.

27 John Smith (1818–85), first professor of chemistry and experimental physics at Sydney University, Smith expressed his creationist views at a meeting of the New South Wales Philosophical Society in 1863 in a debate on Lyell's *Geological Evidences on the Antiquity of Man*, *Sydney Morning Herald*, 12 November 1863.

28 'The History of Australian Tertiary Geology', *Transactions of the Royal Society of Tasmania*, 11 July 1876, p. 78.

29 Presidential Address, 21 January 1876, *Proceedings Linnean Society of New South Wales*, 1877, vol. 1, pp. 95–6.

30 See Chapter 11. Wilson was professor of anatomy and Martin a lecturer in physiology.

CHAPTER TEN
Colonial scientists versus the 'experts'

1 Both Allan Cunningham in New South Wales and Ronald Gunn in Tasmania acquired their training less formally.

2 See Chapter 3, pp. 51–2; the work was Mueller's *Fragmenta Phytographiae Australiae*.

3 Hooker to Mueller, 3 June 1857, Mueller Papers, 1858–70, National Herbarium of Victoria, Melbourne.

4 Bentham had been responsible for classifying the botany of several maritime expeditions. His publications included *A Handbook of British Flora* (1854) and *Flora Hong-Kongiensis* (1861). His most ambitious work was the *Genera Plantarum* (1862–83), prepared in collaboration with Joseph Hooker.

5 Bentham to Mueller, 22 May 1861, Mueller Papers, 1858–70.
6 It is generally thought that Mueller published two volumes of this work. Mueller, however, failed to complete the Victorian Flora and the second volume, *Plants indigenous to Victoria* (Volume II) was prepared by Alfred J. Ewart, government botanist of Victoria after Mueller's death, in 1910.
7 Mueller to Bentham, 24 September 1862, *loc. cit*.
8 Bentham to Mueller, 26 February 1865, Mueller Papers, 1858–70.
9 Leichhardt to Owen, 10 July 1844, Leichhardt Letters, Mitchell Library, Sydney.
10 Report of Gerard Krefft to the Trustees of the Australian Museum, 7 October 1869, Exploration of the Caves and Rivers of New South Wales. Minutes, Reports Correspondence, Accounts, New South Wales Legislative Assembly, Votes and Proceedings, 1882, vol. V, pp. 551–602; and Mozley Moyal, *Scientists*, pp. 206–11.
11 Krefft to Clarke, 19 May 1870, W.B. Clarke Papers, Mitchell Library, Sydney.
12 Owen to Clarke, 1 September 1877, *loc. cit*.
13 Huxley to Macleay, 9 November 1851, *Life and Letters of Thomas Henry Huxley*, New York, 1901, vol. 1, pp. 99–103.
14 Krefft to Parkes, 23 September 1873, Parkes Correspondence, vol. 20, Mitchell Library, Sydney.

CHAPTER ELEVEN
Science in colonial universities

1 D.J. Mulvaney & J.H. Calaby, *So Much That is New: Baldwin Spencer 1860–1929*, Melbourne University Press, 1985.
2 Inaugural Address, 23 March 1887, *Chemistry Pamphlets*,

vol. 3, Victorian State Library, Melbourne.

3 Haswell, a lecturer in zoology and comparative anatomy at Sydney from 1883, was appointed first Challis Professor of Biology in 1889 and held the Chair until 1917. He published his famous *Textbook of Zoology* in 1897 and many papers on the anatomy and taxonomy of various animals, particularly marine invertebrates, *Australian Dictionary of Biography*, vol. 9.

4 See C.H.C. Lamb in *Dictionary of Scientific Biography*, Charles Scribner's, New York.

5 Donald Fleming, 'Science in Australia, Canada and the United States: Some Comparative Remarks', *Proceedings 10th International Congress History of Science*, Ithaca, 1964, vol. 1, pp. 179-96.

6 D. Branagan & G. Holland (eds), *Ever Reaping Something New. A Science Centenary*, University of Sydney, 1985, p. 85.

7 23 November 1891, R. Threlfall Papers, Sydney University Archives, Sydney.

8 Branagan & Holland, *op. cit.*

9 Ann Moyal, *Clear Across Australia*, Thomas Nelson, p. 108.

CHAPTER TWELVE
Experiementers & inventors

1 K.T.H. Farrer, *A Settlement Amply Supplied*, Melbourne University Press, 1980, pp. 11-14.

2 Ann Moyal, *Clear Across Australia*, Thomas Nelson, pp. 72-3.

3 *Australian Dictionary of Biography*, vols 2 and 4.

4 Farrer, *op. cit.*, pp. 192-5.

5 *Australian Dictionary of Biography*, Kernot, vol. 5, pp. 20-2; Warren, vol. 6, pp. 356-7.

6 Farrer to Professor Galloway, 13 July 1894, W.J. Farrer Papers, Mitchell Library, Sydney.

7 *Sydney Mail*, 14 June 1890.
8 Mendel (1822–1884) was the posthumous founder of modern genetic theory. His studies, on the sweet pea plant, were first presented in Brunn in 1865, but were overlooked by contemporaries until 1900 when his great contribution was recognised.
9 13 July 1894, *op. cit.*
10 7 April 1895, Farrer Papers.
11 *Lawrence Hargrave. Australian Pioneer Aeronautical Scientist*, Australian Government Publishing Service, 1984.
12 Farrer Papers.
13 6 October 1892, Lawrence Hargrave Papers, Powerhouse Museum of Science and Industry, Sydney.
14 20 August 1893, *loc. cit.*
15 Hargrave to Chanute, 12 November 1895, *loc. cit.*
16 Letter to Pilcher, 31 July 1896, *loc. cit.*
17 Chanute to Hargrave, 6 August 1899, *loc. cit.*

Select Bibliography

General

Australian Dictionary of Biography (ADB), 1788–1930, 9 vols, Melbourne University Press, Melbourne, 1966.

Basalla, George, 'The Spread of Western Science', *Science*, 1967, vol. 156, pp. 611–22.

Brockway, Lucille, *Science and Colonial Expansion: The Role of the British Royal Botanical Gardens*. Academic Press, New York, 1979.

Carlson, L., 'Bibliography of the History of Australian Science', *Historical Records of Australian Science*, 1982, vol. 5, no. 3. 1983, vol. 5, no. 4; 1984, vol. 6, no. 1; 1985, vol. 6, no. 5. This is a substantial ongoing source on the growing field of the history of Australian science and technology.

Dictionary of Scientific Biography, C.C. Gillespie (ed.), Charles Scribner's, New York, 1976.

Inkster, I., 'Scientific Enterprise and the Colonial "Model": Observations on Australian Experience in Historical Context', *Social Studies of Science* (London), 1985, vol 15.

Kerr, Joan (ed.), *Dictionary of Australian Artists. Painters, Photographers and Engravers, 1770–1870, A-H*. Working Paper 1. Power Institute of Fine Arts, University of Sydney, 1984.

MacLeod, Roy, 'On Visiting the "Moving Metropolis": Reflections on the Architecture of Imperial Science', *Historical Records of Australian Science*, 1982, vol. 5, no. 3.

Moyal, Ann, *Science, Technology and Society in Australia. A Bibliography*, Griffith University, Science Research Centre, Occasional Paper Series, no. 2, 1978.

Mozley, Ann, *A Guide to the Manuscript Records of Australian Science*, Australian National University, Canberra, 1966.

Mozley Moyal, Ann, *Scientists in Nineteenth Century Australia. A Documentary History*. Cassell Australia, Sydney, 1976, (and bibliography).

Reingold, N. & Rothenberg, M., (eds), Scientific Colonialism in Australia and America, Smithsonian Institute, Washington DC, 1986.

Smith, Bernard, *European Vision and the South Pacific, 1768-1850*, 2nd ed. Harper & Row, London, 1985.

Stanbury, Peter (ed.), *100 Years of Australian Scientific Exploration* Holt, Reinhart & Winston, 1975.

Sneddon, George, 'Eurocentrism and Australian Science, Some Examples,' *Search*, 1981, vol. 12.

Stearn, W.T., *The Natural History Museum at South Kensington: A History of the British Museum (Natural History) 1753-1980*, Heinemann, London, 1981.

CHAPTER ONE
The Great South Land

Banks Florilegium, Alecto Historical Editions in association with the British Museum of Natural History, London, 1980.

Beaglehole, J.C. (ed.), *Journal of Captain Cook on his Voyages of Discovery*, vol. 1, *Voyage of the Endeavour 1768–1771*, Cambridge University Press, Cambridge, 1955.

Beaglehole, J.C. (ed.), *The Endeavour Journal of Joseph Banks 1768-1771*, 2 vols, Public Library of New South Wales and Angus & Robertson, Sydney, 1962.

Beaglehole, J.C. (ed.), *The Life of Captain James Cook*, Adam & Charles Black, London, 1974.

Carr, D.J. (ed.), *Sydney Parkinson, Artist of Cook's Endeavour Voyage*, British Museum of Natural History in association with the Australian National University Press, Canberra, 1983.

Carter, H.C., *The Life of Joseph Banks*, British Museum of National History, London, 1986.

Cook Bicentenary Symposium, *Captain Cook, Navigator and Scientist*, Australian National University Press and Australian Academy of Science, Canberra, 1970.

Finney, C.M., *To Sail Beyond the Sunset. Natural History in Australia 1699-1829*, Rigby, Adelaide, 1984.

Miller, David P., 'Sir Joseph Banks: an Historiographical Perspective', *History of Science*, 1981, vol. 19.

Parkinson, Sydney, *A Journal of a Voyage to the South Seas in His Majesty's Ship the Endeavour; faithfully transcribed and edited with preface by Stanley Parkinson from the papers of the late Sydney Parkinson, draughtsman to Joseph Banks Esq.*, Library Board of South Australia, Adelaide, 1972. Australiana Facsimile Editions, no. 34.

Péron, F.E., and Freycinet, L., *Voyage e découvertes aux Terres Australes . . . sur les corvettes Géographe, Le Naturaliste et la goélette Casuarina, pendent les années 1800, 1801, 1802, 1803 et 1804*, vols 1-2, Paris, 1807-1816.

Perry, T.M., *The Discovery of Australia. The Charts and Maps of the Navigators and Explorers*, Thomas Nelson Australia, Melbourne, 1982.

Plomley, N.J.B., *The Baudin Expedition and the Tasmanian Aborigines*, Blubber Head Press, Hobart, 1983.

Scott, Ernest, *Terre Napoléon. A History of French Exploration and Projects in Australia*, Methuen & Co., London, 1910.

Smith, Bernard, *The Art of Captain Cook's Voyages*, Melbourne University Press in association with Australian Academy of the Humanities, 1985, 2 vols.

Stearn, William T., 'A Royal Society Appointment with Venus in 1769; The Voyage of Cook and Banks in the *Endeavour* in 1768–1771 and its Botanical Results', *Notes and Records Royal Society of London*, 1969, vol. 24.

Stearn, William T., 'Franz and Ferdinand Bauer, Masters of Botanical Illustration', *Endeavour*, vol. 19.

Stearn, William T., 'Sir Joseph Banks and Australian Botany', *Records Australian Academy of Science*, 1974, vol. 2, no. 4.

Stearn, William T. (ed.), *The Flower Paintings of Ferdinand Bauer*, introduced by W. Blunt, British Museum (Natural History).

CHAPTER TWO
Under a virgin sky

Brisbane, Sir Thomas, *Reminiscences of General Sir Thomas Makdougall Brisbane*, T. Constable, Edinburgh, 1860.

Burns, T.E. and Skemp, J.R. (eds), 'Van Diemen's Land Correspondents 1827–1849', *Records of Queen Victoria Museum*, Queen Victoria Museum and Art Gallery, NS no. 14, Launceston, 1961.

Carr, D.J. and S.C.M. (eds), *People and Plants in Australia*, and *Plants and Man in Australia*, Academic Press, Sydney, 2 vols, 1981.

Gilbert, L.A., 'Plants and parsons in nineteenth century New South Wales', *Historical Records of Australian Science*, 1982, vol. 5, no. 3.

Henson, Rae, 'A fine field for botanising', *Hemisphere* (European botanical exploration in Australia), September/October 1981, vol. 26.

Huxley, L. (ed.), *Life and Letters of Sir Joseph Dalton Hooker*, 2 vols, John Murray, London, 1918.

McMinn, W.G., *Allan Cunningham, Botanist and Explorer*, Melbourne University Press, Melbourne, 1970.

O'Hagan, J.E., 'Sir Thomas Brisbane, FRS. A Founder of Organised Science in Australia', *Journal Royal Historical Society Queensland*, 1960-1, vol. 6.

CHAPTER THREE
Entrepreneurs & explorers

Aurousseau, Marcel (ed.), *The Letters of F.W. Ludwig Leichhardt*, 3 vols, Cambridge University Press, Cambridge, Hakluyt Society, 1968.

'Botanical Report on the North Australian Expedition under the command of A.C. Gregory', reprinted from *Proceedings Linnean Society*, 20 February 1858, London 1858.

Chisholm, A.H., *An Explorer and his Birds. John Gilbert's Discoveries in 1844-5*, Brown, Prior, Anderson, Melbourne, 1945.

Chisholm, A.H., *Strange New World, the adventures of John Gilbert and Ludwig Leichhardt*, Angus & Robertson, Sydney, 1955.

Chisholm, A.H., *The Story of Elizabeth Gould*, Melbourne, 1944.

Cumpston, J.H., *Thomas Mitchell: Surveyor General and Explorer*, Oxford University Press, London, 1954.

Gould Commemorative Issue, *Emu*, 1938. (Vol. 38 contains thirteen articles on John Gould.)

Heney, H.M.E., *In a Dark Glass: the story of P.E. de Strzelecki*, Angus & Robertson, Sydney, 1961.

Mulvaney, D.J. and Calaby, J.H., *'So Much That Is New', Baldwin Spencer 1860–1929. A Biography*, Melbourne University Press, Melbourne, 1985.

Webster, E.M., *Whirlwinds in the Plain. Ludwig Leichhardt – friends, foes and history*, Melbourne University Press, Melbourne, 1980.

Wills, J.H., 'The Botany of the Victoria Exploring Expedition (Sept. 1860 – June 1861) and, of Relief Contingents from Victoria (July 1861-November 1862)', *Proceedings Royal Society Victoria*, 1962, vol. 75.

CHAPTER FOUR
Navigators & ship's naturalists

Bassett, Marnie, *Behind the Picture: HMS Rattlesnake's Australia-New Guinea Cruise, 1846–50*, Oxford University Press, Melbourne, 1966.

Branagan, D.F., 'The *Challenger* Expedition and Australian Science', *Proceedings Royal Society of Edinburgh*, Series B, 1971/2, vol. 73, no. 10.

Burkhardt, F., Smith, Sydney, *et al.* (eds), *The Correspondence of Charles Darwin*, vol. 1, 1821–1836, Cambridge University Press, Cambridge, 1985.

Darwin, Charles, *The Voyage of the Beagle*, Everyman Library, J.M. Dent & Sons, London, 1959.

Ingleton, G.C., *Charting a Continent*, Angus & Robertson, Sydney, 1944.

Huxley, J. (ed.), *Thomas Henry Huxley's Diary of the Voyage of H.M.S. Rattlesnake*, Chatto & Windus, London, 1935.

Huxley, Leonard, *Life and Letters of T.H. Huxley*, Macmillan, London, 1900; reprinted Gregg International Publishers, Farnborough, 1969.

Iredale, T., 'The Letters of John MacGillivray', *Australian Zoologist*, 1937-40, vol. 9.

Jukes, J.B., *Narrative of the Surveying Voyage of H.M.S. Fly*, 2 vols, T. & W. Boone, London, 1847.

Linklater, Eric, *The Voyage of the Challenger*, John Murray, London, 1972.

Lubbock, Adelaide, *Owen Stanley RN Captain of the Rattlesnake*, Heinemann, Melbourne, 1967.

MacGillivray, John, *Narrative of the Voyage of H.M.S. Rattlesnake during the years 1846-50*, 2 vols, T. & W. Boone, London, 1852.

Marshall, A.J., *Darwin and Huxley in Australia*, Hodder & Stoughton, Sydney, 1970.

Moorehead, Alan, *Darwin and the Beagle Journey*, Hamish Hamilton, London, 1969.

Mozley, Ann, 'James Dwight Dana in New South Wales, 1839-1840', *Proceedings Royal Society NSW*, 1964, vol. 97.

Ross, J.C., *A Voyage of Discovery and Research in the Southern and Antarctic Regions during the years 1839-1843*, 2 vols, John Murray, London, 1847.

Stanton, William, *The Great United States Exploring Expedition of 1838-1842*, University of California Press, Berkeley, 1975.

Wilkes, C., *Narrative of the United States Exploring Expedition 1838-1842*, vol. 1, Ingram, Cooke, London, 1852.

CHAPTER FIVE
Science, societies & the people

A Century of Scientific Process, A History of Several Aspects of Australian Scientific Development with Particular Reference to New South Wales. The Centenary Volume of the Royal Society of New South Wales, Royal Society of New South Wales, Sydney, 1968.

Coppleson, V.M., 'The Life and Times of Dr. George Bennett',

Bulletin of the Post-Graduate Committee in Medicine, University of Sydney, 1955.

Davison, Graeme, 'Exhibitions', *Australian Cultural History,* 1982–3, no. 2.

Fitzpatrick, Kathleen, *Sir John Franklin in Tasmania, 1837–1843,* Melbourne University Press, Melbourne, 1949.

Hoare, M.E., 'All Things are "Queer and Opposite": Scientific Societies in Tasmania in the 1840s', *Isis,* 1969, vol. 60.

Hoare, M. E., 'Science and Scientific Associations in Eastern Australia 1820–1890', Ph.D. Thesis, Australian National University, 1974.

Hoare, M.E., 'The Intercolonial Science Movement in Australasia 1870–1890', *Records of Australian Academy of Science,* 1976, vol. 3, no. 2.

Kohlstedt, Sally G., 'Australian Museums of Natural History: Public Priorities and Scientific Initiatives in the 19th Century', *Historical Records of Australian Science,* 1983, vol. 5, no. 4.

Mercer, P., 'The Tasmanian International Exposition, 1894–95', *Papers & Proceedings Tasmanian Historical Research Association,* March 1981, vol. 28.

Nadel, George, *Australia's Colonial Culture,* Cheshire, Melbourne, 1957.

Pescott, R.T.M., *Collections of a Century. The History of the First Hundred Years of the National Museum of Victoria,* National Museum of Victoria, Melbourne, 1954.

Pescott, R.T.M., *The Royal Botanic Gardens Melbourne, a history from 1845 to 1970,* Melbourne University Press, Melbourne, 1982.

Strahan, R., *Rare and Curious Specimens. An Illustrated History of the Australian Museum 1827-1979,* Australian Museum, Sydney, 1979.

Tregenza, John, *George French Angas. Artist, Traveller, Naturalist,* Art Gallery Board of South Australia, Adelaide, 1980.

Webster, E.M., *The Moon Man: A Biography of Nikolai Miklouho-Maclay,* Melbourne University Press, Melbourne, 1984.

Wheeler, Edward, 'The First Brisbane Congress [ANZAAS], *Search*, May 1981, vol. 12, no. 5, and 'The First Perth Congress', *Search*, May 1983, vol. 4, no. 3/4.

Woodward, J. Francis, *Portrait of Jane. A Life of Lady Franklin*, Hodder & Stoughton, London, 1951.

CHAPTER SIX
The feminine touch

Bassett, Marnie, *The Hentys*, an Australian colonial tapestry, London, 1954.

Carr, J.D., and S.C.M. (eds), *People and Plants in Australia*, Academic Press, Sydney, 1981.

Bischoff, Charitas, *Amalie Dietrich: ein Leben*, Grote, Berlin, 1917. (English translation by A. Liddell Geddie, *The Hard Road: the life story of Amalie Dietrich, 1821–1891*.)

Ellis, Vivienne Rae, *Louisa Anne Meredith. A Tigress in Exile*, Blubber Head Press, Hobart, 1979.

Hasluck, Alexandra, *Portrait With Backround. A Life of Georgiana Molloy*, Oxford University Press, Melbourne, 1955.

Hazzard, Margaret, *Australia's Brilliant Daughter, Ellis Rowan: Artist, Naturalist, Explorer, 1848–1922*, Greeenhouse Publications, Richmond, Victoria, 1984.

Moyal, Ann, 'Collectors and Illustrators. Women botanists of the nineteenth century', in Carr (eds), *Plants and People in Australia*.

Smith, Bernard (ed.), *Documents on Art and Taste in Australia. The Colonial Period, 1770–1914*, Melbourne University Press, Melbourne, 1975.

Rowan, Ellis, *Flower Paintings of Ellis Rowan: from the Collection of the National Library of Australia*, National Library of Australia, Canberra, 1982.

Tardent, Henry A., *Mrs Ellis Rowan: her contribution to art and science in Australia* (a lecture), Wilson & Ferguson, Brisbane, 1927.

Turner, A. Jefferis, 'Amalie Dietrich – A Forgotten Naturalist', *The Queensland Naturalist*, September, 1933, vol. 8.

CHAPTER SEVEN
The conquest of the rocks

Archbold, N.W., 'Western Australian Geology: an historical/review to the year 1870', *Journal Royal Society W.A.*, 1981, vol. 63, no. 4.

Baragwanath, W., 'The Geological Survey 1852–1952 [Victoria], *Victorian Mining and Geological Journal*, 1953, vol. 5.

Bolton, G., *Richard Daintree. A Photographic Memoir*, Australian National University Press, Canberra, 1965.

Branagan, D.F., 'The Geological Society of Australasia 1885–1907', *Journal Geological Society of Australia*, 1976, vol. 23, part 2.

Branagan, D.F., 'Putting Geology on the Map; Edgeworth David and the geology of the Commonwealth', *Historical Records of Australian Science*, 1981, vol. 5, no. 2.

Grainger, Elena, *The Remarkable Reverend Clarke*, Oxford University Press, Melbourne, 1982.

MacMillan, Mona, *Sir Henry Barkly: Mediator and Moderator, 1815–1898*, A.A. Balkema, Cape Town, 1980.

Mozley, Ann, 'Richard Daintree: First Government Geologist of Northern Queensland', *Queensland Heritage*, 1965, vol. 1, no. 2.

Mozley, Ann, 'The Foundations of the Geological Survey of New South Wales', *Proceedings Royal Society N.S.W.*, 1965, vol. 98.

Vallance, T.G., 'Origins of Australian Geology', Presidential

Address, *Proceedings Linnean Society of New South Wales*, 1975, vol. 100.

Vallance, T., 'The Fuss about Coal: Troubled Relations between Paleobotany and Geology', in Carr, D.J. and S.C.M. (eds), *Plants and Man in Australia*, Academic Press, Sydney, 1981.

CHAPTER EIGHT
The weather & the sky

Day, Alan A., 'The Development of Geophysics in Australia', *Proceedings Royal Society N.S.W.*, 1966, vol. 100 (with bibliography).

Doyle, H.A., 'A General History of Geophysics in Australia', *Earth Science History*, Australia volume, 1986.

Gibb, W.J., *The Origins of Australian Meteorology*, Department of Science, Bureau of Meteorology, historical note, Australian Government Publishing Service, Canberra, 1975.

McGregor, P.M., 'Australian Magnetic Observatories', *BMR Journal of Australian Geology and Geophysics*, 1979, vol. 4.

McGregor, P.M., Bond, F.R., and Parkinson, W.D., 'Rossbank Revisited', *Search*, 1985, vol. 16.

Orchiston, W., 'Illuminating Incidents in Antipodean Astronomy: John Tebbutt and the Great Comet of 1881', *Journal of Astronomical Society of Victoria*, December 1981, vol. 34, no. 6.

Orchiston, W., 'John Tebbutt and the Whakatane Eight-Inch Refractor: a Review of the Australian Connection', *Southern Stars*, 1982, vol. 29, no. 8.

Orchiston, W., 'Sydney Observatory, past, present and future', *Bulletin Australian Astronomy*, N.S.W. Branch Bulletin, 1982, 609, supplement: I-VIII.

Russell, H.C., *The Sydney Observatory, History and Progress* (Pamphlet 1882).

Savours, A., and McConnell, A., 'The History of the Rossbank Observatory, Tasmania', *Annals of Science*, 1982, vol. 39.

Tebbutt, J., *Astronomical Memoirs*, F. White, Sydney, 1908.

White, G.L., 'John Tebbutt and the Astronomy at Windsor Observatory', *Proceedings Astronomical Society of Australia*, 1979, vol. 3, no. 5–6.

Wood, Harley, 'Sydney Observatory 1858–1983', *Proceedings Astronomical Society of Australia*, 1983, vol. 5, no. 2.

CHAPTER NINE
Evolution in Australia

Armstrong, P., *Charles Darwin in Western Australia. A Young Scientist's Perception of an Environment*, University of Western Australia Press, Perth, 1986.

Bennett, George, *Gatherings of a Naturalist in Australasia*, London, 1860, Currawong Press, Sydney, 1982, facsimile reprint.

Fletcher, J.J., 'The Society's Heritage from the Macleays', *Proceedings Linnean Society of New South Wales*, 1920, vol. 45.

MacLeod, Roy M., 'Evolutionism and Richard Owen, 1830–1868', *Isis*, 1965, vol. 56, no. 3.

Mozley, Ann, 'Evolution and the Climate of Opinion in Australia, 1850–76', *Victorian Studies*, University of Indiana, 1967, vol. 10, no. 4.

Moyal, Ann Mozley, 'Richard Owen and his Influence on Australian Zoological and Palaeontological Science', *Records Australian Academy of Science*, 1975, vol. 3, no. 2.

Owen, Reverend Richard, *The Life of Richard Owen*, John Murray, London, 1894, 2 vols.

Smith, Bernard, 'Evolution and Australian Nature', *Meanjin Quarterly*, 1959, vol. 18, no. 1.

CHAPTER TEN
Colonial scientists versus the 'experts'

Daley, C. 'The history of *Flora Australiensis*', *Victorian Naturalist*, 1927, vols 43 and 44.
Flora Australiensis. A Description of the plants of the Australian territory, by George Bentham assisted by F. von Mueller, L. Reeve, London, 1863–78.
Kynaston, Edward, *A Man on Edge. A Life of Baron Sir Ferdinand von Mueller*, Allen Lane, Melbourne, 1981.
Powell, J.M., 'National Identity and the gifted imagination: Baron von Mueller, scientist and public servant, 1825–86', *Journal of Intercultural Studies*, vol. 3, no. 1.
Owen, Richard, *Researches on the Fossil Remains of the Extinct Mammals of Australia*, J. Erxleben, London, 1877.

CHAPTER ELEVEN
Science in colonial universities

Branagan, D. and Holland, G. (eds), *Ever Reaping Something New. A Science Centenary*, University of Sydney, 1985.
Branagan, D.F., *Rocks-Fossils-Profs: Geological Sciences and the University of Sydney 1866–1973*, Science Press, Sydney, 1973.
Elkin, A.P., and Macintosh, N.W.G. (eds), *Grafton Elliot Smith: The Man and His Work*, Sydney University Press, Sydney, 1974.
Home, R.D., 'The Problem of Intellectual Isolation in Scientific Life: W.H. Bragg and the Australian Scientific Community, 1886–

1909', *Historical Records of Australian Science*, 1984, vol. 6, no. 1.
Jenkin, John, 'The Bragg Family in Adelaide', University of Adelaide, 1986.
MacMillan, D.S., 'Professor John Smith and the beginnings of photography in Australia', *Proceedings Royal Australian Chemical Institute*, 1959, vol. 26.
Mulvaney, D.S., and Calaby, J.H., *'So Much That is New' Baldwin Spencer, 1860-1929*, Melbourne University Press, Melbourne, 1985.
Osborne, W.A., *William Sutherland. A Biography*, Lothian Book Publishing Co., Melbourne, 1920.
Radford, Joan, *The Chemistry Department of the University of Melbourne; its contribution to Australian Science 1854-1959*.
Radok, R. 'A Profile of Horace Lamb', Mathematics Department, James Cook University, Townsville, 1980.
Smith, S.A., 'The Life and Work of James Thomas Wilson', *Bulletin Post-Graduate Committee in Medicine, University of Sydney*, 1950, vol. 6.

CHAPTER TWELVE
Experimenters & inventors

Blainey, G., *The Rush that never ended,* Melbourne, 1963.
Cawte, Mary, 'William Farrer and the Australian Response to Mendelism', *Historical Records of Australian Science*, 1984, vol. 6, no. 1.
Evans, Lloyd, 'Response to Challenge: William Farrer and the Making of Wheats', *Journal Australian Institute of Agricultural Science*, 1980, Farrer Memorial Oration, 1979.
Farrer, K.T.H., *A Settlement Amply Supplied. Food Technology in*

Nineteenth Century Australia, Melbourne University Press, Melbourne, 1980.

Hudson Shaw, W., and Ruhen, Olaf, *Lawrence Hargrave, Explorer, Inventor and Aviation Experimenter*, Cassell, Sydney, 1977.

Inglis, Amirah, 'Trials of an Inventor in Australia. The Case of Lawrence Hargrave', *Records Australian Academy of Science*, 1961, vol. 1, no. 1.

Lawrence Hargrave. Australian Pioneer Aeronautical Scientist, Australian Government Publishing Service, Canberra, 1984.

Linge, Godfrey J., *Industrial Awakening. A Geography of Australian Manufacturing. 1788 to 1890*, Australian National University Press, Canberra, 1979.

McDonald, W.G., *Lawrence Hargrave of Stanwell Park*, Illawarra Historical Society, Wollongong, 1974.

Moyal, Ann, *Clear Across Australia. A History of Telecommunications*, Thomas Nelson, Melbourne, 1984.

Wheelwright, Francis, *From Digging Stick to Rotary Hoe*, Cassell, Melbourne, 1966.

Wrigley, C.W., 'W.J. Farrer and F.B. Guthrie', *Records Australian Academy of Science*, 1978, vol. 4, no. 1.

Index

Aborigines, assistance to scientists, 19; assaults upon, 45, 52, 64; contact with, 12–13, 26
acclimatization societies, 87
Adelaide Observatory, 122
Adelaide Philosophical Society, 86
Adelaide University, geology and natural sciences, 116, 163; physical sciences, 166, 168–9, 173
aeronautical research, see Hargrave, L.
Agassiz, Louis, 140
agriculture, Brisbane's encouragement of scientific approach, 30; agricultural inventions, 175–7; agricultural colleges in Australia, 178; first Australian chair in, 178, Government encouragement, of, 178, 181; see also Farrer, W.
Albert, Prince Consort, 84
Allen, Sir Harry Brookes, 166
Allport, Mary Morton, 100
Angas, George French, 5, 77, 80
Antarctic, botany of, see Hooker, J.; see also British Expedition; Ross, J.; US Exploring Expedition
anthropology, 26, 53–5, 68, 96
Aplin, Christopher D'Oyly, 112, 114
artists, 4–5, 7 and see Angas, G.F.; Atkinson, L.A.; Bainest, T.; Bevalet; Brierly, O.; Browne, T.; Gill, S.T.; Gould, E. & J.; Huxley, T.H.; Lesueur, A.; Lewin, J.; Lycett, J.; Krifft, G.; Meredith, L.A.; Mitchell, T.;

Index

Oudart, P.; Petit, N.M.; Roughsey, D.; Rowan, E.; Scott, Harriet & Helena; Selleny, J.; Stanley, O.; Stuart, J.; Watling, T.; Westall, W.; Watling, T.

astronomy, 6; influence of Governor Brisbane, 30–3; *Parramatta Catalogue of Stars*, 33; see also Adelaide, Melbourne, Parramatta and Sydney Observatories and Dunlop, J.; Ellery, R.; Rümker, C.; Russell, H.C.; Scott, W.; Tebbutt, J.

Atkinson, Caroline Louisa (Mrs. Calvert) 98

Audubon, John J., 47

Australasian Associations for the Advancement of Science, 85–6, 88, 170

Australian Academy of Science, 88

Australian Chemical Society, 165

Australian Gould League of Bird Lovers, 48

Australian Museum, 80–2; see also Angas, G.F.; Bennett, G. and Krefft, G.

Australian Philosophical Society, 74

Babbage, Benjamin, 112
Bailly, Charles, 25

Banks, Sir Joseph, 1, 3, 10–23, 70, 104

banksia, 16

Barkly, Sir Henry, 108, 129, 152

Bass, George, 19, 29, 104

Baudin, Nicholas, 3, 24–6

Bauer, Ferdinand, 4, 19

Bennett, Dr George, 41, 43, 76; work on monotremes, 132–8, 160; see also Owen, R.

Bentham, George, 150–2, 160

biological sciences, in Australian universities, 162–8; see also botany; evolution

Blackwood, F.P., 60

Bland, William, 176

Blandowski, Wilhelm, 78

Bligh, William, 5

Bosisto, J., 148

botanic gardens, 34, 83; see also Royal Botanic Gardens, Kew

botany, 3, 4–5, 10–13, 15, 16–23, 26–7, 33–8; see also Banks, J.; Bauer, F.; Brown, R.; Hooker, J.; Mueller, F. von; Parkinson, S.

Bragg, Lawrence, 170

Bragg, Sir William, 169–172

Brennan, Louis, 177

Brisbane, Sir Thomas, 30–33, 71

Brisbane Museum, 82

British Admiralty, support of

Index

science, 4, 9–19, 27, 56–69; see also ships
British Association for the Advancement of Science, 136, 153
British Museum, 22, 79; see also Brown, R.; Owen, R.
Brown, H.Y.L., 114–15
Brown, Robert, 19–22; 25, 35
Buchan, Alexander, 4, 10

Caldwell, William Hay, 136–7
Caley, George, 18
Calvert, Mrs Louisa Anne, see Atkinson, Louisa
Calvert, James, 99
Carron, W., 64
Chanute, Octave, 188, 190, 192
Chemical Society of Victoria, 165
chemistry, in Australian universities, 163–6
Chevert Expedition, 77, 184
Clark, Manning, 90
Clarke, Rev. W.B., 74–5, 81, 86, 99; geological work; 67–8, 105–9; meterological work, 118–19; work on fossil fauna, 157–8; see also Clarke Medal
Clarke Medal, 8, 145
Clift, William, 154
climatology, see meteorology
Clunies Ross, Ian, Sir, 2

coal, 105, controversy on age of Australian deposits, 105–10, *passim*; see also Clarke, W.B. and McCoy, F.
Cobb, Nathan, 181–4
colonial exhibitions, 6; see also intercolonial and international exhibitions
comets, see Allport, Mary M., Dunlop, J., and Tebbutt, J.
Commonwealth Bureau of Meteorology, 124
Commonwealth Scientific and Industrial Research Organisation (CSIR and CSIRO) 2, 184
convicts, 6, artists 5, in charge of weather stations, 31
Cook, Captain James, 9–16, 21
Coxen, Charles and Stephen, 40–1
Cunningham, Allan, 22–3, 34
Cunningham, Richard, 52
Cuvier, Georges, 63

Daintree, Richard, 7, 112–13
Dampier, William, 10
Dana, James Dwight, geologist to US Exploring Expedition, 67–9, 107
Darwin, Charles, naturalist on *Beagle*, 57–61; geological theories, 58–61; *Origin of Species* impact in Australia, 55,

86, 139–142; encourages Krefft, 143
Darwin, Dr Erasmus, 132
David, Sir T.W. Edgeworth, 116
Davidson, William, 33
D'Entrecasteaux, Bruny, 24
Denison, Sir William, 74, 115
Depuch, Louis, 25
Dietrich, Amalie, 94–7, 102
Douglass, Dr Henry, 74
Dove, H.W. 118–19
Drummond, James, 33–4, 36, 42, 91
Drummond, Johnson, 42
Dunlop, James, 31–2, 122, 176
Dunn, E.J., 114
D'Urville, Captain, 35

Eardley-Wilmot, Sir John, 74
echidna, see monotremes
education, see mechanics institutes, discipline names, and universities
Edwards, J.E., 176
Elder Exploring Expedition, 53
Elizabeth Bay Houae, 75–6
Ellery, Robert, 123, 129, 137,
engineering, university chairs at Melbourne and Sydney, 178; see also Hargrave, L.
Entomological Society of N.S.W., 77, 87, 97
entomology, 14, 72, 75, 86, 97

Etheridge, R. Jnr, 114
ethnography, see anthropology
European influence on Australian science, 3; see also Blandowski, W.; Dietrich, A.; Krefft, G.; Leichhardt, L.; Mueller, F. von; Neumayer, G.; Strzelecki, P.E. de; and French Scientific Expeditions
evolution, contributions of maritime voyages to theory of, 2, 56–8; Australian contribution and theories of, 36, 38, 59–61, 65, 131; Australian reactions to *The Origins of Species*, 138–145; see also Darwin, C.; Hooker, J.; Huxley, T.H.; Krefft, G. and Owen, R.
explorers, services to science, 5, 48–55; see also Elder exploring expeditions; Horn expedition; North Australian exploring expedition, and Bennett, G.; Leichhardt, L.; Gilbert, J.; Mitchell, T.; and scientific visitors.

Farrer, William, 172–5, 179–183
Feistmantel, Ottaker, 109
Fitzgerald, Robert, D., 143
Fitzroy, Captain Robert, 56, 140
Flinders, Matthew, 4, 19–21, 25

Index

Flora Australiensis, 147–153; see also Mueller, F. von, and Bentham, G.
Florey, Sir Howard, 1
Fossils; see Geology; Palaeontology
Lady Jane, 73, 102, 117
Franklin, Sir John, 66, 72–3
Frazer, Charles, 33–4, 36
French Scientific Expeditions, 23–7
Friend, M., 71
Freycinet, Louis de, 25–6

Galloway, Beverley Thomas, 182
Geological Society of Australasia, 87
geological surveys, 85; New South Wales 110–11, 115; Queensland, 115; South Australia, 115; Tasmania, 112; Victoria, 108, 115; Western Australia, 114
geology, 58–61, 66–7, 82–4, 104–116; see also palaeontology
Gilbert, John, 42–6, 48, 50, 52, 61, 65; see also marsupials
Godeffroy, G.J., 94, 96
Godeffroy Museum of Natural History, 94
gold discoveries and science, 77, 85, 116
Gould, Charles, 108, 112, 114
Gould, Elizabeth, 40–1, 73, 102

Gould, John, 5, 40–8, 108; see also marsupials
great barrier reef, 14–5, 57; early research on, 60–1
government, colonial scientific appointments, 32–3, 86, 109–16; grants for *Flora Australiensis*, 147; finances Wellington Caves Exploration, 155 and *Fossil Mammals of Australia*, 160; Science Board, 6, 87, 146; indifference and utilitarian attitude to science, 72; encouragement of technology, applied science, 177–8 and education 83–5; see also intercolonial and international exhibitions; museums and universities by name
Governors, contribution to science, 72–3; see also Barkly, H.; Brisbane, T.; Denison, W.; Franklin, J.; Hunter, J.
Green, Charles, 10, 16
Gregory, Augustus, 51, 111
Gregory, H.C., 111
Grey, George, 49
Gunn, Ronald Campbell, 36–8, 73
Gurney, Thomas, 9

Haacke, Dr William, 136

Index

Hale, Horatio, 68
Halford, George Britton, 144, 166
Halley, Edmund, 30
Hanson, Richard, 143
Hargrave, Lawrence, 1, 184–92
Hargraves, Edward, 111, 115
Haslar, Museum, 43, 70
Haswell, William, 145
Hearn, Edward, 144
Heathorn, Henrietta, 62
Henderson, Dr John, 71–2
Henslow, J., 58
Herschel, Sir John, 33
Herschel, Sir William, 30
Hill, James Peter, 167
Holmes, William J., 76
Hooker, Joseph D., with British Antarctic Expedition, 36–8, 65; *Flora Tasmaniae*, 5, 36–37, 65, 75, 145; role in *Flora Australiensis*, 147–51
Hooker, Sir William, 35–6, 147–8, 150
Horn expedition, 53–4
Humphrey, Adolarious, 104, 110
Hunter, Governor John, 4, 28, 132, 174
Humboldt, Alexander von, 121
Huxley, Thomas Henry, naturalist on *Rattlesnake*, 5, 61–5, 139–40, 145; friendship with W.S. Macleay, 63, 75, 102; seeks Sydney University chair, 63, 158, 163, 177

Inventions, see Technology and Hargrave, L.
intercolonial exhibitions, 84–5
international exhibitions, 84

Jack, R.L., 115
Jackey Jackey, 64
Jansz, Willem, 10
Jevons, William Stanley, 110–20
Jukes, J.B.; naturalist to HMS *Fly*, 57, 59–60; geological work, 59, 60–1, 107–8
Jussieu, Antoine Laurent, 20–1

Kay, Lieutenant, Joseph, 66; see also Rossbank Magnetic Observatory
Keartland, G.A., 54
Kennedy, Edmund B., 52, 64
Kernot, W.C., 178
Kew, see Royal Botanic Gardens
King, Phillip Parker, 29, 56, 75, 104, 117–18, 122
Koninck, Laurent de, 109
Krefft, Gerard, at Australian Museum, 155, 80–2, 98; work on extinct fossil fauna, 155–160; see also Owen, R.

Index

La Billardière, 24
Lacaille, Abbé Nicholas de, 30
Lamarck, Jean Baptiste de, 26, 140–1
Lamb, Horace, 169
Langley, Samuel Pierpont, 191
La Pérouse, Jean-Francois de, 23–4
Lawrence, Robert William, 36
Lechenault, Jean Baptiste, 25
Leichhardt, F.W. Ludwig,
  exploring and collecting work, 44–5, 50–2, 96, 155;
  meteorological work, 118
Lhotsky, John, 49, 110–1
Lilienthal, O., 191
Lindley, John, 92–3
Linnean Society of London, 21, 139
Linnean Society of NSW, 77, 87
Liversidge, Archibald, 87–8, 116, 136, 163, 178
Lyell, Charles, 58, 139, 154
Lyle, Sir Thomas Rankin, 166, 173

McAlpine, D., 181, 183
McCoy, Sir Frederick, 78; museum builder, 78–80; conflict on coal, 106–8; anti-evolutionist, 142–4; at Melbourne University, 163–4
McKay, H.V., 175
Macleay, Alexander, 75
Macleay, William Sharpe, 63, 64, 75–6, 112, 145, 155
Macleay, Sir William, 98, 144, 184
Macleay, Museum, 77
MacGillivray, J.,
magnetic surveys, 6, 21, 36, 37, 43, 131; see also Rossbank Magnetic Observatory and Neumayer, G.
Maitland, A. Gibb, 115
Mangles, J. Capt., 91–2
marsupials, 12, 15, 29, 131, 156; see also Bennett, G.; Gould, J. & Owen, R., and monotremes
Martin, Sir Charles, 5, 167
Masson, Sir David Orme, 165–6, 167
mathematics, see Pell, M.B.; Lamb, H. and Adelaide, Sydney, Melbourne Universities
Mawson, Sir Douglas, 1
Maximillian, King of Bavaria, 121
mechanics institutes, 7, 83–4, 90, 176
medals, (scientific & technological), 8, 85, 145, 153
Melbourne Botanic Gardens 152
Melbourne Observatory, 121, 129–130
Melbourne University, 162–9; see also McCoy, and Spencer, W. Baldwin

Index

Mendel, Gregor, 181
Menge, Johann, 110
Meredith, Louisa Anne, 99–100
meteorology, 31, 122–4, 132–3.
   See also Clarke, W.B.; Jevons,
   W.; King, P.P., Leichhardt, L.;
   Neumayer, G.; Russell, H.C.;
   Scott, Rev. W.; Tebbutt, J.; and
   Rossbank Magnetic Observatory
Milligan, Dr Joseph, 100
mining, see geological surveys;
   technical museums; technology
Mitchell, Sir Thomas, 49, 52, 59,
   62, 75, 104, 135, 154, 176
Molloy, Georgiana, 90–4, 102
monotremes, generation of 24,
   132–3; platypus, 18, 131–2,
   134; echidna, 135
Mort, Thomas, 177
Mt Stromlo Observatory, 130
Mueller, Sir Ferdinand von, 51,
   99; 142, 147–151; *Flora
   Australiensis*, 147–153; anti-
   Darwinian views, 142–3, 152
Mueller Medal, 153
Murray, R.A., 114
Museums and herbaria, 6, 76–83,
   passim, 85; see also specific
   museums and Royal Botanic
   Gardens, Kew

Napoleon Bonaparte, 24

National Museum of Victoria,
   78–80
Neumayer, George Balthasar, von,
   120, 131
Newbery, James Cosmo, 178
New Guinea, hydrographic surveys
   of, see Ships; HMS *Fly* and
   HMS *Rattlesnake*
New South Wales Geological
   Survey, see Geological Surveys
newspapers and science, 72, 74, 83,
   127
Nicholle, E.D., 177
Nicholson, Dr William, 74
North Australian Exploring
   Expedition, 51–2

Observatories, see specific
   observatories and portable
   observatories
Ornithology, see French Exploring Expedition and Gould,
   E. & J.
Overland Telegraph Line, 53, 123;
   see also Todd, Charles
Owen, Sir Richard, work on
   monotremes, 132–3; on
   marsupials, 135-8;
   antievolutionary views, 139,
   157–8; on extinct fossil fauna,
   158, 160
Oxley, John, 34, 49, 104

Index

palaeontology, 106-8, *passim*, 115, see also Geology and McCoy, F.
Parkes, Sir Henry, 160
Parkinson, Sydney, 4, 10-13, 16-7
Paris Museum, 3, 23, 70
Parramatta Observatory 31-3, 124; see also astronomy
patents, Hargrave's views on, 187-8
Pell, Morris Birkbeck, 169
Pelsaert, Francois, 10, 131
Péron, François, 25-6
Petit, Nicholas Martin, 25
Philosophical Society of Adelaide, 86
Philosophical Society of Australisia, 31, 71
Philosophical Society of New South Wales, 74
Philosophical Society of Queensland, 86
Philosophical Society of Victoria, 85
photography, 7, 53-4
physical sciences, 3-5, 10, 24, 56-69, *passim*; see also astronomy; meteorology; observatories, universities
Pickering, Charles, 68
Pilcher, P.S., 189
Pitman, R.F., 114

Pollock, J.A., 186
Porcher, E.A., 5,
Preiss, L., 93
press, see newspapers & science

Queen Victoria Museum, Launceston, 82
Queensland Philosophical Society, 86
Queensland Geological Survey, see geological surveys
Quiros, 14
Quoy, Jean René, 27

Ramsay, E.P., 82
Rennie, Edward Henry, 165, 173
Ridley, John, 175
Ross, Captain Sir James, 65, 122
Rossbank Magnetic Observatory, 65-6, 81-2, 117, 121; see also Ross J.
Rowan, Marian Ellis, 100-3
Royal Botanic Gardens, Kew, 17-8, 35-7, 93; see also Hooker, Joseph and Hooker, Sir William
Royal Society of New South Wales, 8, 74, 86; see also Clarke Medal
Royal Society of Queensland, 86
Royal Society of South Australia, 86

Index

Royal Society of Tasmania, 86; and Royal Society of Van Diemen's Land, 86
Royal Society of Victoria, 86
Royal Society of Western Australia, 86
Rümker, Christian Carl, 31–2, 122
Russell, Henry Chamberlain, 88, 123, 128, 171, 176, 178, 186

Science Board, 6, 87, 146
scientific community, 70–89 *passim*, and visitors, 57–69
scientific societies, 70–5, 85–7; see also Mechanics Institutes and individual and scientific societies
Scott, Alexander, 97
Scott, Harriett (Mrs Morgan), 97–8, 102
Scott, Helene (Mrs Forde), 97–8, 102, 117
Scott, Rev. William, 125–6
Selwyn, Alfred, 109, 113–4
ships: *L'Astrolabe*, 24; HMS *Beagle*, 56–59; SS *Bramble*, 60; HMS *Britomart*, 61; *La Boussole*, 24; *Chevert*, 77, 184; HMS *Endeavour*, 3, 9–17, 23, 56; HMS *Erebus*, 65, 122; HMS *Fly*, 5, 59–61; *La Recherche*, 24; *L'Esperance*, 24; *Le Géographe*, 24–5; HMS *Investigator*, 19–21, 25, 72, 104; *Le Naturaliste*, 24–5; SS *Peacock* (See US Exploring Expedition); HMS *Rattlesnake*, 5, 57, 61–2; HMS *Terror*, 65; *L'Urania*, 26–7
Smalley, G.R., 128
Smith, Grafton Elliot, 167
Smith, Sir James, 20
Smith, John, 144, 163
Smith, R.B., 175
Smyth, Robert Brough, 113
Solander, Dr Carl, 10, 13, 14, 16–7
Sommer, F. von, 111
South Australian Museum, 52, 77
Spencer, Walter Baldwin, 54–5, 145, 163, 164–5
Spöring, Herman, 10
Stanley, Owen, 5, 57, 61, 64
Stirling, Edward, 53
Stirling, J., 115
Strzelecki, P.E. de, 49, 110
Stuart, Dr James, 76, 91–4
Stuart, John McDonall, 52
Stuart, Sir Thomas Anderson, 166
Sturt, Charles, 75, 104
Stutchbury, Samuel, 111–2, 155
Sutherland, William, 172
Sutton, Henry, 176, 184
Sydney Observatory, 125–7
Sydney School of Arts, 83

Index

Sydney University, 116; sciences at 63, 162–73 *passim*; 186

Tasman, Abel, 10
Tasmanian Geological Survey; see Geological Surveys and Gould, C.
Tasmanian Journal of Natural Science, 72–3, 74
Tasmanian Society of Natural History, 72–3
Tate, Ralph, 53, 162, 163–4
Tebbutt, John, 1, 125–8
Technological museums, 178
Technology, Australian developments and inventors, 174–92, *passim*
Thompson, J.J., 171
Thomson, Dr Alexander, 116, 155–6, 163
Threlfall, Sir Richard, 170, 186
Todd, Sir Charles, 122, 172
Torres, Luis Vaez de, 10
Tupaia, 12
Twelvetrees, W.H., 115

United States Exploring Expedition, 66–9, 75, 91, see also Dana, J.D., and Wilkes, Lieut. C.
universities, 185; see by specific names, Adelaide University, Melbourne University, Sydney University, Universities of Queensland, Tasmania and Western Australia
University of Queensland, 173
University of Tasmania, 172
University of Western Australia, 173

Van Diemen's Land Scientific Society, 71–3
Victorian Geological Survey, see geological surveys and Selwyn, A.
Victorian Magnetic Survey, 121
Vlamingh, Willem de, 10

Wall, Thomas, 64
Wallace, Alfred, 139
Warren, W.H., 178
Waterhouse, G., 52, 77
Watling, Thomas, 5
Watt, J.A., 54
weather, see meteorology
Wellington Caves, NSW, 154–6
Western Australian Museum, 82
Whewell, William, 17
White, John, 28
Wilkes, Lieutenant Charles, 66–8; see also US Exploring Expedition
Wilkinson, C.S., 114–5

Index

Wilson, James T., 166–8
Wilson, William Parkinson, 129, 169
Woodwardian Museum, Cambridge, 106
Woolls, Rev. W., 99
women in science, 90–103; see also mechanics institutes

Woods, Rev. Julian Tenison, 144
Woolfe, Virginia, 98
Wright, Wilbur and Orville, 190–1

zoology, 3–4, 26, 34, 40–9, 79; see also marsupials; monotremes; universities